HINTS ON THE STUDY OF PERSIAN

Hints on the Study of Persian

PESTONJEE KAVASJEE KANGA
JAMSHEDJEE BEJANJEE KANGA

MANOHAR
2026

First published 1916

Reprinted 2026

ISBN 978-81-19139-59-0

Published by
Ajay Kumar Jain *for*
Manohar Publishers & Distributors
4753/23 Ansari Road, Daryaganj
New Delhi 110 002

Printed and bound in India

HINTS

ON THE

STUDY OF PERSIAN

(FOR STANDARDS V., VI. AND VII. OF HIGH SCHOOLS.)

CONTAINING

A complete Accidence and Syntax; Models of Parsing and Analysis; Figures of Speech; Derivations; Moral Maxims and Poetical Quotations; Idioms explained and illustrated; Arabic Plurals; Antonyms; Synonyms; Homonyms; Paronyms; Numerous Model Exercises; and Matriculation Examination Questions with References.

BY

PESTONJEE KAVASJEE KANGA,

PERSIAN TEACHER, SIR J. J. P. B. INSTITUTION AND THE FORT AND PROPRIETARY HIGH SCHOOLS,

AND

JAMSHEDJEE BEJANJEE KANGA,

LATE SENIOR PERSIAN TEACHER, THE NEW HIGH SCHOOL.

NINTH EDITION, REVISED, ENLARGED, & IMPROVED.

Bombay:

PRINTED AT THE

BRITISH INDIA PRESS

1916

PREFACE TO THE NINTH EDITION.

THE previous eight editions of this book, though issued at short intervals, commanded a ready sale in the Presidency and other parts of India, and the eighth edition being out of print, the present one is issued with the necessary alterations in the light of past experience.

P. K. KANGA.

Bombay, June 1916.

PREFACE TO THE SECOND EDITION.

THE Compilers need make no apology for the issue of the second edition within less than six months after the first. The first edition was out in October 1888, and in February 1889 several orders could not be executed, as there were no copies on hand.

In preparing this second edition, our aim has been to enlarge the practical usefulness of the book, and to render it more serviceable by selecting and inserting such words and phrases as are met with in the classical literature of the language; while, on the other hand, special attention has been paid to syntax, the most valuable and interesting portion of the language.

Moreover, we have passed beyond the mere province of Grammarians, and have inserted a variety of good many important things absolutely necessary for students, such as Arabic Plurals, Derivations, Proverbs, Idioms, Adjectives, Antonyms, Synonyms, Homonyms, Paronyms, etc. Besides a complete set of the Matriculation Examination questions with references, numerous Test Questions and Model Exercises are given at the end of every chapter, which, the Compilers venture to trust, will prove a most valuable aid to students. In many respects, therefore, a marked difference may be observed between the first and second editions of this work.

We avail ourselves of this opportunity of tendering our sincere thanks to the Principals, Head Masters, and Persian Teachers of all the High Schools in the Town and Presidency of Bombay for appreciating the worth of the book by introducing it as a text-book in their Schools.

In conclusion, our special thanks are due to Kavasji Edalji Kanga, Esq., Head Master, Moolla Feeroz Madressa, and Fellow of the Bombay University, for the prompt and valuable assistance, and the kind advice, we have received from him in the preparation of this edition.

P. K. KANGA.

J. B. KANGA.

Bombay, March, 1889.

PREFACE TO THE FIRST EDITION.

At the present day, there exist, on this side of India, at least half a dozen books on Persian Grammar. The question, then, may naturally arise—why add one more to the number? Our answer to this question is, that students and candidates for the Matriculation Examination require a book more advanced than almost all the Manuals used in schools at present, and this desideratum we have endeavoured to supply in the following pages to the best of our ability and resources.

As we lay no claim to originality in this book, except in the general arrangement of the subject throughout, it is but fair that we should name the chief sources from which we have drawn our materials. These are—1st, a Grammar of the Persian Language, by M. Lumsden, LL.D., Professor of Arabic and Persian; and, 2nd, a Grammar of the Persian Language, by Duncan Forbes, LL.D., Professor of Oriental Languages. In compliance with the wishes of many experienced and practical Persian teachers, it has been thought absolutely necessary to break up the lists of Compounds, Prefixes, and Suffixes, and to arrange them under their respective classes.

Among the many changes introduced into this book, the most conspicuous are—that the Syntax has been fully and systematically explained; chapters on derivations philologically treated; Proverbs, Idioms, a selection of Adjectives and Contrary Terms have been added; and numerous Model Exercises and Examination Questions have also been added.

In conclusion, we have to acknowledge our deep obligations to Kavasji Edalji Kanga, Esq., Head Master, Moolla Feeroz Madressa, and Fellow of the Bombay University. The kindness shown to us by this gentleman in carefully revising the manuscripts of this work before they passed through the press, and suggesting many useful alterations, is more than we can ever adequately repay.

Our best thanks are due to the esteemed Trustees of the Sir Jamsetjee Jejeebhoy Translation Fund for the support they have given to this work.

P. K. KANGA.
J. B. KANGA.

Bombay, October, 1888.

The works of the following gentlemen were consulted in the preparation of this book :—

M. Lumsden, LL.D.
Duncan Forbes, LL.D.
E. H. Palmer, M.A.
Edward Rehatsek, M.C.E.
Sir William Jones.
Alexander Bain, LL.D.
Joseph Angus, M.A., D.D.
H. M. Hewitt, M.A.
E. B. Eastwick, M.A.
Mirza Mahommed Ibrahim.
Munshi Nizamuddin.
Khan Bahadur Sayed Abdool Fatta Maulvi.

Dictionaries.

Persian, Arabic and English Dictionaries by Francis Johnson, Arthur N. Wollaston and Maulvi Fazl-i-Ali.

Burháni Káti.
Ghiyás-ul-Lughát.
Shams-ul-Lughát.
} Persian Dictionaries.

CONTENTS.

CHAPTER I.

Ancient Dialects of Persia.

In the early period of Persian literature, there were many provincial dialects, distinguished chiefly by the names of the provinces where they were spoken; the principal of which were زبان پهلوي زبان دري and زبان پارسي or زبان فارسي

زبان پهلوي—Pehlvi was at first spoken on the confines of ancient Persia, and afterwards, when Zend ceased to be spoken, in Persia.

زبان دري—It is a dialect made up of Pehlvi, Pâzend and Persian words, only spoken, and not written.

زبان فارسي or زبان پارسي—After Pehlvi, Persian was spoken in its original state. It was pure and simple, without any admixture of Arabic. After the conquest of the Arabs, it became greatly enriched by the introduction of Arabic words. The Persian language is melodious and elegant. A number of admirable works have been written in it by eminent persons.

Arabic Element.

In the seventh century of the Christian era, the Arabs extended their conquests and invaded Persia. In 636 A. D. they gained a decisive victory over the

Persians in the battle of Kadesia, which threw this mighty empire under the Arabian yoke. After this conquest numerous Arabic words were introduced into the Persian language.

Various Persian Handwritings.

In Persia and Arabia the art of printing is as yet very little used; hence their books are written in a variety of different hands. Of these the most common are the *Naskhi* نسخی, the *Tálik* تعلیق, and the *Shikastah* شکسته.

The *Naskhi* and *Tálik* are employed in Europe and India for printing Persian, Arabic, and Hindustani books. The *Naskhi* being the plainest and easiest character to read, is most frequently preferred for printing. The *Shikastah* (*lit. broken-hand*) is a rapid cursory hand much used in correspondence and often not very legible. It is quite irregular and unadapted for printing, but elegant in appearance when properly written.

CHAPTER II.

Orthography = إملا = تهجّي

1. **Orthography** (*Gr. orthos*=correct; *grapho*= I write) = إملا (ملا = he wrote correctly) = تهجّي (هجي = he spelt) explains the nature and sounds of letters, their combination into words and the correct method of spelling words.

Letters of the Alphabet.

حروفِ تهجّي (or) حروفِ هجا

2. حروف (*pl.* of حرف)=**Letters** are *marks* or *characters* used to represent the elementary sounds of language.

3. There are thirty-two letters in the Persian Alphabet. Of these four are peculiar to the Persians, eight are peculiar to the Arabs, and twenty are common to the Persians and the Arabs.

4. The Persians write and read their letters from right to left.

THE ARABIC-PERSIAN ALPHABET.

Letter.	Name.	Pronunciation.	Letter.	Name.	Pronunciation.
ا	الف	*Alef.*	ث	ثي	*Se.*
ب	بي	*Be.*	ج	جيم	*Jeem.*
پ	پي	*Pe.*	چ	چي	*Che.*
ت	تي	*Te.*	ح	حي	*He.*

Letter.	Name.	Pronunciation.	Letter.	Name.	Pronunciation.
خ	خي	*Khe.*	ع	عين	*Ain.*
د	دال	*Daul.*	غ	غين	*Ghain.*
ذ	ذال	*Zaul.*	ف	في	*Fe.*
ر	ري	*Re.*	ق	قاف	*Kāuf.*
ز	زي	*Ze.*	ک	کاف	*Kāf.*
ژ	ژي	*Zhe.*	گ	گاف	*Gāf.*
س	سين	*Seen.*	ل	لام	*Lām.*
ش	شين	*Sheen.*	م	ميم	*Meem.*
ص	صاد	*Saud.*	ن	نون	*Noon.*
ض	ضاد	*Zaud.*	و	واو	*Vawve.*
ط	طوي	*To,e.*	ه	هي	*He.*
ظ	ظوى	*Zo,e.*	ي	يي	*Ye.*

5. In the formation of a word all letters except ا—د—ذ—ر—ز—ژ— and و are joined together; thus لشکر—سلطان—وزير—پادشاه.

6. The seven letters ا—د—ذ—ر—ز—ژ—and و are never connected with those that follow them; as, برادر = brother, داور, = God, سردار.

Note:—**Letters resembling in shape or similar in form such as ب—پ—ت—ث and ج—چ—ح—خ &c., are called حُروفِ مقشابه or مُتَمَثِّل (شبه or مثل = *it resembled.*)**

Letters = حُروف

7. حُروف = *Letters* are divided into *Consonants* = حُروفِ صحيح and *Vowels* = حُروفِ علت.

8. حُروف صحیح = **Consonants** (*con* = together: *sonans* = sounds) are letters which cannot be properly sounded without the help of a *vowel*.

9. The letters ا — و and ي are used as *consonants* as well as *vowels*.

10. In the beginning of a word or a syllable ا — و and ي are used as *consonants*. When they do not begin a word or a syllable they are *vowels*; as وقوف — یاد — وزیر — اسیر.

Note:—In a word when ا — و and ي are proceded by vowels they are called حُرف نیم علّت *Semi-vowels* (*half-vowels*,) as گاو = a cow; بیوه = a widow; نیا = a grandfather.

11. حُروفِ فارسي or عجمي = **Persian Letters.**

The four letters گ — ژ — چ — پ are peculiar to Persian and never occur in the Arabic language. Hence every word in which any one of the four Persian letters occurs, is considered as purely Persian; thus, پاک — چمن — ژیان — گُرگ — گوش.

12. حُروفِ عربي or تازي = **Arabic Letters.**—

The eight letters ق — ع — ظ — ط — ض — ص — ح — ث are peculiar to Arabic and are never used in the Persian language. Hence every word containing any one of the eight Arabic letters is said to be of Arabic origin; as, ثابت — حکم — صاحب — ضامن — طرف — ظلم — عشق — قاصد.

General Rule.

13. A word containing any one of the four Persian letters *is* considered as purely Persian; and a word in which any one of the eight Arabic letters occurs, is said to be of Arabic origin.

حُروفِ عِلّت = VOWELS.

14. حُروفِ عِلّت = **Vowels** are letters which make a complete sound by themselves. The vowel-letters, also called long vowels, are three, *viz.*, ا, و and ي.

Note :—As vowels they cannot begin a word or a syllable

15. اعرابِ ثلاثہ (or) حرکاتِ ثلاثہ (حرکات *pl.* of حرکت = *motion* ثلاثہ from ثلث *three*) the three short vowels or primitive vowels, are ـَـ زبر ; ـِـ زیر ; and ـُـ پیش .

(*a*) ـَـ = زبر = فتح = نصب is always placed above a letter and it is sounded as *short* "*a*," as; خَلق *khalk* = a nation دَم *dam* = breath; مَلَک *malak* = an angel.

N. B.—A letter accompanied by the short vowel ـَـ *zabar* is called مفتوح *or* منصوب.

(*b*) ـِـ = زیر = کسرہ = جر is always placed below a letter and it has the sound of a *short* "*i*," as; گِل *gil* = clay; پِسر *pisar* = a son; مِلک *milk* = property.

N. B.—A letter movable by the short vowel ـِـ *zir* is called مکسور or مجرور.

(c) رفع = ضمّہ = پیش = ـُـ is always written over a letter and it is sounded as *short "u."* as: گُل *gul* = a rose; خُلق *khulk* = nature; دُم *dum* = a tail; مُلک *mulk* = a country.

N.B.—A consonant accompanied by the short vowel ـُـ *pesh* is called مرفوع or مضموم.

16. حُروفِ مُتحرک = **Movable Letters are** those that are accompanied by short vowels; as, پُر *pur* = full; پَر *par* = a wing; دِل *dil* = heart.

17. حُروفِ ساکن or مجزوم = **Quiescent Letters** are those that are not movable by primitive vowels. They are so called, because the sign جَزم (or) سُکون is written over them; as دُختر = a girl; مَردم.

N. B.—As a general rule the initial letter of every word is always movable by a short vowel and the final letter is always quiescent; as, پدر—مرد &c.

دو علت = Diphthongs.

18. دو علت = a diphthong is the *union* of two vowels in one compound sound; hence, diphthongs are also called *compound vowel-sounds.* There are two *diphthongs* in Persian.

I. When a consonant movable by َ *zabar* is followed by the long vowel و, the َ *zabar* and و unite and form a *diphthong*; *viz.*, "*au*" as in the words سَودا *sauda*=madness, سَورت *saurat*=anger; قَول *kaul*=a word, خَوف *khauf*=fear.

II. When a letter accompanied by the short vowel َ *fatah* is followed by the long vowel ی, the َ *fatah* and ی combine and form a *diphthong*, *viz.*, "*ai*" as, in the words قَید *kaid*=confinement, کَید *kaid*=fraud, خَیر *khair*=good, سَیف *saif*=a sword.

N. B.—There are eight vowel-sounds in Persian: three short vowels َ, ِ, ُ, three long vowels ا—و—ی. and two diphthongs.

Orthographical Signs.

علامات اِملای

19. There are certain marks pertaining to *orthography*, which are called *orthographical signs.* The following symbols are used in Persian:—تشدید ّ *tashadid*; مد ٓ; *madda*; تنوین ً *tanwin*; سکون (or) جزم ْ; وصله ٱ; and همزه ء.

I. The sign ّ تشدید (*corroboration*) is placed over a letter when it is doubled; as, جلّاد (جل + لاد)=an executioner; فرّخ (فر + رّخ)=happy.

Note.—The letter having a ّ is called مُشدَّد (*strengthened*).

II. The sign ٓ مد (*extension*) is written over an ا *alif* at the beginning of a word to denote that the *alif* ا is sounded long. This symbol is used to avoid the union of two *alifs* in the beginning of a word; as, آفرین = اافرین = praise; آوردن = ااوردن = to bring; آتش = ااتش = fire.

Note.—The *alif* ا marked with this sign is called الف ممدودہ (*extended alif*). The *alif* ا without a مدّ is called الف مقصورہ (*abridged alif*).

III. The sign ً تنوین (*nunation*) is expressed by doubling the short vowel َ *zabar* and it is generally placed over the letter ا at the end of a word which assumes a *nasal* sound; as سرّاً *sirran*, secretly; صبراً *sabran* = patiently; خالصاً *khalisan*, sincerely; خصوصاً *khasusan* = espccially; حقاً truly.

N.B.—When a word ends in ةً, the letter *alif* ا is not written at the end; حقیقةً *hakikatan*, truly; صورةً *suratan* apparently.

Note.—The letter marked with ً تنوین is called مُنوّن.

VI. The sign ْ سکون (or) جزم (*cutting* or *rest*) is placed over a consonant when it is not accompanied by a short vowel; as, دُکّان — دُخْتَر.

Note.—The letter marked with ْ جزم is called مجزوم (*quiescent*) as opposed to مُتحرّک (*movable*).

V. The sign ٱ وصلہ (*union*) is placed over ا of the definite article ال when it occurs between two nouns, to denote that the last letter of the first word is united with the last letter ل of the article ال and the ا *alif* becomes entirely silent; as دارُالحکومت *daru'l hukumat*=capital.

Note.—The letter ا marked with this symbol is called موصول (*united*).

VI. The sign ـٔ ہمزہ supplies the place of ی in words that end in ہ; as خواجۂ=a master; دادۂ= thou hast given.

Note.—(*a*) When one syllable of a word ends in a vowel and the following syllable begins with a vowel, the ـٔ *hamza* is used over it; as, فائدہ=advantage; طاؤس=a peacock.

(*b*) When two ی come together ـٔ is placed over the first; as, آئین=custom; زائیدن=to bring forth.

Note.—The letter marked with ـٔ is called مہموز.

The Sounds of a few Consonants and Vowels.

تلفّظِ حُروفِ صحیح و حُروفِ علت

نُون غُنّہ=Nasal ن.

20. In a word when the letter ن precedes ب it is sounded like م and it is called نُونِ غُنّہ; as, انبار *ambār*=a heap. جُنبیدن *jumbidan*=to move.

Note.—Final ن preceded by a long vowel has a soft *nasal* sound; as, چُون—چُنان—چُنین.

واو معدولہ = **The Mute or Silent و.**

21. In a word when the letter و is preceded by خ and followed by ا *alif*, it entirely loses its sound; as, خوان *khán* = a table; خواب *kháb* = sleep; خواہر *kháhir* = a sister.

22. واو إشمام ضمہ = The letter و having a slight sound of the short vowel ـُ. Between خ and the letters ب, د, ر, ش, ن, the sound of و is not heard and the letter خ takes a short vowel sound of ـُ as, خوب *khūb* = good; خود *khūd* = a helmet; خون *khūn* = blood; خوش *khūsh* = pleasant.

23. واو معروف (عرف he knew, *i. e., known* or *perceptible* و) when a letter movable by the short vowel ـُ is followed by و, the ـُ *pesh* and و unite and form a long sound; as, قُوت *kūt* = food; نُور *nūr* = light.

24. ہاي ملفوظی (لفظ = *he pronounced*) perceptible ہ. Final ہ preceded by a long vowel ا — و or ي is fully pronounced; as, شاہ *shāh* = a king; پیہ *pih* = fat; گروہ *guroh* = a company.

آنچہ تو داری بحُسن ماہ ندارد ∴ جاہ وجلال تو پادشاہ ندارد

Note.—At the end of a word when ہ is preceded by a consonant movable by a short vowel ـِ *zir*, it is (ملفوظي) pronounced; as, مہ *mih* = great; کہ *kih* = small; سہ *sih* = three.

25. یای مختفی (خفی = *he concealed*) imperceptible ه. Final ه preceded by a letter accompanied by the short vowel ـَـ *zabar*, is not fully pronounced; as دانه *dána*, a grain; خنده *khanda* = laughter; بنده *banda* = a slave.

26. یای معروف (عرف = *he knew, i. e.,* known or perceptible ی). When a letter movable by the short vowel ـِـ *zir* is followed by ی, the ـِـ *zir* and ی combine and produce a long sound; as, مِیر *mír* = a prince; سِیم *sím* = silver; پِیر *pír* = an old man.

CHAPTER III.

CLASSIFICATION OF LETTERS.

تقسیمِ حُروف

N.B.—It must be observed that the four letters peculiar to the Persian, *viz.*, پ—چ—ژ and گ are excluded from the following classifications of letters, for they are all borrowed from *Arabic*.

27. The twenty-eight letters of the Arabic Alphabet are divided into three classes according to their pronunciations, *viz.*, مکتوبي-ملفوظي-مسروري.

(1) حُروفِ مسروري (سرّ, *it was secret*) are pronounced by two letters and are 12 in number, *viz.*, با — تا — ثا — حا — خا — را — زا — طا — ظا — فا—ها—and یا. They are so called because the last letter ا *alif* is not expressed in Persian.

(2) حُروفِ ملفوظی (لفظ, *he pronounced*) are sounded by three letters and are 13 in number; *viz.* الف—جیم—دال—ذال—سین—شین—صاد—ضاد—عین—غین—قاف—کاف—and لام.

(3) حُروفِ مکتوبی (کتب = *he wrote*) are also pronounced by three letters, but their initials and finals are the same: *viz.*, میم—نون and واو.

28. Letters are also divided into two classes, *viz.*, حُرُوفِ منقوطہ *or* مُعجَم (نُقطہ *or* عجم = *a point*), dotted letters, *i.e.*, marked with *diacritical points*; such as ن — پ — ژ &c., and حُرُوفِ غیرِ منقوطہ *or* مُہمل undotted letters, *i.e.*, letters without *diacritical points*; such as ح — ط — د &c.

29. حُرُوفِ مُعجَم = Dotted letters are sub-divided into two classes according to the position of points.

(*a*) حُرُوفِ فوقانی (فوق = *above*) letters dotted above; as, ث — ش — ق — غ — خ &c.

(*b*) حُرُوفِ تحتانی (تحت = *below*) letters dotted below; as, ب — ج — چ — پ — ي.

30. حُرُوفِ منقوطہ = Dotted letters are also sub-divided into three classes according to the number of dots.

(*a*) حُرُوفِ موحدہ (وحد = *one*) = letters with one point; as, خ — ن — ف &c.

(*b*) حُرُوفِ مثناة (ثانی = *two*) = letters that have two dots; as, ت — ق — ي.

(c) حروفِ مُثلثہ (ثلث = *three*) = letters which have three points; as, پ — ژ — چ — ث &c.

31. Letters are also known by the terms شمسی (شمس = *the sun*) *Solar*, and قمری (قمر = *the moon*) *Lunar*.

32. حُروفِ شمسی are those letters before which the letter ل of the Arabic definite article ال assumes the sound of the initial letter of the noun to which ال is prefixed. There are fourteen *shamsī* letters, *viz.*, ت — ث — د — ذ — ر — ز — س — ش — ص — ض — ط — ظ — ل and ن ; *Examples :* دارُالشّفا *dāru'sh-shifā*, a hospital; دارُالضّرب *dāru'z-zarab*, the mint; كريم النفس *karimu'n-nafs* = of a generous soul.

33. حُروفِ قمری are those letters before which the letter ل of the Arabic article ال retains its own sound. The قمری letters are 14 in number, *viz.*, ا — ب — ج — ح — خ — ع — غ — ف — ق — ک — م — و — ہ and ی. *Examples :* دارُالمّرض *dāru'l-maraz* = a hospital; دارُالکُتُب *dāru'l-kutub*, a library.

N.B.—The student should remember that although the letter ل loses its own sound before حُروفِ شمسي and takes that of the letter which follows it, it must always be written in its own form.

34. Classification of Letters according to the Organs of Speech.

حُروفِ شمسی		حُروفِ قمری		
حُروفِ سنیہ = Dentals *or* Tooth-letters *or* Teeth-sounds. ت — ث — د — ذ — ط — ظ — ل — ن.	حُروفِ اسلیہ Linguals *or* Tongue-letters. ر — ز — س — ش — ص — ض	حُروفِ شفوی = Labials *or* Lip-letters *or* Lip-sounds. ب — ف — م — و	حُروفِ لہوی = Palatals *or* Palate-sounds. ج — ی	حُروفِ حلقی Gutturals *or* Throat-letters *or* Throat-sounds. ا — ہ — ح — خ — ع — غ — ق — ک

N. B.—The letters پ — چ — ژ — گ belong to the same classes as their cognate letters (*i.e., letters formed by the same organs* (حُروفِ مُتجانس) *viz.,* ب — ج — ز and ک.

35. Rules for the Permutations of Letters.

قوانینِ تبدیلِ حُروف

(*a*) Labials are interchanged with labials; as, پولاد = فولاد = steel; زبان = زِفان = the tongue; نہیب = نہیو = fear; سفید = سپید white.

(*b*) Palatals are interchanged with palatals; as, جہودی = یہودی = a Jew.

Note.—ج is sometimes changed into گ as لجام = لگام = a bridle; اوج = اوگ = a summit.

(*c*) Gutturals are interchanged with gutturals; as, = قوچ = غوچ = a ram; خستو = ہستو = confessing; اُستاخ = گُستاخ = impudent; اياغ = اياق = a cup.

(*d*) Linguals are interchanged with linguals; as, فرشته = فرسته = an angel; سارک = شارک = a nightingale; کُستی = کُشتی = wrestling.

(*e*) Dentals are interchanged with dentals; as, تراج = دراج = a partridge; اُستاد = اُستاذ = a master.

Note.—Sometimes the letter ا is changed into ی; as ارمغان = یرمغان = a present; اکدش = یکدش = union.

CHAPTER IV.

Words=الفاظ

36. *Words*=الفاظ (*pl.* of لفظ) are articulate sounds, used as *signs* to convey our ideas.

All words=الفاظ=کلمات (*pl.* of کلمہ) are either *primitive* = جامد or اصلی, *derivative* = مُشتق, or *compound*=مُرکب.

I. A *primitive* or *radical*' word = لفظ جامد or اصلی is not derived from another word in the language; as, کار — رحم — باغ &c.

II. A *derivative* word=کلمۂ مُشتق is one that is formed fom a *primitive*, either by prefixing or annexing a syllable; as, کارکن — بیرحم — باغبان &c.

III. A *compound* word=لفظِ مُرکّب is formed by the union of two or more *primitive* words; as, پُشت+خار = خار پُشت; بز + دل = بُزدل; نا + پای + دار = ناپایدار; دار+ال+قرار = دارُالقرار &c.

37. **Classifications of** کلمہ according to the number of letters=حُروف.

I.—ثُنائی (ثان=*two*)=a *biliteral*, *i. e.*, a word consisting of *two* letters; as, حق; خط; صف.

II.—ثلاثي (ثلث = *three*) = *triliteral*, *i. e.*, a word consisting of *three* letters; عقل ; صنم ; ظلم; &c.

III.—رباعي (ربع = *four*) = *quadriliteral*, *i. e.*, a word consisting of *four* letters; as, حساب ; ظالم.

IV.—خماسي (خمس = *five*) a word of *five* letters; as, سلطان; حرارت &c.

V.—خماسي مزيدفيه (مزيد = *increased*; فيه = *in*) a word containing more than *five* letters.

38. Contraction of Words = تخفيف كلمات

The following *contractions* of words have become current in Persian. The *contractions* are made by omitting a letter, generally a vowel and sometimes a consonant:—

اصلي Original.	مخفف Abridged Form.	معني Meaning.	اصلي Original.	مخفف Abridged Form.	معني Meaning.
اندوه	انده	grief.	راه	ره	a road.
اکنون	کنون	now.	شاه	شه	a king.
افغان	فغان	lamentation.	سپاه	سپه	an army.
پنهان	نهان	secret.	فراموش	فرامش	forgotten.
چون	چو	when.	ماه	مه	the moon.
خاموش	خموش	silent.	ناگاه	ناگه	suddenly.
دهان	دهن	mouth.	نگاه	نگه	sight.

QUESTIONS.

I. Give the general rule for the distinction of Persian and Arabic words (13).

II. Separate words purely Persian from those purely Arabic (13) طفل — پیل — ثابت — گرد — ژیان — یقین — قهر — عروس — قد — تواضع — عدل.

III. How do you distinguish between (2-6-7-8-11-12).

(1) حروف تهجّی and حروف متمثّل

(2) حروف علّت and حروف صحیح

(3) حروف تازی and حروف عجمی

(4) حروف متشابه and حروف جدا

IV. What are اعراب ثلاثه? Name and describe them. (15)

V. Name حروف علّت. Under what situations are ا — و ی used as حروف صحیح? (10)

VI. What are the Persian technical terms for *Vowels*, *Diphthongs*, *Consonants*, Primitive Vowels?

VII. What do you understand by مجزوم — متحرک — مرفوع — مجرور — منصوب — مضموم — مکسور — مفتوح?

VIII. What علامات املائی are used in Persian? Name and describe them briefly (19).

IX. What are the names of the following symbols? ـٔ, ـَ, ـٓ, ـّ, and ـِ. How are letters marked with these signs called? (19)

X. Define and illustrate :— حروفِ شمسی — حروفِ تحتانی — حروف مکتوبی — حروف فوقانی

XI. Name the different classes of letters according to—

(1) the position of points. (29)

(2) the number of dots. (30)

XII. Name the organic divisions of the letters of the Alphabet. (34)

XII. Give some general rule for تبدیل حُروف with examples. (35).

XIV. How is the letter ن pronounced when it is followed by ب ? What is its name ? Give examples. (20)

XV. Under what circumstances does the letter ن assume the sound of م ? (20).

XVI. Explain and illustrate :—واوِ معدوله — یای ملفوظی —
واوِ معروف — نونِ غُنّه — (20-21-23-24).

XVII. When does the letter ل of the Arabic article ال take the sound of the initial letter of the noun to which ال is prefixed ? Explain with examples. (32)

XVIII. The *four* letters peculiar to Persian are excluded from the classifications of letters. Why ? Give reasons. (27)

XIX. The letter ل of the article ال changes its natural sound before certain letters. Name those letters and give their technical designation. (32)

XX. Enumerate the different kinds of letters known by the following names :—(34)

حُروفِ سنیه — حُروفِ اسلیه — حُروفِ شفوی — حُروفِ لهوی

حُروفِ حلقی — حُروفِ عجمی — حُروفِ تازی — حُروفِ شمسی

CHAPTER V.

Etymology = صرف

39. *Etymology* (*Gr. etumos*=true and *logos*= word) صرف explains the *Classification, Inflection*, and *Derivation* of words.

Note.—The Term صرف also signifies *accidence.*

40. Classification is the arrangement of words into different *classes* according to their respective properties. These classes are called *Parts of Speech.*

Parts of Speech = اجزاي كلام

41. *Parts of Speech* = اجزای کلام.—There are only three parts of speech in Persian, *viz*, (I) اسم = the *Noun*, (II) فعل = the *Verb*, and (III) حرف = the Particle.

I.—The Term اسم includes Substantives, Adjectives, Pronouns and Participles.

II.—The Term فعل comprises all kinds of Verbs.

III.—The Term حرف includes Adverbs, Conjunctions, Interjections and Prepositions.

Different kinds of Nouns. اقسام اسما

42. Nouns are classified in the following ways:—

I. اسم خاص, **Proper Nouns.**

II. اسم ذات, **Abstract Noun.**

III. اسم عام, **Common Noun.**

IV. اسم الجمع, **Collective Noun.**

V. اسم جنس, **Material Noun.**

VI. اسم تصغیر, **Diminutive Noun.**

VII. اسم آلت, **Noun of Instrument.**

VIII. اسم زمان, **Noun of Time.**

IX. اسم مکان, **Noun of Place.**

43. اسمِ خاص=A proper noun is the name of a particular person or place; as زال — رستم — ایران — شیراز — فریدون &c.

Note.—All proper names are divided into three classes *viz.*, عَلَم — لقب — کُنیت.

(*a*)—Those that are only *proper names* are called عَلَم — as نوشیروان — حاتم.

(*b*)—Those which are *titles of honour* are termed لقب; as مُصلح الدین ; شمس العلما.

(*c*)—Those that begin with ابو = a father, امّ a mother, ابن = a son, are termed کُنیت; as ابوالبشر = the father of man, *i. e.*, Adam; امّ الجیش=the mother of the army, *i. e.*, a standard, ابن ارض (a son of the earth a stranger.

44. اسم ذات—**Abstract Nouns** are the names of *qualities* considered apart from the object in which they are found; as عقل = wisdom; حُسن = جمال = beauty; شفقت = رحمت = mercy; لطف kindness.

RULES FOR

The Formation of Abstract Nouns.

I. **Abstract Nouns** are formed from a

Concrete Noun—

(*a*) By affixing ی; as دوست + ی = دوستي = friendship; دُشمن + ی = دُشمني = enmity; طفل + ی = طفلي = childhood.

(*b*) By affixing ت; as مُحب + ت = مُحبت = affection; مُصاحب + ت = مُصاحبت = familiarity.

(*c*) By affixing يت; as انسان + يت = انسانيت = politeness; اہل + يت = اہليت = worthiness; آدم + يت = آدميت = humanity; جبان + يت = جبانيت = cowardice.

(*d*) By changing the final ه into گ and adding ي; as, بنده—بندگي = servitude; خواجه—خواجگي = mastership.

II. **Abstract Nouns** are formed from an

Adjective—

(*a*) By affixing ی; as صبور + ی = صبوری = patience; راست + ي = راستي = truth; نيک + ي = نيکي = goodness; سخت + ي = سختي severity.

(b) By affixing ت; as, ت + شجاع = شجاعت = bravery; ت + موافق = موافقت = agreement.

(c) By affixing یت; as, یت + جاہل = جاہلیت = ignorance; یت + قابل = قابلیت ability.

(d) By affixing ا; as, ا + گرم = گرما = warmth; ا + سرم = سرما = cold.

(e) By changing the final ہ into گ and adding ی; as, پاکیزہ — پاکیزگی = purity; تازہ — تازگی = freshness.

III By suffixing ی to personal pronouns; as, ی + من = منی = egotism; ی + تو = توی = conceit.

سزا اورا رسد کبریا و منی
کہ ملکش قدیم ست و ذاتش غنی

"Grandeur and egotism are proper for him whose kingdom is ancient, and nature independent."

وحدتی بینی خالی ز دوی ∴ طاہر از کسوت مای و توی

"You will there see a unity which admits of no duality; in which the distinction of persons (literally, *we-ism* and *thou-ism*) can have no place."

IV By suffixing ی to cardinal numerals; as, ی + یک = یکی = unity; ی + دو = دوئی = duality.

اینجا کہ توی دوئی نماید ∴ آنجا ہمہ جز یکی نشاید

"In this world, where you exist, there is the appearance of duality; but in the next world there will be nothing but the unity of God."

45. اسم عام—A Common Noun is the name which is given to every thing of the same kind or class; as شہر = a city; درخت = a tree; چوب = a stick; گل = a flower.

46. I. اسم الجمع = A Collective Noun denotes a number of individuals *united* together as a whole as, فوج = لشکر = an army; رعیت = a subject; گلہ = a flock; رمہ = a herd; طایفہ = a band.

II. اسم جنس A Material Noun denotes substances; as, زر = gold; آب water; شکر = sugar; سیم = silver; پنبہ = cotton.

III. اسم تصغیر = Diminutive Noun. It is a *derivative* from a noun denoting a *small* or a *young* object of the same kind with that denoted by the *primitive*.

Diminutive Nouns are formed by adding چہ *or* یچہ, ک, و and یژہ to nouns.

یاچہ *or* چہ — The particle چہ *or* یچہ is used for small creatures and inanimate objects; as, بزیچہ = a kid, a lambkin; مورچہ = a little ant; سگچہ = a little dog; کوہ چہ = a hillock; کتابچہ = a booklet; جویچہ = a streamlet; باغیچہ a small garden; گلچہ = a floret.

ک—The diminutive suffix ک is used for both animate and inanimate objects; as, مردک =

a little man; پسرک = a little boy; بطک = a duckling; مُرغک = a chicken; رودک = a brooklet = a rivulet; تاجک = a little crown; a coronet.

و—The diminutive suffix و is used for animate and inanimate objects; as, پسرو = a little boy; دُخترو = a little girl; گیسو = a ringlet.

یزه—It is used with inanimate objects; as, دانیزه = (a little grain) a lentil; نایزه = a small reed.

47. اسم آلت — This noun denotes the *instrument* used in the performance of that action represented by the verb from which it is derived: as, مِروحہ (روح = *he reposed*) a fan; مِفتاح (فتح = *he opened*) a key; مِقراض (قرض = *he cut*) scissors; میزان = a balance.

Note.—The initial letter م in the above mentioned instances is termed میم آلت (م denoting *instrument*).

48. اسم زمان—Words denoting *time*; as, روز = day; شب = night; صُبح = morning; شام = evening; فردا = to-morrow.

49. اسم مکان —This noun denotes the *place* where the action represented by the verb from which it is derived, takes place; as, مَشرق (شرق = *he rose*) the place of rising, *i. e.*, the east; مَغرب (غرب = *he set*) the

place of setting, *i. e.*, the west; مُكتب (كتب *he wrote*) a school; مُنزل (نزل *he stayed*) a stage.

Note.—The initial letter م in the aforesaid examples is called ميم ظرفيت (ميم denoting *place*).

N. B.—This force is also expressed in Persian by the suffixes showing *place*.

Suffixes = حُروفِ مُلحقات

Suffixes denoting place.

آباد — احمد آباد (City of Ahmad) Ahmedabad; حیدرآباد = Hyderabad.

بار — دریابار = a sea-port; رودبار = a channel; سنگبار a stoney place.

خانه — کتابخانه = a library; کارخانه = a workshop; شرابخانه = a tavern; سلاح خانه an arsenal.

زار — پنبه زار = a cotton field; کارزار = a battle-field; گلزار = a garden; علف زار a pasturage.

سار — کوه سار — a hilly region; چشمه سار = a fountain; شن — گلشن = a garden.

ستان — پریستان = a fairy-land; گلستان = a garden; گورستان = a grave-yard.

کده — آتشکده = a fire-temple; بتکده = an idol-temple; میکده = a tavern.

دان — گلدان = a flower-pot; شمع دان = a candle-stick; قلم دان a pen-case.

گاه — تماشا گاه = a theatre; خوابگاه = a bed-chamber; رزمگاه = a battle-field; کشتیگاه = a gymnasium; چراگاه a meadow.

لاخ — آتشلاخ = a place abounding in fire; دیولاخ = a place inhabited by demons; رودلاخ = a place abounding in rivers.

50. Compound Nouns = اسمای مُرکّب

Compound Nouns are formed:—

I. By the juxta-position of two nouns of different meanings; as, سیلاب (سیل = a torrent; آب = water) a flood; شبنم (شب = night; نم = moisture) dew. خار پشت = (خار = a thorn; پشت = a back) a porcupine; سنگپشت (سنگ = a stone; پشت = a back) a tortoise; مرغاب (مرغ = bird; آب = water) a duck.

II. By two nouns of the same meaning connected by و; as, مرزو بوم = a native place; مرزو کشور = an empire; زیب و زینت = elegance.

III. By two nouns of different meanings connected by و; as, آب و هوا (*lit. water and air*) climate; کارو بار (*lit.* action and burden) transaction; ردّوبدل (*lit.* rejecting and changing) dispute.

IV. By prefixing a numeral to a noun; as, چارپا (چار = four, پا = foot) a quadruped; یک شنبه = Sunday; هزار پا a milleped.

Questions on the Noun.

I. Name the Principal Parts of Speech in Persian. (41.)

II. Classify the following nouns:—نوشیروان—مهراب—طلا—رحم—لطف—سگچه—قابلیت—طایفه

مُسجد—میزان—گروه—رعیت—مردی—گندُم

III. Give general rules for the formation of Abstract nouns. (44)

IV. Give instances of Abstract nouns formed:—(44)

(a) By suffixing ی to nouns, adjectives, pronouns and numerals.

(b) By affixing یت and ش to nouns and adjectives.

V. Form Abstract nouns from the following *adjectives*:—

تلخ—تازه—بد—سخت—پاکیزه—تیز—

موافق—جاہل—شجاع—صفا—گرم

VI. Give Persian Grammatical terms for:—

Abstract noun; Collective noun; Material noun; Diminutive noun; Proper noun.

VII. Give three examples of each of the following:—

اسم آلت—اسم مکان—اسم زمان (47, 48, 49)

VIII. What suffixes are used to form اسم تصغیر? Give examples. (46 III).

IX. Give Persian words for:—*booklet, brooklet, streamlet, rivulet, floret, coronet, lambkin, duckling, hillock.*

X. What is the force of the initial letter م in the following words:—

مُغرب—مُسجد—مِفتاح—مِروحه—مِنقار—مُشرق.

XI. Form اسم تصغیر from:—

گُل—کو—کوه—زن—رود—جو—باغ

XII. Form words with the following terminations :—(49)

آباد — بار — لاخ — کده — زار — شن — سار

XIII. State general rules for compound nouns and give examples. (50) [(50)

XIV. Give instances of juxta-positional compound nouns.

XV. Separate the following compound nouns and explain their meanings :—

آب و ہوا — مرز و کشور — سیلاب — مرغاب — چارپا

— کاروبار — شبنم — خارپشت — ردّ و بدل — سنگ پُشت

CHAPTER VI.

Inflection = تصریف

51. Nouns are inflected to express *Gender*, *Number* and *Case*.

Gender = جنس

52. Gender = جنس is the distinction made in nouns, to show whether the persons or things of which we speak are *male, female,* or *neither*.

53. The grammatical Genders are :—

I. **The Masculine** = جنسِ مُذکر.

II. **The Feminine** = جنسِ مؤنّث.

III. **The Neuter** = جنسِ غیرذی روح.

IV. **The Common Gender** = جنسِ مُستوی.

I. تذکیر or جنسِ مُذکر (ذکر = *male*) = The *masculine* gender denotes male animals; as, اسپ = a horse; برادر = a brother; پسر = a boy.

II. تانیث or جنسِ مؤنّث (اُنث = *female*) = The *Feminine* gender denotes female animals; as, زن = a woman; خواہر = a sister; دُختر = a girl.

III. جنسِ غیرذی روح (غیر = *without*; ذی = *possessing*; روح = *soul*) = The *Neuter* gender denotes objects *without life*; as, باغ = a garden; میز = a table; چوب = a stick.

IV. جنس مستوی (سو = *alike*) The *Common Gender*. Nouns applied to both sexes *alike, i. e.*, names which are applicable either to males or females, are said to be of the *Common* gender; as, فرزند = a child (*a son or a daughter*); دوست = a friend (*male* or *female*); مُرغ = a bird.

54. **The Feminine** gender of nouns is distinguished from the *Masculine* in two ways.

I. First, by Different Words.

Masculine Gender. جنس تذکیر	Feminine Gender. جنس تانیث
اب = father.	ام = mother.
اسپ = horse.	مادیان = mare.
الاغ = jackass.	آتان = she-ass.
آهو = stag.	غزال = hind.
باب = papa.	مام = mamma.
برادر = brother.	خواهر = sister.
بنده = male slave.	کنیز = female slave.
پدر = father.	مادر = mother.
پسر = boy.	دختر = girl.
تیس = he-goat.	جدی = she-goat.
خروس = cock.	ماکیان = hen.
خُسر = father-in-law.	خوشدامن / خُشو } = mother-in-law.
خواجه = master, lord.	خاتون = mistress, lady.
نوشه = داماد = bridegroom	عروس = bride.
شوهر = husband.	زن = wife.
کدخدا = master of a family.	کدبانو = mistress of a family.
قوچ = ram.	میش = ewe.
مجرد = bachelor.	عزب = maid or spinster.

Note.—This kind of *feminine* is called مؤنث حقیقی.

Second, by Prefixes or Suffixes.

II. By prefixing or suffixing the word نر for the *masculine* and مادہ for the *feminine* to the word denoting the whole class; as:—

Masculine Gender.	Feminine Gender.
جنس مُذکّر	جنس مُونّث
نرآہو=آہونر=deer.	مادہ آہو=آہومادہ=doe.
نربز=بُزنر=he-goat.	مادہ بُز=بُزمادہ=she-goat.
نرببر=ببرنر=tiger.	مادہ ببر=ببرمادہ=tigress.
نرخوک=خوک نر=boar.	مادہ خوک=خوک مادہ=sow.
نرسگ=سگ نر=dog.	مادہ سگ=سگ مادہ=bitch.
نرشیر=شیرنر=lion.	مادہ شیر=شیرمادہ=lioness.
نرقاز=قازنر=gander.	مادہ قاز=قازمادہ=goose.
نرگاو=گاونر=bull.	مادہ گاو=گاومادہ=cow.

Note.—This kind of Feminine is called مُونث لفظي.

55. جنس مُستوِي = **Common Gender.** The following words are used either as *Masculine* or *Feminine.*

Masculine.	Feminine.
بیوہ=widower.	بیوہ=widow.
رود=son.	رود=daughter.
زال=an old man.	زال=an old woman.
زوج=husband.	زوج=wife.
فرس=horse.	فرس=mare.

Feminine of Arabic Words.

56. The *Feminine* of Arabic nouns is formed by adding ہ to the *Masculine*; as :—

Masculine.	**Feminine.**
جنس مذکر	جنس مؤنث
جد = grandfather.	جدہ = grandmother.
خادم = male servant.	خادمہ = female servant.
خال = maternal uncle.	خالہ = maternal aunt.
خیاط = tailor.	خیاطہ = seamstress.
راعی = shepherd.	راعیہ = shepherdess.
زاہد = monk.	زاہدہ = nun.
سلطان = emperor.	سلطانہ = empress.
سید = lord.	سیدہ = lady.
شاعر = poet.	شاعرہ = poetess.
صاحب = master.	صاحبہ = mistress.
عم = paternal uncle.	عمہ = paternal aunt.
فار = rat.	فارہ = female rat.
قیصر = emperor.	قیصرہ = empress.
کلب = dog.	کلبہ = bitch.
مخدوم = master.	مخدومہ = mistress.
مربی = patron.	مربیہ = patroness.
مطرب = , مغنّی = } songster.	مطربہ = , مغنیہ = } songstress.
ملک = king.	ملکہ = queen.
نبی = prophet.	نبیہ = prophetess.
وارث = heir.	وارثہ = heiress.
والد = father.	والدہ = mother.
ولی = benefactor.	ولیہ = benefactress.

Feminine of Turkish Words.

57. The *Feminine* of Turkish nouns used in Persian is formed by affixing م to the Masculine; بیگ=a lord; *Fem.* بیگم=a lady. خان=a prince; *Fem.* خانم=a princess.

Questions on Gender.

I. How many genders are there in Persian? Name them with their English equivalents. (53)

II. The *Feminine* gender of nouns is distinguished from the *Masculine* in two ways. Explain them with examples. (54)

III. How is the *Feminine* of Arabic and Turkish words formed? Give examples. (56-57)

IV. Give the literal and grammatical meanings of جنس and غیرذی روح.

V. What is the technical term for the *Common Gender*? Give two instances of it. (55)

VI. Give with meanings the *Masculine* or *Feminine* as the case may be, of — خانم — مادیان — ماکیان
— داماد — خاتون — خوشدامن — خروس — خواہر
خواجہ — عروس — نوشہ — شوہر.

VII. Form the *feminines* of — مربی — مغنی — بیگ
— میش — آہو — تیس — باب — بندہ — ببر
داماد — غوچ — فار — خوک — خواجہ.

VIII. Some of the following nouns are *Masculine* and some are *feminine*; separate them.

— بندہ — نوشہ — والدہ — عمہ — ضعیفہ — فقیرہ —
خواجہ — جدہ.

IX. Give instances of *Feminines* formed by means of *prefixes* and *suffixes*. (54, II)

X. Mention some words that are used either as *Masculine* or *feminine*. (55)

CHAPTER VII.

Number=عدد

58. **Number=عدد** is the inflection of a noun, to indicate *one* object or *more* than one.

There are two numbers.

I. **The Singular=عددِ واحد**

II. **The Plural=عددِ جمع**

59. عددِ واحد=The *Singular* denotes *one* object and it is always expressed by the noun in its simple form; as, کتاب=a book.

60. عددِ جمع=The *Plural* denotes *more* objects than one; as, کتابها=books.

RULES

61. **For the Formation of the Plural.**

I. Nouns that denote *rational beings* form their *plurals* by adding ان to the *singular*; as, پسر=a boy, *pl.* پسران = boys; زن = a woman, *pl.* زنان = women; مرد = a man, *pl.* مردان=men.

II. Nouns that denote *irrational creatures* form their plurals either by ان or by ها; as, شیر=a lion, *pl.* شیران=lions; اسپ = a horse. *pl.* اسپان=horses; چکاور=a lark, *pl.* چکاورها=larks; کلنگ=a crane; *pl.* کلنگها

بهنگ بسلہ چنگها بنای هشله زنگها

چکاورها کلنگها لکورها هزارها

III. Names of animate objects ending in ا or و form their plurals by inserting ي and then the plural suffix ان; as, دانا = a sage, *pl.* دانایان; گدا = a beggar, *pl.* گدایان; آهو = a deer, *pl.* آهویان; پرستو = a martin, *pl.* پرستویان.

Exception. گاو (و is a semivowel) *pl.* گاوان; نیا *pl.* نیاگان = grandfathers.

IV. Names of animate objects ending in the *imperceptible* ہ form their plurals by changing ہ into گ and adding ان; as بندہ = a slave, *pl.* بندگان; خواجہ = a master, *pl.* خواجگان; خواہندہ = a beggar, *pl.* خواہندگان; مُردہ = a dead man, *pl.* مُردگان.

Note.—When the final ہ is *perceptible* (*preceded by* ا, و *or* ي) the plural suffix is ان; as, شاہ + ان = شاہان = kings.

V. Names of inanimate objects form their plural by ہا; as, کتاب = a book, *pl.* کتابہا; قلم = a pen *pl.* قلمہا; چوب = a stick, *pl.* چوبہا.

Exception.—درخت a tree, *pl.* درختان.

Note.—Parts of the body sometimes form their plural by ان and sometimes by ہا; as, لبان = lips; چشمان = eyes.

اي مہرِ تو در دلہا—وي مُہرِ تو بر لبہا

وي شورِ تو در سرہا—وي سرِّ تو در جانہا

VI. Names of inanimate objects ending in the *imperceptible* ہ sometimes form their plurals by changing ہ into ج, and adding ات; as,

قلعہ = a fortress, *pl.* قلعجات ; کارخانہ = a workshop, *pl.* کارخانجات ; نامہ = a letter, *pl.* نامجات ; نوشتہ (written) a letter, *pl.* نوشتجات

Note.—(*a*) When inanimate nouns end in the *obscure* ہ, it is rejected; as, جامہ = a robe, *pl.* جامہا ; پردہ = a veil, *pl.* پردہا ; پیالہ = a cup, *pl.* پیالہا.

(*b*) When inanimate nouns end in the aspirated ہ it is retained; as, راہ = a way, *pl.* راہہا ; چاہ = a well, *pl.* چاہہا ; کوہ = a mountain, *pl.* کوہہا.

VII. Some inanimate nouns sometimes form their plurals by ات and sometimes by یات as,

عددِ واحد = *Singular.*	عددِ جمع = *Plural.*
اِتفاق = accident.	اتفاقات
باغ = garden.	باغات
تقصیر = error.	تقصیرات
مُراد = desire.	مُرادات
عطر = perfume.	عطریات
غزل = ode.	غزلیات
نقل = story.	نقلیات

62. Plural of Arabic Feminines.—Arabic *feminine* nouns form their plurals by rejecting the final ہ and adding the suffix ات; as, ملکہ = a queen, *pl.* ملکات ; والدہ = mother, *pl.* والدات ; سیّدہ = a lady, *pl.* سیّدات.

63. Plural of Compound Nouns.--Compound nouns form their plurals by adding the suffix to the second part of the word; as, چارپا = a quadruped, *pl.* چارپایان ; صاحبدل = a pious man, *pl.* صاحبدلان.

Two Plurals with different meanings.

64. Some nouns have *two plurals* with separate meanings :—

Singular.		*Plural.*
سر —		سران = generals.
		سرها = heads.
گردن —		گردنان = chiefs.
		گردنها = necks.
رقیب —		رقیبان = guardians.
		رقیبات = serpents.
امر —	*Ar.*	أمور = affairs.
	Ar.	اوامر = commands.
بیت —	*Ar.*	بیوت = houses.
	Ar.	ابیات = couplets.
حاجب —	*Ar.*	حُجّاب = porters.
	Ar.	حواجب = eyebrows.
عین —	*Ar.*	اعیان = nobles.
	Ar.	عیون = eyes.
غریب —	*Ar.*	غُربا = poor persons.
	Ar.	غرائب = strange things.

Plural with Numerals.

65. When nouns, expressing a *number* or *quantity,* are preceded by numerals, the plural suffix is not used; as, هزار اسپ=a thousand horses; ده پادشاه =ten kings; چهل من=forty maunds; چهل سال= forty years.

Dual Number= مُثنّی or عددِ تثنیه

66. مُثنّی or عددِ تثنیه (ثنی=*it was two-fold*) is the *dual* number of the *Arabic* language. It is formed by affixing ان for the *nominative*, and ین for the *oblique* cases; as, دار a house; داران = two houses, دارین of, to, or in two houses.

67. In Persian the *dual* number with the suffix ین is sometimes used to denote *a pair of things*; as,

Examples.

Singular=عدد واحد	*Dual*=عدد تثنیہ
جانب=a side.	جانبین=both sides.
طرف=a side.	طرفین=both sides.
قمر=the moon.	قمرین=the sun and the moon.
کون=the world.	کونین=both worlds.
نعل=a shoe.	نعلین=a pair of shoes.
والد=father.	والدین=parents.

68. جمع الجموع *or* منتہی الجموع = *The extreme* of plurals or plural of plurals. It is the last form of the plural number from which no other plural can be formed; as

Examples.

عدد واحد	عددِ جمع	جمع الجموع
امر=an affair.	امور	امورات
بیت=a house.	بیوت	بیوتات
جوہر=a jewel.	جواہر	جواہرات
خرج=expense.	اخراج	اخراجات
صاحب=a master.	اصحاب *pl.* صحب	اصاحیب
فرقہ=a sect.	افراق *pl.* فرق	افاریق
فعل=action.	افعال	افاعیل
قول=a word.	اقوال	اقاویل

Questions on Number.

I. Give Persian words for singular, plural and dual numbers, (58, 66).

II. Give general rules for forming the plural in Persian, (61)

III. State the different modes of forming the *plural* of nouns ending in ه and give examples. (61 VI).

IV. How is the *plural* of nouns ending in vowels formed ? Give instances. (61. III)

V. Mention some nouns that have two plurals with separate meanings. (64).

VI. How do you form the plural of *Arabic feminines?* Give examples. (62).

VII. What do you understand by the *Dual* number ? What terminations are used for it ? (66).

VIII. How are عدد تثنیه and مُنتهی الجمع otherwise called? (66, 68.)

IX. What do you understand by the term جمع الجُموع ? Give some examples, (68).

X. Give with meanings the plurals of — بازو — غزل —
بادپا — کُشته — آشنا — کارخانه — نیا — گاو —
نقل — مُراد — خوبرو — نوشته

CHAPTER VIII.

حالت = Case.

60. حالت (*lit. state.*)=Case is either the *form* or *state* of a noun or pronoun, to express the *relation* which it bears to other words.

Note—All other forms of the noun except the nominative are called *Oblique cases.*

70. In Persian the *oblique* cases are formed by means of *prefixes* and *suffixes*.

71. The following six cases are used in Persian:—

I. حالت فاعلي = **The Nominative.**

II. حالت مفعولي = **The Accusative.**

III. حالت مفعولي = **The Dative.**

IV. حالت جري = **The Objective.**

V. حالت اضافت = **The Genitive.**

VI. حالت ندا = **The Vocative.**

72. حالت فاعلي = **The Nominative** is the case which denotes the person or thing about which we are speaking; as, كتاب از دست أفتاد; أستاد رفت

73. حالت مفعولي = **The Accusative** case is generally formed by adding the termination را; as, او مرا ديد ;أستاد شاگرد را طلبيد

RULES

74. For the Insertion of the Termination را

I. When we wish to render the object definite or particular, را is added; as,

قاضي جلّاد را طلبيد ;مغل طوطي را خريد

II. When the action described by the verb is such as might be performed by either the subject or the object, the termination را is added to avoid ambiguity; as, رستم سهراب را بيفگند ;شير فيل را كشت

III. When a personal pronoun or its substitute خود is used as the object of a verb, the termination را is added; as,

نگه دار مارا ز راه خطا ;مرا نمي شناسي

فلان شخص خود را پنهان كرده است

75. Rules for the Omission of را.

I. When the nature of a sentence is such as to enable the reader or hearer to comprehend the sense clearly without را, it is omitted; as,

دوستي طعام فرستاد ;شخصی خطی می نوشت

II. When a conjunctive personal pronoun is used as the object of a verb, the termination را is dispensed with; as, ديروز ديدمش ;پادشاه خلعتم بخشيد

Position of the Termination را.

76. When the object of a verb is connected with another noun or governed by an adjective, the termination را is added to the latter noun or adjective; as, پادشاه خراسان سلطان محمود سبكتگين را بخواب ديد ;اين گدای شوخ چشم مُبذر را برانيد

77. حالت مفعولی — The **Dative** Case is formed either by prefixing the particle به or by suffixing را; as, به هرمز چندین گفت نوشیروان; آستاد شاگرد را انعام داد

Note—In a sentence where the Dative and the Accusative both occur together, if the Accusative be indefinite, the Dative is formed by را; as, شخصی مال خود صرّافی را سپرد but if the Accusative be definite, it takes را, and then the Dative must be formed by prefixing the particle به; as,

امیری پسر را به ادیبی داد—پادشاه آن خلعت را به وزیر داد

78. حالت جری — The **Objective** case is formed by prefixing any of the prepositions از, در, با and برای to the Nominative; as, ازقلم; درباغ; باشمشیر;

79. حالت ندا — The **Vocative** Case. It is formed by prefixing either ای or یا to the Nominative; as, یاخدا; ای دوست; یارحیم, O Merciful God.

II. In poetry the Vocative is frequently formed by suffixing ا to the Nominative; as, کریما, O Merciful! پروردگارا, O God! خسروا, شهریارا O king!

* الها قادرا پروردگارا — کریما منعما آمرزگارا *
* که را دا دلیرا شهانوذرا — گوا تاجدارا مهادا ورا *

80. حالت اضافت — (*lit. relation*). The **Genitive** or Possessive Case is formed by prefixing the short vowel ـِ *zir* to the noun in the Possessive Case; as, اسپِ پادشاه, the horse *of* the king; خلعتِ وزیر, the robe *of* the minister; مالِ سوداگر. Hence, every possessive construction must have three parts, *viz.*, the first *or governing noun* is termed the مضاف

and the second *or the noun governed* is called مضاف الیہ and the *vowel* زیر is called کسرۂ اضافت.

It undergoes changes in the following cases:—

I. If the مضاف ends in the long vowel ا or و the letter ی is used instead of زیر ـِ; as, پای دوست—موی سر—روی پسر—بوی گل

II. If the مُضاف ends in the long vowel ی or the imperceptible ہ, the mark ـٔ *hamza* is used; as, جامۂ برادر — خانۂ پدر

N. B.—**When the مُضاف ends in the perceptible ہ the short vowel زیر ـِ is used ; as, سپاہِ دُشمن—راہِ صواب—شاہِ ایران**

Note.*—Hence there are three علامت اضافت (*pl.* علامات) signs of the Genitive case, *viz.*, ـِ *zir.*, ; ي and ـٔ *hamza.

81. When two or more nouns follow each other in the possessive case, the sign of the possessive is affixed only to the last مُضاف as, اسپ وفیل و شُترِ وزیر

82. اقسامِ اضافت = **Different kinds of Izafat :—**

I. إضافتِ بیاني *or* توضیحي

II. إضافتِ تمليکي *or* تخصیصي

III. إضافتِ توصیفي *or* موصوفي

IV. إضافت مقلوبي *or* قلب إضافت

V. إضافتِ ظرفي VI. إضافتِ استعارہ

VII. إضافتِ تشبیہی VIII. إضافتِ ابنی

IX. فک إضافت

83. توضیحی or إضافت بیاني is that kind of possessive construction in which the مُضاف الیہ denotes the *substance* or *material* of which the مُضاف is made; as, تخت عاج = a throne of ivory; دیوار خشت = a wall of bricks; خاتم طلا = a ring of gold; طوق سیم = a chain of silver.

48. تخصیصی or إضافت تملیکی (ملک = *property*) is that in which the مُضاف الیہ is the *owner* of the مُضاف; as, گنج قارون = the treasure of Kārun; رخش رستم = the charger of Rustam; خانۂ دہقان = the house of a peasant; قصرسلطان = the palace of the king.

Note.—Sometimes the مُضاف is the owner of the مُضاف الیہ; as, خاقان چین—سلطان روم—قیصرہند.

85. موصوفي or إضافت توصیفی (وصف = *qualified*) is that which expresses the relation between the موصوف (the noun *qualified*) and the صفت *adjective*); as, روز روشن = a bright day; باغ خرم = a delightful garden; گرد دلیر = a brave hero; تیغ تیز = a sharp sword; شب تار = a dark night.

سال خرم فال نیکو مال وافر حال خوش

اصل ثابت نسل باقي تخت عالي بخت رام

بادت اندر ہرد و گیتي برقرار و بردوام

Note.—When compound adjectives are used, the إضافت is termed إضافت توصيفي مرکب; as, اسپ باد پا a fleet steed; مرد سنگدل = a merciless man, دہرِ جفا پیشہ = cruel world.

86. إضافت تشبیہی (شبہ = *it resembled*) it is a kind of *simile* (*i.e.*, *comparison of two things*) in which the مُضاف الیہ is compared to the مُضاف; as, آینہ دل = دل چون آینہ = the heart which resembles a mirror; شیر مرد = مرد چون شیر = a man who resembles a lion; گلرخ = رخ چون گل = cheeks like roses; غنچہ لب = لب چون غنچہ = lips like rosebuds.

Note.—In the example آئینہ دل , دل is the thing compared = مُشبہ and آئینہ is the thing compared to = مُشبہ بہ

إضافت استعارہ is that which indicates a metaphor; as, دستِ عقل, the hand of wisdom, سرِ ہوش, the head of intelligence.

87. (*a*) اضافت ظرفي — (ظرف = *a vessel*) is that kind of possessive construction in which the مُضاف الیہ is the *receptacle* of the مُضاف; as, آبِ دریا = the water of the sea; میوۂ باغ — ریگِ صحرا.

(*b*) Sometimes the مُضاف is the *receptacle* of the مُضاف الیہ, as, کیسۂ زر = a purse of gold; کوزۂ آب = a pitcher of water; شیشۂ شراب = a bottle of wine.

Note.—In the aforesaid instances the thing contained is called مظروف and the *vessel* or the *receptacle* is called ظرف.

اضافت ابنی is that in which the relation between the father and the son is expressed by the omission of the word بن; as, حجاج بوسف, *i. e.*, حجاج بن یوسف

88. قلب اضافت or اضافت مقلوبی (قلب = *inverted*) is that kind of possessive construction in which the ordinary form of اضافت is inverted, *i. e.*, the مضاف is preceded by مضاف الیہ and the علامت اضافت is omitted, as, عالم پناہ = پناہ عالم = the asylum of world; سپاہ سالار = سالار سپاہ = the general of an army; گلاب = آب گل = rose-water; شہریار = یار شہر = (the friend of a city) a king.

89. فک اضافت — There are certain words such as سر — صاحب — قایم — نایب and ولي which do not admit of the علامت اضافت, when they are used in a possessive construction; this kind of اضافت is called فک اضافت as, صاحب دل = a pious man, صاحب ہنر = a skilful man, سرمایہ (سر = source, مایہ = wealth) capital; قایم مقام = a successor; ولي نعمت = (ولي a master; نعمت = favour) a patron.

Note.—When the words سر = *head* and صاحب = *owner* are used in a restricted sense, the علامت اضافت is used; as سرِ دوست, صاحبِ خانہ.

تصریف = Declension.

90. Persian nouns do not undergo any change in the terminations of their *oblique* cases, whether they be singular or plural, masculine or feminine.

		عدد واحد *Singular.*	عدد جمع *Plural.*
Nom.	حالت فاعلی	دوست a friend	دوستان
Acc.	مفعولي ,,	دوست را a friend	دوستان را
Dat.	مفعولی ,,	به دوست or دوست را } to a friend	به دوستان or دوستان را
Obj.	جری ,,	از دوست با دوست } with a friend	از دوستان با دوستان
Gen.	اضافت ,,	ـِ دوست of a friend	ـِ دوستان
Voc.	ندا ,,	اي دوست O friend!	اي دوستان

Note.—In like manner may be declined every substantive in the Persian language. The only questions are, in the first place, whether ـِ , ي, or ـٔ should be used as the sign of the Genitive Case; and secondly, whether ان or ها is to be added in plural.

Questions on Case.

I. What does حالت literally signify? What is its grammatical name? (69)

II. Name all the cases. How are they generally formed in Persian? (70, 71) [Give examples. (78, 77)

III. How are the accusative and the dative cases formed?

IV. State the general principles that regulate the insertion of the termination را and illustrate by examples. (74)

V. Give rules for the omission of را (75)

VI. Where is the termination را placed, when the object of a verb is connected with another noun or qualified by an adjective? (76)

VII. How are the dative and the accusative formed when both occur together in a sentence? (77, *Note*).

VIII. What cases are formed by prefixing prepositions and suffixing ا to the nominative ? (78. 79)

IX. What two ways are there of expressing the vocative case ? What is the distinction observed in their usage ? (79)

X. How is the حالت إضافت formed ? What are its principal parts ? (80)

XI. How are the words connected by علامت إضافت called in Persian ? How are they placed in a genitive construction ? (80)

XII. What is generally used as علامت إضافت ? Notice the changes it undergoes in some cases, giving examples. Enumerate علامت إضافت with examples.

XIII. Name the different kinds of إضافت (82)

XIV. Define and illustrate ظرفي — توضيحي — توصيفي — استعاره — تشبيهي — تمليكي — مقلوبي

XV. Explain fully فک إضافت. (89)

XVI. Mention some words that do not admit of علامت إضافت when they are used in a genitive construction.

XVII. Distinguish between مُضاف and مُضاف اليه, صفت and موصوف, مشبه and مشبه به, ظرف and مظروف.

XVIII. Name and explain the following Izáfats :—

کاسهٔ بلور — تیغ آهن — سفجار پسر — شیشهٔ گلاب — گلاب —
مزرع گندم — شب تار — لعل لب — زاد بوم —
اورنگ زیب — دشمن صعب — لاله رخ — صندوق کتب —
گدای مُبذر — کدخدا — طوق سیم — صاحب غرض
سنبل زلف — شاهنامه — ناخدا — سیماب — شهریار

CHAPTER—IX.

صفت = Adjective.

91. صفت (*lit. quality*). An *Adjective* is a word used with a noun to denote some *quality* or other *attribute* belonging to the person or thing represented by the noun; as, مرد نیک=a good man; گیاه سبز= green grass; روي زیبا=a beautiful face. In these instances نیک—سبز and زیبا are adjectives, and مرد - گیاه and رو are nouns qualified by these adjectives, and they are called موصوف.

92. إسم موصوف (وصف=*qualified*). The noun qualified by an adjective is called اسم موصوف; as, روز روشن=a bright day; روز is موصوف and روشن is صفت; باغ خرم=a delightful garden, باغ is موصوف and خرم is صفت.

93. Position of the صفت—In a sentence the صفت is generally placed after the موصوف and they are both connected by the short vowel ِ- *zir*, which is called کسرۂ توصیفی; as, مرد شجاع=a brave man; شب تار=dark night; عمر عزیز=precious life.

94. It undergoes changes in the following cases :—

(*a*) If the موصوف ends in long vowels ا or و, the letter ي is used instead of ِ *zir*; as, گداي کور=a blind beggar; روی زیبا = a beautiful face; پای دراز = a long leg; موی سفید = white hair; هوای خوش = pleasant air.

(b) If the موصوف ends in the imperceptible ه, the mark ء hamza is placed over it; as, جامۀ سفید = a white robe; پنجۀ تیز = a sharp claw; چشمۀ شیرین = a sweet stream. But if the موصوف ends in the perceptible ه, the short vowel ـِ zir, is used, as شاهِ عادل

کوهِ بلند — ماهِ روشن — راهِ راست —

Note.—(a) In Poetry the adjective sometimes precedes the noun; as,

هشیوار دستور بردست شاه * او دشمن نامور رستم است
جز از پاک ایزد نترسم ز کس

(b) Some adjectives may be placed indifferently *before* or *after* the qualified nouns; as, دهقان پیر — پیرزن — مال بسیار — بسیار کس, تمام روز — اعقاد تمام, نیک مرد, نوجوان, شیرین زبان, حاضر جواب.

(c) Sometimes substantives are used as adjectives; as مرد دزد — مرد درویش — مرد باغبان.

مراتب تفضیل = Degrees of Comparison.

95. **Comparison** is the inflection of an adjective to denote the *increase* or *decrease* of the quality implied in the adjective.

96. There are two *degrees of comparison*, *viz.*, the *Comparative* = صفت تفضیل and the *Superlative* = صفت مبالغه.

97. اصلی or صفت ماحض (ماحض, *it was pure*). The **Positive** state *or* form is the simple quality itself, and is therefore *not a degree*; as, تلخ = bitter; زشت = ugly; سخت = severe.

98. صفت تفضیل (فضل, *he excelled*). The **comparative** degree expresses a *greater* degree of the quality than the positive. It is formed by adding the suffix تر to the *Positive*, as, شیرین تر = sweeter, بزرگتر = greater, خوبتر = better.

99. The word *"than"* after the Comparative degree is expressed by از; as,

شهد شیرینتر از شکر است * شیر زیانتر از پلنگ است

Note.—The Adjective به is often used in the *positive form* when denoting *comparison*, and it is generally followed by که or از; as, خاموشي به از سخن بد است

بازوی بخت به که بازوی زور * معزولی به که مشغولي

یک طلعت زیبا به از هزار خلعت دیبا * اندکی جمال به از بسیاری مال

100. صفت مبالغه (بلغ = *it was superior*). The **Superlative** degree expresses the *highest* degree of the quality. It is formed by adding the suffix ترین to the *Positive*, as بزرگترین = greatest; شیرینترین = sweetest; خوبترین = best.

Note.—Somtimes the termination ترین is contracted into ین; as, برترین = برین = highest; بهترین = بهین = best; کهترین = کهین = smallest; مهترین = مهین = greatest.

مهین سلاطین روي زمین و بهین خواقین دنیا و دین*

Note.—The *Superlative* governs the genitive; as,

کمترین جانوران خر است * بهترین خزائن جهان هنر است

کرم و سخاوت بهترین خصایل انسان است *

(*b*) The Superlative is sometimes used like a simple adjective to express *pre-eminence* in some quality, in which case the *Izafat* is not used; as,

نگویم گرامیترین گوهري — سپردم به نامیترین شوهری

"I will not say that I have given the most excellent lady to the most illustrious husband."

Arabic
Comparative and Superlative.

101. The **Comparative** and **Superlative** degrees of Arabic adjectives are formed by prefixing the letter *alif* ا to the triliteral root.

Note.—If we reject *servile letters* from Arabic words we get their triliteral roots. The *servile letters* are س — ت — ا — م — ن — و and ي. It must be remembered that the *servile letters* may be used as *radical letters* of the triliteral root.

Arabic Comparative and Superlative.

Adjectives.	Triliteral Roots.	Comparative or Superlative.
جميل = beautiful.	جمل	اجمل
جليل = glorious.	جلّ	اجلّ
حسين = beautiful.	حسن	احسن
حقير = contemptible.	حقر	احقر
حقيق = true.	حقّ	احقّ
خالص = sincere.	خلص	اخلص
ذليل = mean.	ذلّ	اذلّ
رحيم = merciful.	رحم	ارحم
سعيد = happy.	سعد	اسعد
سافل = low.	سفل	اسفل
شريف = noble.	شرف	اشرف
شجاع = brave.	شجع	اشجع
عظيم = great.	عظم	اعظم
عادل = just.	عدل	اعدل
عزيز = precious.	عزّ	اعزّ
فاضل = excellent.	فضل	افضل
فقير = poor.	فقر	افقر
قليل = little.	قلّ	اقلّ
كبير = great.	كبر	اكبر
كامل = perfect.	كمل	اكمل
مبارك = blessed.	برك	ابرك
مشهور = celebrated.	شهر	اشهر

Double Comparative.

102. Sometimes we meet with both forms (*Arabic* and *Persian*) united; as, افضل تر = more excellent; اصعبتر = more difficult; اعظمتر = greater.

103. صفت مرکب = **Compound Epithets.**—*Compound Adjectives* are formed :—

I. By the *juxtaposition* of two nouns; جفا پیشه (جفا tyranny, پیشه = profession) tyrannical; بزدل (بز = a goat, دل = heart) timid; پری رو (پری fairy, رو face) beautiful; سنگدل (سنگ = stone, دل = heart) cruel; سرو قد (سرو = cypress, قد = stature) tall; بادپا (باد = wind; پا = foot) fleet.

II. By prefixing an adjective to a noun; as, خوبرو , خوب صورت , (خوب = good, رو = صورت = face) beautiful; نیک سیرت (نیک = good, سیرت = conduct) virtuous; پاک دامن پاک = pure, دامن = skirt) chaste.

III. By suffixing an imperative to a noun; as; زور آور , strong; دلگیر (دل = heart, گیر = seize) sorry; سرفراز (سر head; فراز = exalt) eminent; کاردان (کار = action; دان = know) skilful; دلپسند = pleasant.

IV. By suffixing a past participle to a noun; as, جهان دیده (جهان, world, دیده seen), experienced; سال خورده (سال = year, خورده = eaten) old; دل شکسته (دل, heart, شکسته broken) disappointed; جنگ آزموده (جنگ battle, آزموده, tried) veteran; کار آزموده (کار, work. آزموده , tried) skilful.

104. There is an extensive class of adjectives formed by means of *prefixes* = حروف وصل and *suffixes* = حروف ملحق.

Adjectival Prefixes.

با — *with, possessing*; as بامال = rich; باهوش = intelligent; بادل = generous.

بي — *without*; as, بیچاره, helpless; بیوقوف ignorant, بی رحم cruel; بیوفا ungrateful.

کم — *little, nothing*, as, کم خرد = کم فهم = stupid; کم بخت = unfortunate; کم زور = weak.

نا — *not*; as, ناچیز = worthless, ناأمید = hopeless; نابینا = blind; ناپسند = disagreeable; ناخوش = unhappy; ناپاک = impure.

هم — *together, same* هم دل = هم قدم = هم نشین = هم دم = intimate, همدرد = sympathetic.

Adjectival Suffixes,

105. Denoting *possession* and *fulness.*

سار — شرمسار = bashful; شاخسار = umbrageous.

گین — خشمگین angry; غمگین = sorrowful; سهمگین = horrible; اندوه گین = melancholy.

مند — هنرمند = skilful; دردمند = afflicted; سودمند = profitable; خردمند = عقلمند = wise.

ناک — خطرناک = dangerous; هولناک = dreadful; غمناک = melancholy; دردناک = painful.

دار — مالدار, زردار = rich; ابردار = cloudy; خاردار thorny.

وار — سوگوار = mournful; تقصیروار = faulty; امیدوار = hopeful.

ور — هنرور = skilful; کینه‌ور = revengeful; نامور = famous.

Adjectival Suffixes.

Denoting *likeness, similitude,* or *resemblance.*

آسا — مرد آسا = like a man, manly; مُشک آسا = like musk, odoriferous.

چرده — سیه چرده = blackish; زرد چرده = yellowish.

دیس — ماه دیس = like the moon; خوردیس = like the sun.

سا — عنبرسا = resembling ambergris; سحرسا magical.

سار — خاکسار = (earth-like) humble; گاوسار = like an ox.

سان — گُربه سان = (cat-like) deceitful. لاله سان = tulip-like

فام — گُلفام = rose-like, of a rose colour; لعلفام = ruby-coloured.

گون — گُلگون = rose-coloured, لاله گون = of a tulip colour. مَیگون (wine-coloured) reddish.

وار — دیوانه وار = like a mad man; ذرّه وار = (like an atom) humble.

وش — غُنچه وش = like a rose-bud; قمروش = ماه‌وش = moon-like.

Adjectival Suffixes,

106. Denoting *worthiness* or *fitness*.

آنہ — امیرانہ = princely; خسروانہ = شاہانہ = kingly = royal. دیوانہ (fit for a demon) mad.

وار — شاہوار (befitting a king) royal.

107. Adjectival Suffixes denoting *relation*.

اني — جسماني (*belonging* or *relating* to the body) corporal; نوراني = luminous, bright; نفساني = sensual.

ي = انساني human; ارضي = (*pertaining* to the earth) earthly; شیرازی = *of* or *relating* to Shiraz; مصری = Egyptian.

Adjectival Suffix denoting *material*.

ین = *made of*; as, زرین = golden; آتشین = fiery; چوبین = wooden; پشمین = woollen.

108. تصغیرِ صفت = **Diminutive of Adjectives.**

چہ — سبکچہ = somewhat light.

ک — تلخک = somewhat bitter; تیزک = somewhat sharp; زردک = somewhat yellow; سفیدک = somewhat white; سُرخک = somewhat red; شیرینک = somewhat sweet; گرمک = somewhat hot; خوشترک = somewhat pleasanter.

Questions on the Adjective.

I. Distinguish between صفت and موصوف (91,92).

II. Where is the صفت placed in a sentence? How is it generally joined with موصوف? (93).

III. When do you use ی and ـِ between موصوف and صفت ? (94.)

IV. Name the degrees of comparison, and state how they are formed in Persian and Arabic. (98, 100, 101)

V. What particles are used in Persian to express the word "*than*"? Use them in sentences. (99).

VI. Give instances of superlatives formed by the suffix ین and by the prefix ا. (100, 101).

VII. What adjective is used to denote comparison without the suffix تر ? (99 *Note.*)

VIII. How many servile letters are there in Persian? Name them. (101 *Note.*)

IX. How do you find the triliteral root of a word? Give examples. (101 *Note.*)

X. Mention some adjectives that take for their comparatives both the suffix تر and the prefix ا (102).

XI. Give the meanings and Arabic superlatives of the following adjectives :—ذلیل — خالص — جمیل — عالم — قلیل — رحیم — شجاع — حقیر — سعید — شریف — کامل — مبارک — صغیر.

XII. Give with meanings the positive forms of اشرف — اظهر — احق — اجل — اضعف — افقر.

XIII. What parts of speech are combined to form compound adjectives? Give examples. (103).

XIV. How are the adjectives implying "*possession*," "*similitude*" and "*fitness*" formed in Persian?

XV. Convert, by the use of affixes, the following nouns into adjectives. سهم — اُمید — غم — آرزو — نام — مُشک — خشم — سوگ — شاخ — هنر — سود.

XVI. **Give examples :—**

(*a*) **Of adjectives positive in form but used comparatively. (99)**

(*b*) **Of adjectives forming their superlatives by ین**

XVII. **Give as many examples as you can of the following four kinds of compound epithet :—(103)**

(*a*) **Noun + noun, (*b*) noun + participle, (*c*) noun + imperative, (*d*) adjective + noun.**

XVIII. **In the following, separate the prefixes and give meanings of the prefixes and words :— همدرد — کمفهم — همدل — ناپایدار — باهوش — بیوفا — کمزور — بامال — ناسپاس — بیحیا**

XIX. **Enumerate and give examples of suffixes denoting "*fulness*" and "*resemblance*" (105)**

XX. **Do adjectives ever form their diminutives? If so, how? Give examples. (108)**

XXI. **Pick out and explain all the prefixes and suffixes in the following words :— امیدوار — ماه وش — بیوفا — گربه سان — غمگین — کمخرد — نا امید — گاو سار — ماه دیس — هولناک — لاله گون — باخرد — قمروش — ذره وار**

CHAPTER X.

Pronouns = ضمایر

109. ضمیر = A Pronoun is a word used *instead of a noun*, to avoid repeating it in the same sentence; as, چون پادشاه بر تخت نشست او وزیر خود را طلبید.

110. ضمایر = Pronouns may be divided into the following classes ;—

I. إسم ضمیر = **Personal.**

II. إسم موصول = **Relative.**

III. إسم إستفهام = **Interrogative.**

IV. إسم مشترک = **Reflexive.**

V إسم إشاره = **Demonstrative.**

VI. إسم إضافت = **Possessive.**

VII. إسم تنکیر = **Indefinite.**

VIII. إسم مبهم = **Distributive.**

IX. إسم مقابل = **Reciprocal.**

111. Personal Pronouns are the *substitutes* for the names of *persons*. There are three *personal* pronouns; namely, من = I, تو = thou, او = he *or* she.

Personal Pronouns are of two kinds, *viz.* :—

I. ضمایرِ منفصل (فصل = he *separated*) Disjunctive Personal Pronouns; *namely*, من = I *pl.* ما = we; تو = thou *pl.* شما = you; او = he *pl.* ایشان = they.

II. ضمایرِ متصل (وصل = *he united*) Conjunctive Personal Pronouns; *namely*, م، ت، ش، *pl.* مان، تان، شان.

112. Disjunctive Personal Pronouns = ضمایرِ منفصل = من — تو — او are used both as *masculine* and *feminine*; as, من = I (a *man* or a *woman*), تو = thou (a *boy* or a *girl*); او = *he* or *she*.

113. Disjunctive Personal Pronouns have *two* numbers, the *singular* and *plural*; and *three* persons in each number; *namely* :—

I. متکلم (کلم = *he spoke*) *lit.* a speaker, *i. e.*, the first person; as, من = I *pl.* ما = we.

II. مخاطب (خطب = *he addressed*) *lit.* one spoken to by another, *i. e.*, the second person; as, تو = thou *pl.* شما = you.

III. غایب (غیب = *he was absent*) *lit.* absent, *i. e.*, the third person; as, وی *or* او = he *pl.* ایشان = they.

Declension of Personal pronouns.

تصریفِ ضمایر

114. مُتِکَلِّم = First Person.

واحد = *Singular.*		جمع = *Plural.*
حالتِ فاعلی **Nominative.**	من = I.	ما = we.
حالتِ مفعولی **Accusative.**	مرا = me.	مارا = us.
حالتِ مفعولی **Dative.**	مرا = me. بمن = to me.	مارا = us. بما = to us.
حالتِ جرّی **Objective.**	ازمن = from me. بامن = with me.	ازما = from us. باما = with us.
حالتِ اِضافت **Genitive.**	ـِ من = my.	ـِ ما = our.

115. مُخاطب = Second Person.

واحد = *Singular.*		جمع = *Plural.*
حالتِ فاعلی **Nominative**	تو = thou	شُما = you.
حالتِ مفعولی **Accusative**	تُرا = thee.	شُمارا = you.
حالتِ مفعولی **Dative**	تُرا = thee. بتو to thee.	شُمارا = you. بشُما = to you.

واحد = *Singular.*		جمع = *Plural.*
حالت جرّی Objective	از تو = from thee. باتو = with thee.	از شُما = from you. با شُما = with you.
حالت ندا Vocative	ای تو = O thou!	اي شُما = O you!
حالت إضافت Genitive	ـِ تو = thy.	ـِ شُما = your.

116. غایب = **Third Person.**

واحد = *Singular.*		جمع = *Plural.*
حالت فاعلي Nominative	او = he or she.	ایشان = they.
حالت مفعولي Accusative.	اورا = him.	ایشانرا = them.
حالت مفعولي Dative	اورا = him. بہاو = to him	ایشانرا = them. بہ ایشان = to them.
حالت جرّی Objective	از او = from him. با او = with him.	از ایشان = from them. با ایشان = with them.
حالت إضافت Genitive	ـِ او = his.	ـِ ایشان = their.

117. ضمایرِ متّصل = **Conjunctive Personal** *Pronouns.* When they are joined to nouns, they correspond either with the Possessive or the Dative Case; as, اسپم = اسپ من; پادشاه خلعتم بخشید اسپم گریخت

خلعت مرا =. In the first instance م is called میم إضافت, and in the second it is called میم مفعول. ت and ش are also used in the same way.

تنش روشن خطش جوشن رخش گلشن لبش شکر

118. When a noun ends in ا or و the letter ی is inserted between the noun and the *pronominal suffix*; as پای من=پایم, my foot; so, پایت and پایش; روی من=رویم, my face; so, رویت and رویش; گلویم, گلویت and گلویش; my, thy and his throat.

119. When a noun ends in ه, the letter ا is inserted between the noun and the *pronominal* termination; as, خانهٔ من=خانه ام, my house; in the same manner خانه ات and خانه اش; جامه ام, جامه ات and جامه اش; my, thy and his robe.

120. When these *pronominal terminations* are joined to a verb, they correspond with the Dative or Accusative Case of the personal pronouns, and are called ش مفعول and م, ت; as, دادم ترا = دادمت, I gave thee; پرسیدند اورا = پرسیدندش, they asked him; زرم مرا بخشید=زرم بخشید=he gave me money.

121. The plural terminations مان, تان, and شان are sometimes used in poetry to denote the possessive, as well as the dative and accusative; as, داور روزی رسان توفیق و نصرت شان دهاد "May the All-provident God give them glory and victory"

زبون گشت رومی ز پیکار شان
اجل خواست کردن گرفتار شان

"The Grecians were defeated in their battle, and *Death* desired to make them his prey."

عمر تان مدام بادا = "May your life be perpetual." جهان دیده پیری زمان بر کنار = An old experienced man had sat apart from us.

اگر ایزد دعای شان شنودی

Relative Pronouns.

122. اسم موصول (وصل *he joined*).—It stands for a noun previously expressed, *i.e.*, "ANTECEDENT" = موصول به the words که = who and چه = which, are considered as relative pronouns.

123. The pronoun که has for its antecedent (موصول به) either an animate or an inanimate object; as, پادشاهی که طرح ظلم فگند—پای دیوار ملک خویش بکند, درختی که اکنون گرفتست پای—بنیروی شخصی برآید زجای

The pronoun چه is used only for inanimate objects, and it is always preceded by such words as آن, چنان, چندان, هر.

Compound Relatives.

124. ضمایر موصول مرکب—The compound words هرکه, هر آنکه, and هرچه, هرآنچه, correspond to the words "*whosoever,*" "*whatsoever,*" or "*whichsoever,*" the former generally denoting rational beings, and the latter inferior animals, or inanimate objects; as, هرکه دست از جان بشوید—هرچه در دل آید بگوید

Interrogative Pronouns.

125. اسم استفهام—(فهم, *he understood*) —The Interrogative Pronouns are used in asking questions; they are که = who; چه = what, which; کدام = which; چند = how many, how much.

(*a*) کہ is used for persons ; as, نیکبخت کیست پدرت کیست ;ادب از کہ آموختی.

(*b*) چہ is used for things; as, دلت چہ مي خواہد ہنرت چیست ; امروز چہ خوردي

(*c*) کدام is used both for persons and things; as, کدام پسر حاضر است ; کدام عمل نیک دردنیا کردی

(*d*) چند is used for number and quantity; as, چند کتاب فارسی خواندۀ ; چند روز گذشت؟ این غرور وخشم چند ; این ستم وبیداد چند؟

Note.—Interrogation is usually expressed in Persian by the tone of the voice. In writing, however, the interrogative particle آیا is prefixed to a question, or the word یا نہ affixed to it ; as, آیا سبق خواندۀ ;طعام خوردي یا نہ

Possessive Pronouns = ضمایر مضاف الیہ.

126. The possessive pronouns, *mine, thine, his, hers*, &c., are expressed in Persian by the phrases آنِ من or از آنِ من = *mine*; آنِ تو or از آنِ تو = *thine*; آنِ او or از آنِ او = *his or her*; آنِ ما, or از آنِ ما = *our*; از آنِ شما = *your*; از آنِ ایشان = *their*.

Note.—The phrase از آن is also used with nouns, and signifies "belonging to;" این خانہ اوّل از آنِ کہ بود ؟ گفت از آنِ جدم ; چون او بگذشت از آنِ کہ شد ؟ گفت از آنِ پدرم*

Reflexive Pronouns ضمایر مشترک

127. The invariable word خُود exactly corresponds with the reflexive pronoun "*self.*"

Various Usages of خود

(*a*) It is employed equally for the first, second and third persons in the singular as well as the plural; as:—

واحد = Singular.	جمع = Plural.
من خود = I myself.	ما خود = we ourselves.
تو خود = thou thyself.	شُما خود = you yourselves.
او خود = he himself, or she herself.	ایشان خود = they themselves.

(*b*) It is employed as a substitute for a possessive pronoun if it be of the same person with the nominative of the sentence; as, I write *my* letter, من خط خود مي نویسم; *he* went to *his* place, او بجائ خود رفت ; من جامهٔ خود میخواهم

(*c*) It is also used without any personal pronoun as the nominative of a verb, and the verbal suffix clearly expresses the sense; as, خود کردم, I myself did it; خود کردهٔ. In the third person singular, ش is sometimes added to it for the sake of emphasis; as, خودش گفت he himself said.

Note.—Sometimes, instead of خود the words خویش and خویشتن are used; as, بچشم خویش دیدم — خویشتنرا بزرگ پنداری ;پای دیوار مُلک خویش بکند

Demonstrative Pronouns اِسم اِشارہ

Demonstrative Pronouns point out the things to which they refer. They are divided into

I اِسم اشارہ قریب (شار, *he pointed*; قریب *near*). It is used to point out an object near the speaker; as, این, this.

II. إسم إشارہ بعید (بعید, *remote*).—It is used to point out an object distant from the speaker; as, آن, that.

129. Different Uses of این and آن

(*a*) These pronouns are used both for animate and inanimate objects, and are applicable to all genders and numbers and always precede the substantive to which they refer; as این مرد this man; این مردان these men; آن کتاب that book, آن کتابها, those books; آن زن, آن زنان.

(*b*) When این and آن are both used together in a sentence to represent persons or things that are *near* and *distant* from the speaker, they signify "*the latter*" and "*the former*" respectively; as,

سگ و دربان چو یافتند غریب
این گریبانش گیرد و آن دامن

Indefinite Pronouns.

130. The Indefinite Pronouns speak of *persons* or *things* in a vague or general manner; these are کسي — هیچ = any; هریک every one; چند, some.

Distributive Pronouns.

131. The Distributive Pronouns denote the persons or things that make up a number considered *separately*; they are هر each, every, either.

Reciprocal Pronouns.

132. The Reciprocal Pronouns denote the mutual influence which the agents and objects have upon each other; these are, *each other* = هریک = *one another*.

Questions on the Pronouns.

I. Classify the pronouns with their English equivalents. (**110**)

II. How are اسم ضمیر and اسم اشارہ sub-divided?

III. Name the three persons and give their literal and grammatical meanings. (113)

IV. Explain the terms مُنفصل and مُتصل (111)

V. Decline من—تو and او in both numbers. (114-116)

VI. How are conjunctive personal pronouns used with nouns ending in ا , و and ہ? give examples. (118,119)

VII. What are the plural forms of م — ت — ش ?
Use them in sentences. (121)

VIII. How are "*mine, thine, his, our, yours, their, whose, whosoever, whatsoever*" expressed in Persian?

IX. What does "از آن" signify? Use it in a sentence. (126)

X. Explain the different uses of خود with examples. (127)

XI. What do you know of the words خویش — خودش and خویشتن? Form sentences. (127)

XII. State the various usages of the Demonstrative Pronouns این and آن. (129)

XIII. What do you understand by ضمیر مُضاف الیہ — اسم تنکیر — ضمیر مُشترک — موصول بہ — اسم مُبہم

XIV. State the difference in usage between the interrogative pronouns کہ — چہ , and کدام . (125)

XV. What Interrogative pronoun is used to denote both number and quantity? (125)

First Parsing Model.

I. — فریدون مرا زر بخشید

فریدون — اسم خاص — جنس تذکیر — حالت فاعلي — متعلق بفعل "بخشید"

مرا — اسم ضمیر مُتکلم — جنس مُذکر — عدد واحد — حالت مفعولي متعلق بفعل "بخشید"

زر ــــ اسم جنس ــ جنس غیر ذي روح ــ حالت
مفعولي متعلق بفعل "بخشید"

باخشید ــــ فعل

Second Parsing Model.

II.ــــ مرد ضریر سگی داشت کہ اورا رہ نمود

مرد ــــ اسم عام ــ جنس مذکر ــ عدد واحد ــ
حالت فاعلي متعلق بفعل "داشت"

ضریر ــــ صفت منسوب بموصوف "مرد"

سگی ــــ اسم عام ــ جنس تذکیر ــ عدد واحد
حالت مفعولي متعلق بفعل "داشت"

داشت ــــ فعل

کہ ــــ اسم موصول ــ جنس مذکر ــ حالت
فاعلي متعلق بفعل "نمود"

اورا ــــ اسم ضمیر غایب ــ جنس مذکر ــ عدد واحد
حالت مفعولي متعلق بفعل "نمود"

رہ ــــ اسم عام ــ جنس غیر ذي روح ــ عدد واحد
حالت مفعولي متعلق بفعل "نمود"

نمود ــــ فعل

CHAPTER XI.

فعل = Verb.

فعل—(*lit.* an *action*). A verb is a word which *affirms* or *asserts* something.

133. اقسام افعال = **Classification of Verbs.**

I. فعل متعدي = **Transitive.**

II. فعل لازمي = **Intransitive.**

III. فعل معروف = **Active.**

IV. فعل مجهول = **Passive.**

V. فعل مجبور = **Causal.**

VI. فعل معاون = **Auxiliary.**

VII. فعل ناقص = **Defective.**

VIII. فعل بيفاعل = **Impersonal.**

IX. فعل مشترک = **Reflexive.**

X. فعل نفي و نهي = **Negative and Prohibitive.**

XI. فعل مسمي = **Denominative.**

XII. فعل سماعي = **Strong** *or* **Irregular.**

XIII. فعل قياسي = **Weak** *or* **Regular.**

XIV. فعل مركب = **Compound.**

134. فعل متعدي = **Transitive Verb.**—When the action denoted by the verb is directed towards some object, the verb is termed transitive; as, آن سوداگر اسپي را خريد ; استاد شاگرد را طلبيد

135. فعل لازمي = **Intransitive Verb.**—When the action denoted by the verb is not directed towards some object, the verb is termed intransitive; as, استاد مي آيد ;پادشاه بشكار رفت.

136. فعل معروف (عرف = *he knew*). **Active Verb.**—When the subject of a verb is expressed, the verb is called active; as, پادشاه بر تخت نشست.

137. فعل مجهول (جهل = *it was unknown*).—**A Passive Verb** is that of which the nominative or agent is not expressed.

RULE

For the Formation of the Passive Voice.

138. The Passive Voice = صيغهٔ مجهول is formed by adding the various tenses of شدن to the past participle of a *transitive* verb.

N. B.—Intransitive Verbs have no Passive Voice.

Tenses.	Examples.	Meanings.
Infinitive.	پرسيده شدن	to be asked.
Past tense.	پرسيده شد	was asked.
Imperfect.	پرسيده مي شد	was being asked.
Perfect.	پرسيده شده است	has been asked.
Pluperfect.	پرسيده شده بود	had been asked.
Future.	پرسيده خواهد شد	will be asked.
Future perfect.	پرسيده شده باشد	shall have been asked.
Aorist.	پرسيده شود	may be asked.
Present.	پرسيده مي شود	is asked.

Note.—The word صیغه literally signifies "*the form*," and is applicable to many other terms; as, صیغهٔ ماضي = past *tense*; صیغهٔ امر = imperative *mood*; صیغهٔ معروف = active *voice*; صیغهٔ امکاني = potential *mood*.

139. فعل مجبور **Causal or Causative Verb** is formed by adding the termination انیدن or اندن to the imperative of a verb; as,

Infinitives.	Imperatives.	Causal Verb.
پریدن, to fly.	پر	پراندن or پرانیدن
پوشیدن, to cover.	پوش	پوشانیدن
ترسیدن, to fear.	ترس	ترسانیدن
جستن, to jump.	جه	جهانیدن
خوردن, to eat.	خور	خورانیدن
دویدن, to run.	دو	دوانیدن
رسیدن, to reach.	رس	رسانیدن

140. فعل معاون (عون = be *helped*). **Auxiliary Verb.**—An Auxiliary *or* Helping Verb is one which assists other verbs in forming their *voice*, *mood*, or *tense*.

Auxiliary Verbs.	Tenses formed by the help of the auxiliary verbs.	Examples.
هستن	Perfect tense.	پرسیده است
بودن	Pluperfect tense.	پرسیده بود
خواستن	Future tense.	خواهد پرسید
باشیدن	Future perfect.	پرسیده باشد
توانستن	Potential mood.	توانست پرسید
شدن	Passive voice.	پرسیده شد

Note.—Some of these verbs (خواستن — شدن) are also capable of being used independently; as,

دلت چه میخواهد؟ * وقت جوانی بشد از دست من

شد غلامی که آب جو آرد * از من چه میخواهی؟

141. فعل ناقص (نقص = *it was defective*')— **Defective Verb.**—Verbs that have not the full *complement* of tenses are called defective.

Infinitives.	Meanings.	Forms in use.
آغشتن	to mix.	آغشته
آغاشتن	to accumulate.	آغاشته
خستن	to wound.	خسته
بایستن	to become.	باید — بایسته
شایستن	to be worth.	شاید — شایسته

N.B.—In Persian there exists a number of verbs, some of the regular forms of which (chiefly the *Imperative*, *Aorist*, and *Present*) seldom or never occur.

Infinitives.	Forms wanting or not in use. *Imp.*; *Aor.*; *Pres.*	Verbs substituted in the forms wanting.
ابشتن = to conceal	,, ,, ,,	پوشیدن
الفاختن = to collect.	,, ,, ,,	اندوختن
آختن = / آهیختن = } to draw	,, ,, ,,	برکشیدن
آغشتن = to mix.	,, ,, ,,	آمیختن
آغاشتن = to accumulate.	,, ,, ,,	گرد کردن

Infinitives.	Forms wanting or not in use. *Imp.; Aor.; Pres.*	Verbs substituted in the forms wanting.
آغوشیدن = to embrace.	,, ,, ,,	در آغوش کردن / در بر کشیدن
آلفتن = to be confounded.	,, ,, ,,	آشوفتن
برشتن = to fry, roast.	,, ,, ,,	بریان کردن
خستن = to wound.	,, ,, ,,	فگاردن
سرشتن = to knead; to create.	,, ,, ,,	عجین کردن
شیفتن = to be distracted.	,, ,, ,,	آشوفتن
مُشتن = to rub.	,, ,, ,,	مالیدن

142 فعل بي فاعل = **Impersonal Verb.**—The infinitives بایستن and شایستن are called impersonal verbs, because باید and شاید are used impersonally with nouns and pronouns in the accusative case; as,

آدمیرا صبر باید * پادشاه را کرم باید

مارا خردمندي كافي باید كه تدبیر مملکت را شاید

143. فعل مشترک (شرک = *he divided*).—**Reflexive Verbs** are those which are used transitively as well as intransitively; as,

Infinitives.	Transitive.	Intransitive.
آموختن	to teach.	to learn.
آمیختن	to mix.	to associate.
پختن	to cook.	to ripen.
تاختن	to attack.	to run.
ریختن	to pour.	to flow.
نمودن	to show.	to appear.

144. فعل نفي — **Negative Verb.**—A verb is rendered negative by prefixing the particle نہ (or ن); as, نہ رسید, he did not reach; نکردہ است, he has not done; نخواہد آمد, he will not come.

This ن is called نون نفي. With the imperative, م is used to express prohibition; as, مکن don't do; مخور, don't eat. This م is called ميم نهي.

145 نون نفي and ميم نهي — **Negative** ن **and Prohibitive** م.—The distinction between the negative particles م and ن used for prohibition and negation is this, that م is used for the negative imperative only, and ن for all other tenses.

Note.—(*a*) When verbs beginning with الف are preceded by باي زايد (the redundant ب), نون نفي (the negative ن) or ميم نهي (the prohibitive م), the ا is changed into ي; as اندیشیدن; so, میندازـ نینداخت ـ بینداخت ـ انداخت ـ بیندیش ـ میندیش.

(*b*) When the same particles (ب, ن and م) are prefixed to the verbs beginning with الف ممدوده, the first ا is changed into ي and the second ا is retained; as, آموخت میاموزـ نیاموخت ـ بیاموخت, &c.

145. a. افعال مسمي = **Denominative Verbs** are those that are formed from nouns by adding یدن; as, جنگ + یدن = جنگیدن = to fight; خواب + یدن = خوابیدن = to sleep; ستیز + یدن = ستیزیدن = to quarrel; فہم + یدن = فہمیدن = to understand; طلب + یدن = طلبیدن = to call; پسند + یدن = پسندیدن to approve.

146. افعال قیاسي — **Weak or Regular Verbs,** *i. e.*, those whose imperatives are formed according to the established rules ; as, آموختن ; افتادن.

147. افعال سماعی — **Strong or Irregular Verbs,** *i.e.*, those whose imperatives are not formed according to the rules; as, دادن ; کردن

148. Compound Verbs = افعال مرکب are formed—

I. By prefixing a noun to an infinitive; as, امید داشتن = to hope; ستم کردن = to oppress; سوگند خوردن = to swear; غم خوردن = to grieve; ثنا کردن = to praise; حسد بردن = to envy; عرض نمودن = to request; صلاح دادن = to advise.

II. By prefixing an adjective to an infinitive; as, پاک کردن = to purify; خوش کردن = to please; دراز کردن = to lengthen; روشن ساختن = to illuminate; پر کردن = to fill; آزاد کردن = to free; خشک ساختن = to dry; تمام ساختن = to complete.

III. By prefixing a preposition to an infinitive; as, در آمدن = to enter; درخواستن = to propose; دریافتن = to think; برگشتن = to return; بر آوردن = to produce.

IV. By prefixing an adverb to an infinitive; as, بالارفتن = to ascend; فروخوردن = to swallow; فرود آمدن = to descend; باز گشتن = to return; باز کردن = to open.

Inflection of Verbs.—Verbs are inflected for voice, mood, tense, number and person.

Number and Person.

149. Verbs have number and person. To denote the number and person of a verb, the following suffixes are used:—

Verbal Suffixes or Personal Terminations.

Person.	Singular.	Plural.
مُتكلم 1st person.	م	يم
مُخاطب 2nd person.	ی	يد
غايب 3rd person.	د or ت	ند

Note.—In the past and the past imperfect tenses د or ت is used for the third person singular, because the infinitive always ends in دن or تن; as, كرد , مى كرد , آموخت , مي آموخت. In the aorist and the present د is always used for the third person singular; as, كند, آموزد, مي كند.

N.B.—In all tenses, formed by the help of the auxiliary verbs, the verbal suffixes are added to the auxiliary and not to the principal verb; as, رفت خواهم, رسيده باشند, خواهی آمد, ميتوانيم ساخت, آورده بودند.

Sometimes the verbal suffixes م and ي are added to nouns, pronouns and adjectives to represent the full forms هستم and هستي, respectively; as, ماری تو كه هركرا بينی بزني

منم سلطان اين مُلك ; تو حكيم كاملي

The Three Tenses = ازمنهٔ ثلاثه

150. As time is divisible into Past, Present and Future, we have three primary tenses in Persian, which are called ازمنه ثلاثه (ازمنه *pl.* of زمان, time, tense and ثلث three); these are:—

I. زمان ماضي **Past Tense,** which shows an action already done; as, رفت=he went.

II. زمان حال **Present Tense,** which shows an action as being done; as, ميرود = he is going.

III. زمان مستقبل **Future Tense,** which shows an action to be done; as, خواهد رفت = he will go.

151. زمان ماضي **The Past Tense,** (3rd pers. sing.) is formed by the omission of the final letter ن from the infinitive; as, پرسيدن P.T. پرسيد.

Singular=واحد	**Plural**=جمع
1st pers. پرسيدم I asked.	پرسيديم we asked.
2nd pers. پرسيدي thou askedst.	پرسيديد you asked.
3rd pers. پرسيد he asked.	پرسيدند they asked.

152. زمان حال—**The Present Indefinite or the Present Imperfect Tense** is formed by prefixing the particle مي (*sometimes* همي), and adding the verbal suffixes to the imperative; as, پرسيدن imperative پرس.

Singular = واحد	**Plural**=جمع
1st pers. مي پرسم I ask *or* I am asking.	مي پرسيم, we ask *or* we are asking.
2nd pers. مي پرسي thou askest *or* thou art asking.	مي پرسيد, you ask *or* you are asking.
3rd pers. مي پرسد he asks *or* he is asking.	ميپرسند, they ask *or* they are asking.

153. زمان مستقبل (قبل, *before*). — **The Future Tense** is formed by prefixing خواه (*the imperative* of خواستن), with personal terminations to the past tense of the principal verb.

Singular = واحد	Plural = جمع
1st pers. خواهم پرسید, I will ask.	خواهیم پرسید, we will ask.
2nd pers. خواهی پرسید, thou wilt ask.	خواهید پرسید, you will ask.
3rd pers. خواهد پرسید, he will ask.	خواهند پرسید, they will ask.

Note.—In poetry the infinitive is sometimes used instead of the past tense; as, — که خواهی شدن ناگهان پایمال

که خواهم شدن سوی ایران زمین

که خواهد کردنت روزی فراموش ; مرا کسی نخواهد خریدن به هیچ

154. مضارع. — **The Aorist** (which expresses *indefinite time*) is formed by adding the personal terminations to the imperative of a verb; as, پرسیدن imperative پرس.

Singular = واحد	Plural = جمع
1st pers. پرسم, I may ask.	پرسیم, we may ask.
2nd pers. پرسی, thou mayst ask.	پرسید, you may ask.
3rd pers. پرسد, he ma ask.	پرسند, they may ask.

N. B.—The principal use of this tense is to express an infinitive clause; as, نمیخواهم که روي او ببینم = "I do not wish *to see his face.*" آمقان خواست که چوبي بردارد وکودکانرا بزند • آن پسر خواست که گلها بچیند و به خانهٔ خود برد • من میخواهم که به خانهٔ روم و طعام بخورم •

Note.—It has sometimes the force of the future tense; as,
دلا گر کني راستي اختیار — شود خلق دنیا ترا دوستدار
گریک سخن قبول کني هرچه بخواهی ترا بدهم

155. PRESENT TENSES = از منهٔ حال

The Present Indefinite } = حال زمان
The Present Imperfect }

The Present Perfect = ماضی قریب

PAST TENSES = از منهٔ ماضی

The Past Indefinite = ماضی مطلق

The Past Imperfect = ماضی استمراري

The Past Perfect = ماضی بعید

The Habitual Past = ماضی مستعمل

The Desiderative *or* } ماضی تمنا =
The Optative Past }

The Subjunctive Past = ماضی شرطیه

The Potential Past = ماضی إمکاني

156. FUTURE TENSES = از منهٔ مستقبل

The Future Indefinite = زمان مستقبل

The Future Perfect = ماضی متشکی

The Future Perfect Continuous } ماضی استمراری متشکی

157. Varieties of ماضی=اِقسام ماضی

I. ماضی مطلق=**The Past Indefinite.**

II. ماضی اِستمراری=**The Past Imperfect.**

III. ماضی مستعمل=**The Habitual Past.**

IV. ماضی قریب=**The Present Perfect.**

V. ماضی بعید=**The Past Perfect.**

VI. ماضی متشکی=**The Future Perfect.**

VII. ماضی اِستمراری متشکی = **The Future Perfect Continuous.**

VIII. ماضی تمنیِّ = { **The Desiderative (or) The Optative Past.**

IX. ماضی شرطیہ=**The Subjunctive Past.**

X. ماضی اِمکاني=**The Potential Past.**

158. ماضی مطلق = **The Past Indefinite** is already explained (*vide* Article 151).

159. ماضی اِستمراری , (مر= *continued*).— **The Past Imperfect** is formed by prefixing the particle مي (*sometimes* ہمي) to the Past Tense; as,

Singular = واحد	**Plural** = جمع
1st pers. مي پرسیدم=I was asking.	می پرسیدیم = we were asking.
2nd pers. می پرسیدي = thou wast asking.	می پرسیدید = you were asking.
3rd pers. می پرسید = he was asking.	مي پرسیدند = they were asking.

160. ماضی مستعمل، (عمل *he practised*).—**The Habitual Past** is formed by suffixing ي to all the persons of the Past Tense except the 2nd pers.; as,

Singular=واحد	**Plural**=جمع
1st pers. پرسیدمي = I used to ask.	پرسیدیمي = we used to ask.
2nd pers. Not used.	Not used.
3rd pers. پرسیدی = he used to ask.	پرسیدندی = they used to ask.

N.B—The four following tenses are compounded of the Past Participle and Auxiliaries. This Participle (اسم مفعول) is formed by adding ة to the Past Tense, as, پرسید, past participle پرسیدة, asked or having asked.

161. ماضی قریب (قرب, *it approached*).—**The Perfect Tense** represents an action *or* event that has only *just now* been completed. It is formed by adding the terminations ام — ای — است (*for the singular*) and ایم — اید — اند (*for the plural*) to the past participle of the principal verb; as,

Singluar=واحد	**Plural**=جمع
1st pers. پرسیدة ام = I have asked.	پرسیدة ایم = we have asked.
2nd pers. پرسیدۀ = or پرسیدة ای = thou hast asked.	پرسیدة اید = you have asked.
3rd pers. پرسیدة است = he has asked.	پرسیدة اند = they have asked.

Note.—When ام and است are combined with the words چہ - کہ or رلہ, the ة is often rejected, and the ا *alif* is changed into ی; as, کیست = کہ است, who is he? چہ است

=چيست what is it ? نہ است=نيست, it is not. كہ ام= كيم = who am I ? نہ ام = نيم = I am not.

162. ماضي بعيد (بعد, *it was distant.*)—**The Pluperfect** expresses an action *or* event which *was past* before some other *past* action *or* event mentioned in the sentence. It is formed by adding بود (*the past tense of* بودن *to be*) with personal terminations to the past participle of the principal verb; as,

Singular=واحد	**Plural**=جمع
1st pers. پرسيده بودم, I had asked.	پرسيده بوديم = we had asked.
2nd pers. پرسيده بودی, thou hadst asked.	پرسيده بوديد = you had asked.
3rd pers. پرسيده بود, he had asked.	پرسيده بودند = they had asked.

163. ماضی متشكی (شك *he doubted*).—**The Future Perfect** denotes that a future action *or* event will be *completed before* another future action *or* event. It is formed by adding باش (*the imperative of* باشيدن *to be*) with verbal suffixes to the past participle of the principal verb; as,

Singular=واحد	**Plural**=جمع
1st pers. پرسيده باشم= I shall have asked.	پرسيده باشيم = we shall have asked.
2nd pers. پرسيده باشي= thou shalt have asked.	پرسيده باشيد = you shall have asked.
3rd pers. پرسيده باشد, he shall have asked.	پرسيده باشند= they shall have asked.

164. ماضی استمراری متشکی = **The Future Perfect Continuous Tense** is formed by prefixing the particle مي to the future perfect; as,

Singular = واحد	**Plural** = جمع
1st pers. می پرسیده باشم, I shall have been asking.	می پرسیده باشیم = we shall have been asking.
2nd pers. می پرسیده باشی thou shalt have been asking.	می پرسیده باشید = you shall have been asking.
3rd pers. می پرسیده باشد, he shall have been asking.	می پرسیده باشند = they shall have been asking.

165. ماضی تمنا (منی = *desire*).—**The Optative** or *Desiderative Past* expresses the desire of doing that which is indicated by the *verb*.

It is formed by prefixing the particle کاش or کاشکی to the Habitual Past; as,

Singular = واحد	**Plural** = جمع
1st pers. کاش پرسیدمی, would I had asked.	کاش پرسیدیمی = would we had asked.
2nd pers. Not used.	Not used.
3rd pers. کاش پرسیدی, would he had asked.	کاش پرسیدندی = would they had asked.

166. ماضی شرطیہ (شرط = *condition*).—**The Subjunctive Past** is formed by prefixing the particle اگر to the Past Imperfect.

Singular = واحد	Plural = جمع
1st pers. اگر می پرسیدم, If I asked.	اگر می پرسیدیم = If we asked.
2nd pers. اگر می پرسیدی If thou askedst.	اگر می پرسیدید = If you asked.
3rd pers. اگر می پرسید, If he asked.	اگر می پرسیدند = If they asked.

Note.—Sometimes the Aorist is also used in the Subjunctive Mood (صیغه شرطیه); as,

Singular = واحد	Plural = جمع
1st pers. اگر پرسم, If I ask.	اگر پرسیم = If we ask.
2nd pers. اگر پرسی, If thou askest.	اگر پرسید = If you ask.
3rd pers. اگر پرسد, If he ask.	اگر پرسند = If they ask.

N.B.—Sometimes the Habitual Past is used in (صیغه شرطیه) as; اگر این خر نبودی پیش بیطار نرفتي

اگر من پذیرفتمی تاج و تخت—نبودی ترا این بزرگی و بخت *

167. ماضی اِمکانی (مکنه, *power*).—**The Potential Past** is formed by prefixing the past tense of توانستن to the past tense of a verb; as,

Singular = واحد	Plural = جمع
1st pers. توانستم پرسید, I could ask.	توانستیم پرسید = we could ask.
2nd pers. توانستی پرسید, thou couldst ask.	توانستید پرسید = you could ask.
3rd pers. توانست پرسید, he could ask.	توانستند پرسید = they could ask.

168. ماضي معطوفه (عطف = conjunction).—The Conjunctive Past is formed by prefixing the past participle of a verb to the past tense of another verb; as طلبيده گفت = طلبيد و گفت, having called he said, or he called and said; پرسيده رفتند, having asked they went. In this instance the letter ه has the same force as that expressed by the conjunction و; thus, پسرش خمر خورده عربده کرده خون کسي ريخته گريخت; أستاد آمده شاگردان را درس داده بازرفت

The Potential Mood = صيغه إمكاني

169. The Potential Mood is formed by prefixing the respective tenses of توانستن to the past tense of a verb. The following tenses are used in صيغهٔ إمكاني

I. صيغهٔ إمكاني باماضي, **Potential Past.**

II. صيغهٔ إمكاني با إستمراري, **Potential Imperfect.**

III. صيغهٔ إمكاني بامضارع, **Potential Aorist.**

IV. صيغهٔ إمكاني باحال, **Potential Present.**

صيغهٔ إمكاني با ماضي, is the same as ماضي إمكاني (*vide* article 167).

170. صيغهٔ إمكاني با إستمراري — **The Potential Imperfect** is formed by prefixing the Past Imperfect of توانستن to the past tense of a verb; as.,

Singular = واحد	Plural = جمع
1st pers. مي توانستم پرسيد, I could ask.	مى توانستيم پرسيد = we could ask.
2nd pers. مى توانستى پرسيد thou couldst ask.	مى توانستيد پرسيد = you could ask.
3rd pers. مى توانست پرسيد, he could ask.	مى توانستند پرسيد = they could ask.

171. صيغهٔ اِمكانى با مضارع—The Potential Aorist is formed by prefixing the Aorist of توانستن to the past tense of a verb; as,

Singular = واحد	Plural = جمع
1st pers. توانم پرسيد, I can ask.	توانيم پرسيد, we can ask.
2nd pers. تواني پرسيد, thou canst ask.	توانيد پرسيد, you can ask.
3rd pers. تواند پرسيد, he can ask.	توانند پرسيد, they can ask.

172. صيغهٔ اِمكانى با حال—The Potential Present is formed by prefixing the present tense of توانستن to the past tense of a verb; as,

Singular = واحد	Plural = جمع
1st pers. مي توانم پرسيد, I can ask.	مي توانيم پرسيد, we can ask.
2nd pers. مي تواني پرسيد, thou canst ask.	مي توانيد پرسيد, you can ask.
3rd pers. مي تواند پرسيد, he can ask.	مي توانند پرسيد, they can ask.

Participles.

173. إسم مفعول — **The Past or Perfect Participle** expresses the *completion* of an action. It is formed by adding ه to the past tense; as, کرده = done *or* having done; گفته, said *or* having said; آورده, brought *or* having brought; طلبیده called *or* having called.

Note.—In Arabic إسم مفعول is formed by prefixing م and inserting و between the second and third letters of the triliteral root; as, مظلوم, oppressed; مکتوب, written; مخلوق created; محکوم, ordered; مقتول, slaughtered; معلوم, معروف, known; مقبول, accepted.

إسم حالیه — **The Present or Imperfect Participle** expresses the *continuance* of an action. It is formed by adding ان to the imperative; as, ان + دو = دوان = running; ان + کن = کنان = doing; ان + ترس = ترسان = fearing; ان + نویس = نویسان = writing. دیدندش گریزان و افتان و خیزان

صیغهٔ امر The Imperative Mood.

174. امر is divided into the following classes:—

I. امر حاضر = **Simple Imperative.**

II. امر مدامی = **Continuative Imperative.**

III. امر نهي = **Prohibitive Imperative.**

IV. امر غایب = **Imperative in the third person.**

V. امر دعا or تمنا } **Optative** or **Desiderative** } **Imperative.**

175. امر حاضر (حاضر, *present*).—It is the word of command and, therefore, in its simplest form is always in the second person singular or plural; as, خوان, read thou, *pl.* خوانید; خور, eat thou, *pl.* خورید; پرور, nourish thou, *pl.* پرورید.

176. امر مداومی (دام, he *continued*).—**Continuative Imperative** *or* the Imperative *of Duration, i.e.,* the command to keep an action continued. It is formed by prefixing the particle می to امر حاضر; as, میخوان = go on reading; می خور = go on eating; مي پرس = go on asking; مینویس = go on writing.

177. امر نہی **Prohibitive Imperative.**—It is formed by prefixing the negative particle م to امرحاضر; as, مکن *pl.* مکنید = do not do; مپرس *pl.* مپرسید = do not ask. مخور *pl.* مخورید = do not eat.

Note.—This م is called میم نہي = prohibitive م and it is used for the negative imperative only. In all other tenses the negative is formed by prefixing the particle ن, which is called نون نفي = Negative ن; as, نگفت, نرود, نبود, نکرد.

178. امر غایب (غیب, *absent*)—Imperative in the third person singular or plural; as, رود = he shall go *or* let him go; کند = he shall do *or* let him do; پرسد = he shall ask, *or* let him ask; رسد = he shall reach, *or* let him arrive.

179. امر تمنّا = **Optative** *or* **Desiderative Imperative.**—It expresses the desire of doing that which is indicated by the *verb.* It is formed by inserting the letter ا between the last two letters of امرغایب, as, رواد = may he go! رساد = may he arrive! بخشاد = may he bestow! آمرزاد = God grant he may forgive!

Note.—The Negative Optative is formed by prefixing م or ن to the optative; as, نماناد = ن + ماناد = may he not remain! *i. e.*, may he perish! نکناد = may he not do!

Formation of the Imperative.

180. Every Infinitive = مصدر ends in دن or تن, as, طلبیدن = to call, انداختن = to throw. Hence the two terminations دن and تن are called علامت مصدر, *i.e.*, the sign of the Infinitive.

181. Infinitives in دن are preceded by ا, ر, ن, و, and ي. (These letters may be grouped into the word روانی = a course.)

Note.—There are three other letters, *viz.*, ت, ز, and م which also precede دن, but as there is only one infinitive of each kind, they are excluded from the general rule; as, ستدن to take (Imp. ستان); زدن, to strike (Imp. زن); آمدن to come. (Imp. آی).

182. Infinitives in تن are always preceded by خ, س, ش, and ف.

Rules for the Formation of the Imperative.

183. General Rule.—In order to form the Imperative, the termination دن or تن must be rejected from the Infinitive, and the following rules should be applied :—

Rule I. When ا precedes the termination دن it is rejected; as, افعال قیاسی = *Weak or Regular.*

افتادن = to fall, *Imp.* افت; ایستادن = to stand, *Imp.* ایست; فرستادن, = to send, *Imp.* فرست; نهادن = to put, *Imp.* نه.

Exceptions—Strong or Irregular Verbs.

افعال سماعي	Meanings.	Imperatives.
آمادن	to prepare.	آمای or آما
دادن	to give.	ده
زادن	to be born.	زا or زای
ستادن	to take.	ستان
گشادن	to open.	گشا or گشای

Note.—There are some infinitives in which a letter or two may occasionally be omitted; as, ایستادن = اِستادن = ستادن = to stand; افتادن = فتادن = to fall; نگریستن = نگرستن = to look; انگندن = فگندن = to throw.

Rule II. When خ precedes the termination تن it is changed into ز. *Examples*—

افعال قياسي	Imp.	افعال قياسي	Imp.
آموختن, to teach.	آموز	پیختن, to sift.	پیز
انداختن, to throw.	انداز	توختن, to draw, seek.	توز
اندوختن, to collect.	اندوز	تاختن to run.	تاز
انگیختن, to excite.	انگیز	دوختن, to sew.	دوز
آمیختن, to mix.	آمیز	ریختن, to pour.	ریز
افروختن, to kindle.	افروز	ساختن, to make.	ساز
آویختن, to hang.	آویز	سوختن, to burn.	سوز
		گریختن, to flee.	گریز
باختن { to play. to lose.	باز	گداختن, to melt.	گداز
پرداختن, to engage.	پرداز	نواختن, to cherish.	نواز
پختن, to cook.	پز	افراختن, to exalt.	افراز

Exceptions— افعال سماعي = Strong Verbs.

سيختن = to weigh, *Imp.* سنج; شناختن = to recognise, *Imp.* شناس; فروختن = to sell, *Imp.* فروش; گسيختن = to break, *Imp.* گسل; دوختن = to milk, *Imp.* دوش.

Rule III. When ر precedes the termination دن it is retained. *Examples*—

افعال قياسي	Imp.	افعال قياسي	Imp.
افسُردن, to congeal, to wither.	افسُر	سپُردن or سپاردن, to entrust.	سپار or سپر
افشُردن to squeeze.	افشُر	سُتردن, to shave.	ستر
افشاردن, to press.	افشار	شُمردن, to reckon.	شُمر
آزاردن or آزردن, to injure.	آزر or آزار	گُستردن, to spread.	گُستر
بُردن, to carry.	بُر	گُذاردن to perform.	گذار
پروردن, to nourish.	پرور	پژمُردن, to wither, to fade.	پژمر
خوردن, to eat.	خور		

Exceptions— افعال سماعي, Strong Verbs.

كردن = to do, *Imp.* كُن; مُردن to die, *Imp.* مير.

Rule IV. (*a*) When س precedes the termination تن, it is sometimes changed into ه. *Examples*—

جُستن = to jump, *Imp.* جه; خواستن = to desire, *Imp.* خواه; رُستن = to escape, *Imp.* ره; كاستن = to lessen, *Imp.* كاه.

(*b*) س is sometimes changed into وی. *Examples*—
جُستن=to seek, *Imp.* جُوی ; رُستن=to grow, *Imp.* رُوی; شُستن=to wash, *Imp.* شُوی.

(*c*) س is sometimes changed into ی; as, آراستن, to adorn, *Imp.* آرای; پیراستن to adorn, *Imp.* پیرای.

(*d*) س is sometimes rejected. *Examples*—
دانستن=to know, *Imp.* دان; زیستن=to live, *Imp.* زی; گریستن = to weep, *Imp.* گری; مانستن = to resemble, *Imp.* مان; نگریستن = to behold, *Imp.* نگر.

Exceptions—افعال سماعي=Strong Verbs.
بستن = to bind, *Imp.* بند; پیوستن = to join, *Imp.* پیوند; خاستن=to rise, *Imp.* خیز; شکستن = to break, *Imp.* شکن; گُسستن = to break, *Imp.* گُسل; نشستن = to sit, *Imp.* نشین; ریستن=to spin, *Imp.* ریس.

Rule V. When ش precedes the termination تن, it is changed into ر. *Examples*—

افعال قیاسي	Imp.	افعال قیاسي	Imp.
انباشتن, to fill.	انبار	گُذشتن, to pass.	گُذر
انگاشتن, to suppose.	انگار	گُذاشتن, to leave.	گُذار
پنداشتن, to think.	پندار	گُماشتن, to send.	گُمار
داشتن, to keep.	دار	نگاشتن, to paint.	نگار
کاشتن, to sow.	کار		

Exceptions—افعال سماعي=Strong Verbs.

افراشتن, to exalt.	افراز	گشتن, to turn.	گرد
آغاشتن, to heap up.	آغاش	نوشتن, to write.	نویس
کُشتن, to kill.	کُش	هِشتن, to leave.	هِل

Rule VI. (*a*) When ف precedes the termination تن, it is changed into پ, *Examples*—

آشوفتن, to be disturbed	آشوب	شتافتن, to hasten.	شتاب
تافتن {to shine. to twist.	تاب	فریفتن, to deceive.	فریب
		کوفتن, to knock.	کوب
روفتن, to sweep.	روب	یافتن, to find.	یاب

(*b*) ف is sometimes changed into و. *Examples*— رفتن = to go, *Imp.* رو ; کافتن = to dig, *Imp.* کاو ; گفتن = to say, *Imp.* گو ; شنفتن = to hear, *Imp.* شنو.

(*c*) ف is sometimes retained; as, بافتن = to weave, *Imp.* باف ; شکافتن = to split, *Imp.* شکاف ; شگفتن = to blossom, *Imp.* شگف ; نهفتن = to conceal, *Imp.* نهف.

Exceptions—افعال سماعی = Strong Verbs. پذیرفتن = to accept, *Imp.* پذیر ; خفتن = to sleep, *Imp.* خسپ ; گرفتن = to catch, *Imp.* گیر ; سفتن = to bore, *Imp.* سنب.

Rule VII. When ن precedes the termination دن, it is retained. *Examples*—

افگندن, to throw.	افگن	راندن, to drive.	ران
افشاندن, to sprinkle.	افشان	ستاندن, to take.	ستان
آگندن, to fill.	آگن	کندن, to dig.	کن
پراگندن, to disperse	پراگن	ماندن, to remain.	مان
خواندن, to read.	خوان	نشاندن, to plant.	نشان

Exceptions—گندن = to stink = to rot, *Imp.* گند.

Rule VIII. When و precedes the termination دن, it is changed into ی[1].

Examples—

افعال قیاسی	Imp.	افعال قیاسی	Imp.
افزودن, to increase.	افزای	ربودن, to rob.	ربای
اندودن, to plaster.	اندای	زدودن, to polish	زدای
آسودن, to repose.	آسای	فرسودن, to rub.	فرسای
آلودن, to pollute.	آلای	سودن, to rub.	سای
آزمودن, to try.	آزمای	ستودن, to praise.	ستای
آمودن, to fill.	آمای	فرمودن, to order.	فرمای
بخشودن, to bestow.	بخشای	گشودن, to open.	گشای
پیمودن, to measure.	پیمای	نمودن, to show.	نمای

Exceptions—افعال سماعی = Strong Verbs. تنودن = to draw, *Imp.* تنو; درودن = to reap, *Imp.* درو; زنودن = to neigh, *Imp.* زنو; شنودن = to hear, *Imp.* شنو; غنودن = to slumber, *Imp.* غنو

Rule IX. When ی precedes the termination دن, it is rejected. *Examples*—

افعال قیاسی	Imp.	افعال قیاسی	Imp.
آمرزیدن, to forgive.	آمرز	تراشیدن, to shave.	تراش
آرمیدن, to rest.	آرم	تکیدن, to run.	تک
آشامیدن, to drink.	آشام	جوشیدن, to boil.	جوش
بخشیدن, to bestow.	بخش	جنگیدن to fight.	جنگ
بریدن, to cut.	بر	جنبیدن to move.	جنب
بوئیدن, to smell.	بوي	چریدن, to graze.	چر
پرسیدن, to ask.	پرس	چسپیدن, to stick.	چسپ
پوزیدن, to apologize.	پوز	چمیدن, to strut.	چم
پوسیدن, to spoil.	پوس	چکیدن, to drop.	چک
پوشیدن to cover.	پوش	خزیدن, to creep.	خز
پوئیدن, to search.	پوي	خلیدن, to prick.	خل
ترسیدن, to fear.	ترس		

افعال قیاسی	Imp.	افعال قیاسی	Imp.
خمیدن, to be crooked.	خم	شمیدن, to smell.	شم
خلیمیدن, to blow the nose.	خلیم	شکیبیدن, to be patient.	شکیب
خائیدن, to chew.	خای	غلطیدن, to roll.	غلط
خاریدن, to scratch.	خار	غُریدن, to roar.	غُر
خوشیدن, to dry.	خوش	فهمیدن, to understand.	فهم
خرامیدن, to strut.	خرام	کندیدن, to dig.	کند
خراشیدن, to scratch.	خراش	گُنجیدن, to hold.	گنج
خوابیدن, to sleep.	خواب	گزیدن, to bite.	گز
خُسپیدن, to sleep.	خُسپ	لغزیدن, to slip.	لغز
خندیدن, to laugh.	خند	لیسیدن, to lick.	لیس
خریدن, to purchase.	خر	مکیدن, to suck.	مک
دُزدیدن, to steal.	دُزد	مالیدن, to rub.	مال
درخشیدن, to shine.	درخش	نکوهیدن { to despise. to reproach.	نکوه
درویدن, to reap.	درو		
دویدن, to run.	دو	نوردیدن { to fold. to travel.	نورد
دریدن, to tear.	در		
دمیدن, to blow.	دم	نیوشیدن, to hear.	نیوش
رقصیدن, to dance.	رقص	نوشیدن, to drink.	نوش
رمیدن, to be afraid.	رم	وزیدن, to blow.	وز
زاریدن, to cry.	زار	ورزیدن, to practise.	ورز
سنجیدن, to weigh.	سنج	هراسیدن, to fear.	هراس
سرفیدن, to cough.	سرف	هراشیدن, to vomit.	هراش
سفلیدن, to sneeze.	سفل	هلیدن, to leave.	هل
سگالیدن, to think.	سگال		

Exceptions—افعال سماعي=Strong Verbs.
آفریدن = to create, *Imp.* آفرین; چیدن; = to cull, *Imp.* چین: دیدن = to see, *Imp.* بین; شنیدن to hear, *Imp.* شنو; گزیدن = to select, *Imp.* گزین.

Note.—**It should be remembered that most of the imperatives given as exceptions to the preceeding rules are not, strictly speaking, irregular verbs; because they have their corresponding regular infinitives in** یدن **still in use; in fact, we should consider the infinitives as anomalous or irregular and the imperatives regular. For the imperatives are the original verbs, while the infinitives have assumed different forms.**

Examples—

Infinitives.	Imperatives.	Infinitives.
بستن=to bind.	بند	بندیدن
خفتن=to sleep.	خسپ	خسپیدن
سختن=to weigh.	سنج	سنجیدن
سفتن=to bore.	سنب	سنبیدن
گسیختن=to break.	گسل	گسلیدن
گشتن=to turn.	گرد	گردیدن
هشتن=to leave.	هل	هلیدن

N.B.—**From the examples given above it may be easily perceived that almost all the imperatives have their regular infinitives ending in** یدن.

گردان=Conjugation of a Causal Verb in the Active Voice.

مصدر=Infinitive; ترسانیدن = to frighten.

Past Tense=ماضی مطلق

Singular=واحد	**Plural**=جمع
1st pers. ترسانیدم = I frightened.	ترسانیدیم = we frightened.
2nd pers. ترسانیدی = thou frightenedst.	ترسانیدید = you frightened.
3rd pers. ترسانید = he frightened.	ترسانیدند = they frightened.

Past Imperfect=ماضی إستمراري

Singular=واحد	**Plural**=جمع
1st pers. می ترسانیدم , I was frightening.	می ترسانیدیم , we were frightening.
2nd pers. می ترسانیدی , thou wast frightening.	می ترسانیدید , you were frightening.
3rd pers. می ترسانید , he was frightening.	می ترسانیدند , they were frightening.

Perfect Tense=ماضی قریب

Singular=واحد	**Plural**=جمع
1st pers. ترسانیدۀ ام , I have frightened.	ترسانیدۀ ایم , we have frightened.
2nd pers. ترسانیدۀ , thou hast frightened.	ترسانیدۀ اید , you have frightened.
3rd pers. ترسانیدۀ است , he has frightened.	ترسانیدۀ اند , they have frightened.

Pluperfect=ماضی بعید

Singular=واحد	**Plural**=جمع
1st pers. ترسانیدۀ بودم , I had frightened.	ترسانیدۀ بودیم , we had frightened.
2nd pers. ترسانیدۀ بودی , thou hadst frightened.	ترسانیدۀ بودید , you had frightened.
3rd pers. ترسانیدۀ بود , he had frightened.	ترسانیدۀ بودند , they had frightened.

Future Tense = زمان مستقبل

Singular = واحد	Plural = جمع
1st pers. خواهم ترسانید, I will frighten.	خواهیم ترسانید, we will frighten.
2nd pers. خواهی ترسانید, thou wilt frighten.	خواهید ترسانید, you will frighten.
3rd pers. خواهد ترسانید, he will frighten.	خواهند ترسانید, they will frighten.

Future Perfect = ماضی مشکّی

Singular = واحد	Plural = جمع
1st pers. ترسانیده باشم, I shall have frightened.	ترسانیده باشیم, we shall have frightened.
2nd pers. ترسانیده باشی, thou shalt have frightened.	ترسانیده باشید, you shall have frightened.
3rd pers. ترسانیده باشد, he shall have frightened.	ترسانیده باشند, they shall have frightened.

Aorist = مضارع

Singular = واحد	Plural = جمع
1st pers. ترسانم, I may frighten.	ترسانیم, we may frighten.
2nd pers. ترسانی, thou mayst frighten.	ترسانید, you may frighten.
3rd pers. ترساند, he may frighten.	ترسانند, they may frighten.

Present Tense=زمان حال

Singular=واحد	**Plural**=جمع
1st pers. مي ترسانم, I frighten.	مي ترسانيم, we frighten.
2nd pers. مي ترساني thou frightenest.	مي ترسانيد, you frighten.
3rd pers. مي ترساند, he frightens.	مي ترسانند, they frighten.

Imperatives.

ترسان—امر حاضر=frighten.

مترسان—امر نهی=do not frighten.

ميترسان—امر مدامي=go on frightening.

ترساند—امرغايب=he shall frighten.

ترساناد—امر دعا=may he frighten!

Conjugation=گردان

of a Transitive Verb in the Passive Voice.

GENERAL RULE.

صيغهٔ مجهول = **The Passive Voice** is formed by adding the different tenses of شدن to the *past participle* of a *transitive* verb.

N.B.—Intransitive Verbs have no *Passive Voice.*

مصدر = **Infinitive.** طلبيده شدن to be called.

I.—Passive Voice. Past Indefinite.

صيغهٔ مجهول ماضی مطلق

It is formed by adding the past tense of شدن to the past participle of a *transitive* verb.

Singular=واحد	Plural=جمع
1st pers. طلبیده شدم, I was called.	طلبیده شدیم, we were called.
2nd pers. طلبیده شدي, thou wast called.	طلبیده شدید, you were called.
3rd pers. طلبیده شد, he was called.	طلبیده شدند, they were called.

II.—Passive Voice. Past Imperfect.

صیغهٔ مجهول ماضی استمراري

It is formed by adding the past imperfect of شدن to the past participle of a *transitive* verb.

Singular=واحد	Plural=جمع
1st pers. طلبیده مي شدم, I was being called.	طلبیده مي شدیم, we were being called.
2nd pers. طلبیده مي شدی, thou wast being called.	طلبیده مي شدید, you were being called.
3rd pers. طلبیده مي شد, he was being called.	طلبیده مي شدند, they were being called.

III.—Passive Voice. Perfect Tense.

صیغهٔ مجهول ماضی قریب

It is formed by adding the perfect tense of شدن to the past participle of a *transitive* verb.

Singular=واحد	Plural=جمع
1st pers. طلبیده شده ام, I have been called.	طلبیده شده ایم, we have been called.
2nd pers. طلبیده شدهٔ, thou hast been called.	طلبیده شده اید, you have been called.
3rd pers. طلبیده شده است he has been called.	طلبیده شده اند, they have been called.

IV.—Passive Voice. Pluperfect Tense.

صیغهٔ مجهول ماضی بعید

It is formed by adding the pluperfect of شدن to the past participle of a *transitive* verb.

Singular=واحد	Plural=جمع
1st pers. طلبیده شده بودم, I had been called.	طلبیده شده بودیم, we had been called.
2nd pers. طلبیده شده بودی, thou hadst been called.	طلبیده شده بودید, you had been called.
3rd pers. طلبیده شده بود, he had been called.	طلبیده شده بودند, they had been called.

V.—Passive Voice. Future Tense.

صیغهٔ مجهول زمان مستقبل

It is formed by adding the future tense of شدن to the past participle of a *transitive* verb.

Singular=واحد	Plural=جمع
1st pers. طلبیده خواهم شد, I will be called.	طلبیده خواهیم شد, we will be called.
2nd pers. طلبیده خواهی شد, thou wilt be called.	طلبیده خواهید شد, you will be called.
3rd pers. طلبیده خواهد شد, he will be called.	طلبیده خواهند شد, they will be called.

VI.—Passive Voice. Future Perfect Tense.

صیغهٔ مجهول ماضی مشکی

It is formed by adding the future perfect of شدن to the past participle of a *transitive* verb.

Singular=واحد	**Plural=جمع**
1st pers. طلبیده شده باشم, I shall have been called.	طلبیده شده باشیم, we shall have been called.
2nd pers. طلبیده شده باشی, thou shalt have been called.	طلبیده شده باشید, you shall have been called.
3rd pers. طلبیده شده باشد, he shall have been called.	طلبیده شده باشند, they shall have been called.

VII.—Passive Voice. Aorist.

صیغهٔ مجهول مضارع

It is formed by adding the Aorist of شدن to the past participle of a *transitive* verb.

Singular=واحد	**Plural=جمع**
1st pers. طلبیده شوم, I may be called.	طلبیده شویم, we may be called.
2nd pers. طلبیده شوی, thou mayst be called.	طلبیده شوید, you may be called.
3rd pers. طلبیده شود, he may be called.	طلبیده شوند, they may be called.

VIII.—Passive Voice. Present Tense.

صیغهٔ مجهول زمان حال

It is formed by adding the present tense of شدن to the past participle of a *transitive* verb.

Singular=واحد	Plural=جمع
1st pers. طلبیدہ می شوم, I am called.	طلبیدہ می شویم, we are called.
2nd pers. طلبیدہ می شوی, thou art called.	طلبیدہ می شوید, you are called.
3rd pers. طلبیدہ می شود, he is called.	طلبیدہ می شوند, they are called.

IX.—Passive Voice. Potential Past.

صیغۂ مجہول ماضی إمکانی

It is formed by prefixing the past tense of توانستن to the past tense *passive voice* of a *transitive* verb.

Singular=واحد	Plural=جمع
1st pers. توانستم طلبیدہ شد, I could be called.	توانستیم طلبیدہ شد, we could be called.
2nd pers. توانستی طلبیدہ شد, thou couldst be called.	توانستید طلبیدہ شد, you could be called.
3rd per. توانست طلبیدہ شد, he could be called.	توانستند طلبیدہ شد = they could be called.

X.—Passive Voice. Potential Aorist.

صیغۂ مجہول و إمکانی با مضارع

It is formed by prefixing the Aorist of توانستن to the past tense *passive voice* of a *transitive* verb.

Singular=واحد	Plural=جمع
1st pers. توانم طلبیدہ شد, I can be called.	توانیم طلبیدہ شد, we can be called.
2nd pers. توانی طلبیدہ شد, thou canst be called.	توانید طلبیدہ شد, you can be called.
3rd pers. تواند طلبیدہ شد, he can be called.	توانند طلبیدہ شد, they can be called.

گردان = Conjugation of a Compound Verb.

مصدر = Infinitive.

عرض نمودن = to request.

Past Tense ماضی مطلق

Singular = واحد	Plural = جمع
1st pers. عرض نمودم , I requested.	عرض نمودیم , we requested.
2nd pers. عرض نمودی , thou requestedst.	عرض نمودید , you requested.
3rd pers. عرض نمود , he requested.	عرض نمودند , they requested.

Past Imperfect = ماضی استمراری

Singular = واحد	Plural = جمع
1st pers. عرض مینمودم , I was requesting.	عرض مینمودیم, we were requesting.
2nd pers. عرض مینمودی thou wast requesting.	عرض مینمودید, you were requesting.
3rd pers. عرض مینمود he was requesting.	عرض مینمودند, they were requesting.

Perfect Tense = ماضی قریب

Singular = واحد	Plural = جمع
1st pers. وعرض نموده ام I have requested.	عرض نموده ایم, we have requested.
2nd pers. عرض نمودهٔ , thou hast requested.	عرض نموده اید, you have requested.
3rd pers. عرض نموده است. he has requested.	عرض نموده اند, they have requested.

Pluperfect=ماضی بعید

Singular=واحد	Plural=جمع
1st pers. عرض نموده بودم =I had requested.	عرض نموده بوديم = we had requested.
2nd pers. عرض نموده بودي =thou hadst requested.	عرض نموده بوديد = you had requested.
3rd. pers. عرض نموده بود =he had requested.	عرض نموده بودند = they had requested.

Future Tense=زمان مستقبل

Singular=واحد	Plural=جمع
1st pers. عرض خواهم نمود =I will request.	عرض خواهيم نمود = we will request.
2nd pers. عرض خواهي نمود =thou wilt request.	عرض خواهيد نمود = you will request.
3rd pers. عرض خواهد نمود =he will request.	عرض خواهند نمود = they will request.

Future Perfect=ماضی متشکی

Singular=واحد	Plural=جمع
1st pers. عرض نموده باشم =I shall have requested.	عرض نموده باشيم = we shall have requested.
2nd pers. عرض نموده باشي =thou shalt have requested.	عرض نموده باشيد = you shall have requested.
3rd pers. عرض نموده باشد =he shall have requested.	عرض نموده باشند = they shall have requested.

Aorist=مضارع

Singular=واحد	Plural=جمع
1st pers. عرض نمايم = I may request.	عرض نمائيم = we may request.
2nd pers. عرض نمائي = thou mayst request.	عرض نمائيد = you may request,
3rd pers. عرض نمايد = he may request.	عرض نمايند = they may request.

Present Tense=زمان حال

Singular=واحد	Plural=جمع
1st pers. عرض مينمايم = I request.	عرض مينمائيم = we request.
2nd pers. عرض مينمائي = thou requestest.	عرض مينمائيد = you request.
3rd pers. عرض مينمايد = he requests.	عرض مينمايند = they request.

Imperatives.

امرحاضر — عرض نماى = request.
امرنهى — عرض منماى = do not request.
امر مُدامي — عرض مينماى = go on requesting.
امرغايب — عرض نمايد = he shall request.
امردعا — عرض نماياد = may he request!

Questions on Verbs.

I. Name the varieties of افعال with their English equivalents. (133)

II. What parts of speech are prefixed to simple infinitives to form compound verbs? (148)

III. Give four examples of each of the following four kinds of compound verbs:—(*a*) Noun + Infinitive; (*b*) Adjective + Infinitive; (*c*) Preposition + Infinitive; (*d*) Adverb + Infinitive. (148)

IV. Explain the follwing :—

لازمي — معروف — مجهول — متعدي — معاون

V. How are the following formed? Give examples.

صيغه مجهول — فعل مجبور — صيغه امکاني

VI. What verbs are called افعال معاون ? Why are they so called? Which of these are Principal Verbs as well as Auxiliaries? (140)

VII. Name the tenses that are formed by the help of the Auxiliary Verbs. (140)

VIII. Convert the following in افعال مجبور :—

آموختن—سوختن—فهميدن—خوردن—نوشتن
— پروردن — دادن

IX. Give a complete list of افعال ناقص with their meanings and the forms that are used at present.

X. What are Impersonal Verbs? How are they used in Persian? Illustrate by sentences. (142)

XI. What is افعال مشترک ? What verbs are used as such? Name them. (143).

XII. How are Negative Verbs formed in Persian? (144).

XIII. What two negative particles are there in Persian? Give their grammatical names. (144).

XIV. Show by examples the difference between نون نفی and ميم نهي and give their English meanings. (145)

XV. Classify the following infinitives:—

ترسيدن — ترسانيدن — رستن — رشتن — بايستن —
باشيدن — شايستن — برشتن — خواستن — خاستن

XVI. What do you understand by ازمنهٔ ثلاثه? State how they are all formed. Give examples. (150)

XVII. What terminations are used to denote the number and person of a tense? (149)

XVIII. What auxiliary verbs are used in the formation of زمان مستقبل — ماضی مشکی — صیغه امکانی — فعل مجهول — ماضی بعید — ماضی قریب (140)

XIX. Name اقسام ماضی, with their English equivalents. (157)

XX. Give and illustrate the rules for the formation of all kinds of ماضی (from 158 to 168).

XXI. What do you understand by صیغه امکانی? How many varieties of صیغه امکانی are there in Persian? Name them and state how they are all formed. (169 to 172).

XXII. How are اسم مفعول and اسم حالیه formed? Give examples (173)

XXIII. Give the Arabic forms of اسم مفعول from the following triliteral roots :—(173 Note)

خلق — قتل — عرف — کتب — جهل — رحم — فهم — نقل

XXIV. Conjugate شناختن in the following tenses :—

(a) ماضی مشکی — ماضی استمراری —(صیغه معروف)
زمان حال — ماضی استمراری مشکی — زمان مستقبل

(b) ماضی قریب — مضارع — ماضی مشکی —(صیغه مجهول)
زمان مستقبل — ماضی بعید

XXV. How many moods are there in Persian? Name them.

XXVI. What verbal forms are used to express wishes? Explain and illustrate them with examples (165, 179).

XXVII. Form امر دعا, امر نهی and امر مدامی from
دادن — کردن — پرسیدن — پروردن — بخشیدن

XXVIII. How are امر تمنّی ,امر نهی and امر مدامی formed? Give examples. (**176, 177, 179**).

XXIX. How many varieties of صیغه امر are there? Name them. (**174**).

XXX. How do you express the following in Persian :—

(*a*) O! would that I knew. (*b*) We shall have frightened. (*c*) Would that they beheld thy face. (*d*) Thou hast been sent. (*e*) He was being asked. (*f*) Would to God I had not obtained. (*g*) Thou canst not throw. (*h*). You might have seen. (*i*) Would that I too had been with them. (*j*) Would to God I had known. (*k*) We had been recognised. (*l*) Thou shalt have been forgiven. (*m*) Would he had learnt. (*n*) They could not arrive. (*o*) I will be entrusted. (*p*) He must have reached. (*q*) Would to heaven he had arrived. (*r*) Would that I had obtained happiness. (*s*) He can be recognised. (*t*) They can be taught. (*u*) They could not be asked.

XXXI. Give the following tenses of دادن

(۱)—صیغه معروف مستقبل متکلم جمع

(۲)—صیغه شرطیه ماضی استمراری غایب واحد

(۳)—صیغه مجهول ماضی بعید متکلم واحد

(۴)—صیغه امکانی باحال مخاطب جمع

(۵)—صیغه مجهول ماضی متشکی متکلم واحد

(۶)—صیغه مجهول زمان مستقبل مخاطب واحد

(۷)—صیغه امکانی بااستمراری غایب جمع

(۸)—ماضی استمراری مخاطب جمع

(۹)—ماضی استمراری متشکی غایب جمع

(۱۰)—ماضی امکانی غایب واحد

(۱۱)—صیغه مجهول ماضی امکانی مُتکلم واحد

(۱۲)—صیغه مجهول امکانی بامضارع غایب جمع

XXXII. How are Denominative verbs formed in Persian? Give instances. (145)

XXXIII. Give Persian infinitives with their imperatives:—

To sow, to sew, to sleep, to hear, to bore, to break, to adorn, to fear, to weigh, to strut, to scratch, to cut, to shave, to fill, to dig, to throw, to exalt, to rub, to rob, to leave, to send, to take.

XXXIV. What are علامت مصدر? What termination are used as such? Name them. (180)

XXXV. State the various modes of forming the Imperative in Persian, exemplifying each. (183)

XXXVI. Give as many exceptions as you can to the following rules:

(*a*) خ is changed into ز; (*b*) ش into ر; (*c*) و into اي; (*d*) س into ه and وی; (*e*) ف into ب and و (183)

XXXVII. Mention those infinitives that do not form the imperatives like اُفتادن and بخشیدن (183)

XXXVIII. Give the meanings and the imperatives of the following infinitives, and state the rules by which they are formed:—

آفریدن — بردن — بستن — پیوستن — پیختن — تنودن
جُستن — جَستن — چیدن — خاستن — خواستن — خفتن —
دیدن — رُستن — رَستن — رقصیدن — شکستن — شستن —
شناختن — عطسیدن — غنودن — فریفتن — فروختن — کاستن
— کوفتن — گزیدن — مردن — کاشتن — وزیدن — ورزیدن
— هشتن — هراشیدن — هراسیدن (183)

XXXIX. What are weak verbs? Classify خفتن — آفریدن — سفتن — یافتن — ستودن — دادن — چیدن هشتن — فروختن as weak or strong verbs. (146, 147)

CHAPTER XII.

Verbal Nouns.

184. In Persian all words derived from the verbs and generally used as *gerunds* are called اسم مصدر. Its varieties are—

I. اصلی or مصدر حقیقی—When an Infinitive itself is used as a verbal noun, it is called مصدر حقیقي or اصلی; as, پادشاهی بکشتن اسیري اشارت کرد
خوردنش تندرستی آرد بار ;ساقیا آمدن عید مبارک بادت
سوارانرا از گفتن او تهور زیاده گشت

II. حاصل مصدر—It is formed by adding ش to the Imperative of a verb; as,

Infinitives.	Imperatives.	حاصل مصدر
آسودن=to rest.	آساي	آسایش=rest.
بخشیدن=to bestow.	بخش	بخشش=gift.
پرستیدن=to worship.	پرست	پرستش=worship.
خواستن=to desire.	خواه	خواهش=desire.
دادن=to give.	ده	دهش=gift.
دانستن=to know.	دان	دانش=knowledge.
ستودن=to praise.	ستاي	ستایش=praise.
کوشیدن = to endeavour.	کوش	کوشش=endeavour.
کشتن=to kill.	کش	کشش=slaughter.

III. مصدر معنوی — It is formed —

(*a*) By adding ار ‌ ـُ to the past tense third person singular; as,

گفت + ار = گفتار = speech; کرد + ار = کردار = action; دید + ار = دیدار = sight; کشت + ار = کشتار = massacre.

(*b*) By adding ه to the imperative; as, لرزه = trembling; خنده = laughter; گریه = weeping; اندیشه = anxiety; ناله = lamentation.

(*c*) By adding اک to the imperative; as, خور + اک = خوراک = food; سوز + اک = سوزاک = burning; جوشاک = boiling; پوش + اک = پوشاک = dress.

(*d*) The past tense of a verb is used as مصدر معنوی; as, گفت عالم = the advice of a wise man; گشاد کار = the accomplishment of one's object; شناخت یار = the knowledge of one's friend.

(*e*) The Past Participle is used as مصدر معنوی; as, دو صد گفته; = two hundred speeches; دادهٔ او = his gift; نوشتهٔ او = his letter; کردهٔ خویش = your own deed.

(*f*) The Imperative is used as مصدر معنوی; as, سوز جگر = the anguish of the heart; گداز دل = affliction of the heart.

185. مصدر ترکیبی = Compound Verbal Nouns.

(*a*) The past tense of two verbs together; as, آمد و شد = آمد و رفت = intercourse; گفت و شنود = conversation; داد و ستد = خرید و فروخت = traffic; رفت و گذشت = past; نشست برخاست = etiquette; نوشت و خواند = correspondence.

(*b*) The past tense of a verb with its imperative as, گفتگو = conversation; جستجو = inquiry; شست و شو.

=washing; رفت وروب=sweeping; بست وبند – control; تاخت و تاز=assault; کوفت و کوب=beating.

(*c*) The imperatives of two verbs together; as, سوز وساز = anguish of mind; گیر و دار=bustle, hubbub; تک و پو = diligent search; خیز و گیر (*lit. rise and catch*) =children's game; خور و پوش = food and raiment.

Noun of Agency=اسم فاعل

Rules for

186. The Formation of اسم فاعل

I. It is formed by adding نده to an imperative; as, نده + پرست = پرستنده = a worshipper; نده + خواه=خواهنده = a beggar; نده + رو = رونده = a traveller; نده + نویس=نویسنده= a writer.

II. It is formed by adding ا *alif* to an imperative; as, ا + دار = دارا = a possessor; ا+ جوي = جويا = a seeker; ا + شنو= شنوا = a hearer; ا + گوي = گويا = a speaker.

Note.—In Arabic اسم فاعل is formed by inserting ا *alif* between the first two letters of the *triliteral* root; as, ظالم = a tyrant; خالق = the Creator; حاکم = a governor; کاذب = a liar, قاتل = a murderer, ناظر = an inspector; کاتب = a writer.

187. Noun Suffixes denoting the Agent.

بان — گله بان = a shepherd; میزبان = a host; پاسبان=a watchman; باغبان = a gardener; دربان=a porter; گاوبان=a herdsman.

چي — جارچي = a crier; بوستانچي = a gardener.
چي — خزانچي = a treasurer; كتابچي = a librarian; نقارچي = a drummer; عرابچي = a carter.
كار — جفاكار = a tyrant; صلاح كار = an adviser; خطاكار = a sinner; زيان‌كار = an injurer.
گار — ستمگار = a tyrant; گنهگار = a criminal; مددگار = a supporter; خدمتگار = a servant.
گر — سوداگر = a merchant; جادوگر = a magician; كاردگر = a cutler; كفشگر = a shoe-maker; درودگر = a carpenter; آهنگر = a blacksmith; كوزه‌گر = a potter; زرگر = a goldsmith.
وان — ساروان = a camel-driver; فيلوان = an elephant-keeper; رزوان = a keeper of a vineyard.

188. اسم فاعل تركيبى—**Compound Noun of Agency.** It is formed by suffixing the imperative of a verb to a noun; as, جفاگستر = a tyrant; سخن‌چين = a tale-bearer; دروغگو = a liar; كاركن = a manager; تيرانداز = an archer; خبرنويس = a reporter.

Verbal Adjectives.

189. In Persian, اسم فاعل (*noun of agency*) اسم حاليه (*Present Participle*) and اسم مفعول (*Past Participle*) are used as *Adjectives* and they are called صفت مشتق = *Derivative Adjectives.*

I. اسم فاعل is used as an Adjective; as, جانور درنده = devouring animal; مركب تازنده = a fleet horse; دولت پاينده = everlasting wealth; آفتاب تابنده = the shining sun.

II. اسم حالیہ is used as an Adjective; as, ماہ تابان=the glittering moon; مہر درخشان =the shining sun; آب روان=a running stream; آسیای گردان = a revolving mill; چشم گریان=a weeping eye.

III. اسم مفعول is used as an Adjective; as, دل شکستہ=a (*broken*) disappointed heart; نان سوختہ=a burnt bread; شلغم پختہ = a boiled turnip; عمر گذشتہ = a past life.

Questions

on Verbal Nouns and Adjectives.

I. How many varieties of اسم مصدر are there? Name them. (184)

II. How are the following formed? Give examples. حاصل مصدر—مصدر ترکیبی—اسم فاعل ترکیبی.

III. Give instances of verbal nouns of the same nature as روفت و روب—خوانه و نوشت—خور و خواب

IV. What is اسم فاعل? How is it formed in Persian and Arabic? Give examples. (186)

V. Enumerate and give examples of suffixes denoting the agent. (187)

VI. What parts of speech are used as Verbal Adjectives? Give examples. (189)

VII. Give words ending in —بان—گار—وان—کار چی—گر. (187).

VIII. What do you understand by اسم مصدر—صفت مشتق and حاصل مصدر?

IX. Name some verbal nouns formed by adding ہ—ش and اک to imperatives. (184, III).

X. Give two instances of each of the following :—

(*a*) Past tense used as a verbal noun.

(*b*) Past participle used as a verbal noun.

(*c*) Imperative used as a verbal noun. (**184**. III.)

Third Parsing Model.

1.—دزدي بر خانۀ درويشي رفت ودر گوشۀ بنشست *

دزدي = اسم عام — جنس مذكر — عدد واحد — حالت فاعلي — متعلق بافعل "رفت" *

بر = در — حرف جر

خانۀ = اسم عام — جنس غيرذي روح — عدد واحد — حالت جرى *

درويشى = اسم عام — جنس تذكير — عدد واحد — حالت اضافت *

رفت = فعل لازمى — ماضى مطلق — غايب — واحد — متعلق بافعل "دزدي" *

و = حرف عطف

در = حرف جر

گوشه = اسم عام — جنس غير ذي روح — عدد واحد — حالت جري

بنشست = فعل لازمي — ماضي مطلق — غايب — واحد — متعلق بافعل "دزدي" *

Fourth Parsing Model.

چون درويش اورا ديد خيلى ترسيد *

چون = حرف زمان

درويش = اسم عام — جنس مذكر — عدد واحد — حالت فاعلي — متعلق بافعل "ديد" *

اورا = اسم ضمیر غایب — جنس مذکر — عدد واحد — حالت مفعولي *

دید = فعل متعدی — ماضي مطلق — غایب — واحد متعلق بافاعل "درویش" *

خیلي = حرف مقدار *

ترسید = فعل لازمي — ماضي مطلق — غایب — واحد متعلق بافاعل "درویش" *

CHAPTER XIII.

حرف = Particle.

190. حرف is the last of the three heads under which all parts of speech are classified by Persian grammarians. Particles, including Adverbs, Prepositions, Conjunctions, and Interjections are called حروف مرکب (*lit.*, letters combined together), in contradistinction to حروف مفرد single letters.

191. حروف مرکب are divided into :—

I. حروف تمیز = **Adverbs.**

II. حروف عطف = **Conjunctions.**

III. حروف اصوات = **Interjections.**

IV. حروف جر = **Prepositions.**

192. Classification of Adverbs = حروف تمیز

I. حروف زمان = Adverbs of Time : بعد = پس = after ; حالا = کنون = اکنون = now : هرگز = ever; هنوز = yet ; همیشه = always ; باز = again گاهی = sometimes ; پیش = قبل = before ; هرگاه = whenever ; چون = when.

II. حروف مکان = Adverbs of Place : بالا = فراز = فوق = above ; فرود = پائین = تحت, below ; درون = اندرون = within ; بیرون = without ; = هر کجا = wherever.

III. حروف استفهام = Adverbs of Interrogation, *or* Interrogative Adverbs : چون how ;

چرا = why ; کو = where ; کي = how or when.

کی باشد و کي باشد و کی باشد و کي
من باشم و وی باشد و می باشد ولی

Note.—In this example the reiteration of the word کي denotes the earnest desire, entertained by the speaker, for the arrival of that period of time in which he shall enjoy the united pleasures of love, music and wine.

IV. حروف تشبیه = Adverbs of Comparison, *or* Comparative Adverbs ; مثل , مانند , گویا , چنان , چنین , همچون , همچو , چون , چو , چنانکه , چنانچه , همچنان , همچنین , in the same manner, as, like.

V. حروف اثبات = Adverbs of Affirmation, *or* Affirmative Adverbs ; همانا , هر آئینه , certainly ; البته ; verily ; بیشک , لاشک , بی‌شبه , بی سخن , undoubtedly.

VI. حروف ختم کلام , Adverbs of Conclusion, في الجمله , القصه , الغرض , in short ; آخر , آخرالامر , عاقبت , عاقبت‌الامر , at last.

VII. حروف مقدار = Adverbs of Quantity : بس , enough ; کم , اندک , قدری , خورده , برخی , قلیل , a little ; خیلي = بسیار = much ; فراوان = وافر = abundantly ; کافی = sufficiently.

VIII. حروف سیرت = Adverbs of Quality ; دلیرانه , bravely ; عاقلانه = دانشورانه = prudently.

IX. حروف قبول Adverbs of Consent = بان = نعم = بلی = آری = yes.

X. حروف اشتباه = Adverbs of Doubt: مگر = باشد = شاید = perhaps; تواند = possibly.

193. Adverbs from Nouns.—By prefixing a Preposition to a Noun; as, بخوبی = perfectly; بشدت = severely; درنهان = secretly; بشر = maliciously; بغایت = extremely.

194. Adverbs from Pronouns.

(*a*) By prefixing Demonstrative Pronouns to Substantives; as, اینسو = این طرف = hither; آنسو = آنطرف = thither; اینجا = here; آنجا = there.

(*b*) By prefixing Interrogative Pronouns to Substantives; as, کجا = where; کدام طرف = whither; چگونه (*in what manner*), how.

195. Adverbs from Adjectives.—Adjectives without undergoing any change are used as adverbs; as, خوب = درست = well; سخت = severely, پاک = entirely; مشکل = scarcely; نادر = rarely; تنگ = tightly; تمام = totally.

Questions on the Adverb.

I. Name the principal divisions of حروف مرکب with their English equivalents. (191).

II. From what parts of speech are adverbs generally Formed? Give examples. (193, 194, 195)

III. Give examples of Demonstrative and Interrogative Adverbs. (194)

IV. Classify the following adverbs:—هنوز — بس — مگر — شاید — همچو — مثل — کی — هان — القصه — بالا — البته — قدری — نعم — همانا

V. Give instances of Adjectives used as Adverbs (195)

VI. Give examples of Prepositional and Pronominal Adverbs. (**193,194**)

VII. Give Persian words for—*Interrogative, Comparative, Affirmative* Adverbs.

VIII. How are Adverbs of *Consent, Quality, Quantity* and *Conclusion* called? Give examples.

حروف عطف = Conjunctions.

A **Conjunction** is a word which joins two sentenecs.

196. Conjunctions are divided into:—

I. حروف شرط = **Conditional**; as, اگر ,گر ,ار.

II. حروف علت or حروف سببی **Causative**; as, کہ, زیراکہ, because; لاجرم, لهذا, بنابرین, therefore.

III. حروف استدراک = **Adversative**; as, اما = ولیکن = ولي = لیکن = لاکن = but.

IV. حروف تردید = **Alternative**; as, کہ = یا either, or; خواه = whether.

فریدون آمد کہ سهراب ∴ گلستان خوانم کہ بستان

V. حروف جملہ = **Concessive**; as, ورچہ = گرچہ = اگرچہ = although = though.

گرچہ تو امیر و ما اسیریم ∴ ورچہ تو بزرگ و ما حقیریم•

گرچہ تو غني و ما فقیریم ∴ دلداري دوستان ثواب است•

VI. حروف معیت = **Copulative**; as, و and, نیز = هم = also.

Note.—(*a*) When two nouns are connected by و, the first (or the thing with which something else is joined) is called

معطوف عليه, and the second (or the thing joined with something else) is called معطوف.

Questions on the Conjunction.

I. What do you understand by حروف عطف? (196)

II. How do you classify conjunctions? (196)

III. Mention *two* conjunctions that denote opposition, *two* condition, *two* cause, and *two* concession. (196)

IV. Give Persian technical terms for Copulative, Adversative, Alternative, Causative and Concessive conjunction. (196)

V. Classify the following :—(196)

گرچه — یا — نیز — اما — ار — خواه — لاجرم — و — که — لهذا — ولي

VI. Distinguish between معطوف اليه and معطوف (*note*)

حروف اصوات = Interjections.

An **Interjection** is a word which expresses sudden feeling.

197. Interjections are classified into :—

I. حروف ندا = **Exclamatory**; as, ایا, یا, ای, oh!

II. حروف تحسین or انبساط = Interjections expressing *praise* or *admiration*; *as*, واه = شاباش = آفرین = bravo! well done! زهی = مرحبا = welcome!

زهی خط و زهی خال و زهی زلف سیه فام
زهی قد و زهی خد و زهی جسم خوش اندام

III. حروف دعا or تمنا = Interjections expressing *wish* or *prayer*; as, کاش, کاشکي, اندیک

would to God! خواستم, would! ناخواستم may God forbid!

IV. تاسف *or* افسوس حروف = Interjections expressing *regret* or *sorrow*; as, آه = دریغا افسوس = alas! دردا = وای = oh misery! حسرتا = oh pity!

∴ وای دریغا وای دریغا وای دریغ

∴ کانچنان ماهی پنهان شد زیر میغ

V. حروف تنبیه = Interjections expressing *warning*; as الا = تا = زنهار = هرگز, beware!

VI. حروف إستحقار = Interjections expressing *disgust* or *hatred*; as, أف = fie! تفو = fie for shame!

Questions on the Interjection.

I. How are Interjections called in Persian? (197)

II. How may Interjections be classified? (197)

III. How are the following expressed in Persian? Oh pity! Well done! Welcome! Would to God! May God forbid! Fie for shame! Beware! (197)

IV. Give grammatical terms for Interjections expressing *warning, grief, disgust, praise* and *wish.* (197)

V. Classify the following :— اندیک — آیا — الا — آه — هرگز — کاش - وای — واه واه — أف — (197)

VI. How are Interjections expressing *praise, grief, desire, hatred* and *warning* called? Give examples.

حروف جر = Prepositions.

A Preposition is a word placed before a noun or pronoun to show the relation between it and some other word in the sentence.

198. Simple Prepositions are از (*in poetry frequently* contracted into ز)=from=by; با=with; بر = on = upon; در = in = into; بی = without; تا = till = until.

These prepositions are termed حروف معنوی (*real particles*).

199. Position of Prepositions.—Prepositions are placed before the simple nominative forms of *Nouns* and *Pronouns*; as, درخانه = in the house; بردرخت = on a tree; بامن = with me.

ای مهر تو در دلها — وی مهر تو بر لبها *
وی شور تو در سرها — وی سر تو در جانها *

Note.—Certain prepositions, such as بالا = *above*, پیش = *before*, نزد = *near*, زیر = *beneath*, require the *izafat*, or the sign of the genitive case, between them and the noun which they govern; as,

بالای سر—زیر درخت—پیش پادشاه—نزد طبیب

200. حروف إستثنا = **Prepositions of** *Exception*, *i.e.*, prepositions meaning *except*; as, الّا=جز=سوای= مگر = ورای = غیر=except. غیر is followed by از; as, نداریم غیر از تو فریادرس

Note.—A person or thing that is excepted is called مُستثنی I. and that from which مُستثنی is excepted is called مُستثنی منه II. ; as, تمام رعیت پیش پادشاه رفتند مگر سهراب
I II

201. Redundant Particles = حروف زاید. Some particles, such as, فرا , فراز , مر &c., are used redundantly in a sentence without affecting the sense and they are called حروف زاید.

حرف التنکیر=**Indefinite Article.**

202. An **Indefinite Article** is expressed by adding یای تنکیر to a noun; as, = شخصي *a* man; درختي=*a* tree; پادشاهي=*a* king.

حرف التعریف **Definite Article.**

203. The **Definite Article** is expressed by یای تنکیر followed by the relative که; as,

درختي که اکنون گرفتست پای
پادشاهي که طرح ظلم فگند

درختي که=the tree; پادشاهي که=the king.

CHAPTER XIV.

Syntax=نحو

204. نحو = **Syntax** treats of the correct method of arranging words into sentences.

Words are related to each other, by way of *Concord*=موافقت.

205. موافقت=**Concord** is the agreement of one word with another in *gender*, *number*, *person*, or *case*.

206. جمله = **A Sentence** is a collection of words so arranged as to express one complete *thought*.

Every sentence consists of two parts; the *subject* and the *predicate*.

207. مبتدا *or* موضوع *or* مسندالیه=the *subject*, *i. e.*, the person or thing about which something is said; it is also termed فاعل (*lit.* "*the doer of an action*") the Nominative.

208. خبر *or* محمول *or* مسند به=the *predicate* is that which we say or affirm respecting the subject, and is expressed by the verb; as,

آن پسر مست است and آن پسر میدود

209. رابط = (ربط = he *joined*) the *Copula* *i. e.*, the word which unites the *subject* and the *predicate*. The words است and بود are used as رابط; as, نوشیروان معلم بود ;سهراب وکیل است

210. رابط اثبات *and* رابط نفی = *Affirmative Copula* and *Negative Copula.* What is said about the subject is sometimes *affirmed* or *denied*; hence the copula may be either *affirmative* or *negative*; as,

نوشیروان عادل است ;سهراب طبیب نیست

RULES FOR

211. The arrangement of words in a sentence.

Rule I. In a simple sentence the subject is placed first, then the object, and lastly, the predicate; as,

وزیر اسپرا خرید ;پادشاه وزیر را طلبید

N. B.—(*a*) In poetry the subject is sometimes placed last; as, راست نخواهد شد این پشت کوز ;سود ندارد همه اسباب راست

(*b*) Sometimes the object stands emphatically first; as اورا تو به ده درم خریدی ;ترا من خردمند پنداشتم

(*c*) In poetry the verb is sometimes placed first for the sake of emphasis, thus شد غلامی که آب جو آرد

نیاموزد بهایم از تو گفتار ;بدوزد شره دیدهٔ هوشمند

زنند جامهٔ ناپاک گازران بر سنگ ;نخورد شیر نیم خوردهٔ سگ

Rule II. Words and phrases denoting time place, manner and cause are generally placed before the subject; thus, روزی در شهری درویشی بردکان بقالی رفت

در موسم تابستان روزی شامگاه گروهی مردمان در باغ رفتند ;در آن زمان بسبب عنفوان جوانی پادشاه در سیر و شکار مشغول می شد ;در شهری انبار پنبه بدزدی رفت

Rule III. When a personal pronoun is the subject of a verb, it is expressed in the verbal **suffix**, hence the subject is usually omitted.

اگر با او مناقشه خواهی کرد سزا خواهی یافت

فردا از آن طرف خواهم رفت و ترا سلام خواهم کرد

Rule IV. When a clause stands as the object of a verb, it is placed last; thus, آن مرد گفت مرا احمق میپنداری * پادشاهی در خواب دید که تمام دندانهای او افتاده بود ; شنیدم که ملکرا دشمنی صعب روی نمود ; آن شخص نوشت که مردکی در خط من نظر میکند *

Rule V. When the object of a verb is qualified by a relative clause, the object is placed before the verb, and the qualifying phrase after it; thus, طوطی را دیدم که برسر درختی نشسته بود * سرهنگزاده را دیدم که عقل و خرد داشت ; پادشاهی را شنیدم که بکشتن اسیری اشارت کرد ; پارسای را دیدم که زخم پلنگ داشت ; دهقانی را دیدند که تخم میکاشت

Rule VI. In Persian the indirect form of construction is dispensed with. The exact words of the speaker are reproduced, and they are introduced by the word که ; thus, او مرا گفت که منم سلطان این ملک دو برادر مال خود پیرزنی را سپردند و گفتند که حالا بسفر میرویم هرگاه ما هر دو خواهیم آمد مال خواهیم گرفت ; لقمان گفت که هرچه نه دانم بپرسیدن آن ننگ ندارم

N.B.—When a Person has occasion to relate what he has heard from another, the usage of the Persian language requires that it should be done in the direct construction.

212. In Persian the subject of a proposition may be either a *noun*, a *pronoun*, an *infinitive*, or a *clause*.

(*a*) **Noun.** لشکر شکست یافت ؛ پادشاه بر تخت نشست

(*b*) **Pronoun.** او مرا دید ؛ من ترا میشناسم

(*c*) **Infinitive.** { خوردنش تندرستی آرد بار / نوشیدنم پای رفتن ببست }

(*d*) **Clause.** { هرچه رود بر سرم رواست / هرچه زود بر آید دیر نپاید }

213. In Persian the Object or *Complement* of a transitive verb may be either a *noun*, a *pronoun*, an *infinitive*, or a *clause*.

(*a*) **Noun.** شیر فیل را کشت ؛ شخصی خطی مینوشت

(*b*) **Pronoun.** نگه دار مارا از راه خطا ؛ مرا میشناسی

(*c*) **Infinitive.** خروشیدن ترکان شنید

امیری گفتن آغاز کرد ؛ بادی مخالف وزیدن گرفت

(*d*) **Clause.** هرچه در میان آید بخورد ؛ هرچه در دل آید بگوید

هرچه از دونان بمنت خواستی در تن افزودی و از جان کاستی

214. Rules for the Concord *or* **Agreement of a Verb with its Subject.**

Rule I. When the subject denotes a rational object, the verb agrees with it in number and persou; as, غلامی از نزد صاحب خود گریخت ؛ من اورا خاموش گردانم ؛ عاصیان از گناه توبه کنند ؛ چگونه دل داری که میگری

Rule II. Two or more nouns in the singular denoting animate objects require the verb to be put in the plural number; thus, روباه و شیر و مرد نزد قفس رسیدند* شیری و مردی در یک خانه تصویر خود دیدند*

Rule III. When the subject denotes an inanimate object, the verb generally remains singular whether the subject be singular or plural; thus, چشمانش در چشم خانه همی گردید* درختان شگفت و گلهای چمن بباد رفت؛ دانها خشک شد؛ واقعها در پیش است

Rule IV. Two or more nouns in the singular denoting inanimate objects require the verb to be put in the singular; thus, خرابی و بدنامی آید زجور* علم و سخاوت بهترین خصایل انسان است* درشتی و نرمی بهم به است* زر و سیم از سنگ همی آید*

Rule V. When the subject of a verb denoting an animate object is preceded by a numeral adjective, it always remains singular in form, but takes a plural verb; but if it denotes an inanimate object, the verb is put in the singular; thus, ده درویش در گلیمی بخسپند* چهار کس بطریق تفرج در باغ رفتند* چهل سال عمر عزیزت گذشت* صد من روغن کفایت کند*

Rule VI. Nouns of multitude, denoting animate objects, sometimes take the verb in the singular and sometimes in the plural, according to the unity or plurality of the idea conceived in the mind of the speaker; thus, شهنشاه عادلرا رعیت لشکر است خلقی بر او گرد آمدند و تقویت کردند* رعیت چو بیخ اند و سلطان درخت* طایفهٔ دزدان بر سر کوهی نشسته بودند* جماعتی آهنگ گریز کردند*

N.B.—When a *collective noun* conveys *unity* of idea, the verb should be *singular*; as, رعیت چون لشکر است but when it conveys *plurality* of idea, the verb must be *plural*; as, رعیت چو بیخ اند و سلطان درخت

Rule VII. Arabic plurals, denoting rational beings, take the verb in the plural; but if they denote inanimate objects, the verb is put in the singular: as, حکما از تاویل آن فرو ماندند؛ بدریا در منافع بیشمار است * ارکان دولت وصیت ملک بجا آوردند * اکابر میگویند که فواید سفر بسیار است ارکان دولت بپسندیدند *

Rule VIII. When nominatives of different persons are joined by و, the verb is plural and agrees with the first rather than with the second and with the second rather than with the third; as, من و تو هر دو خواجه تاشانیم—بندهٔ بارگاه سلطانیم من و او چون دو مغز بادام صحبت داشتیم * من و رفیقي سالها سفر کرده بودیم * من و تو مثل شیر و شکر هستیم *

Rule IX. When inferiors speak to or of their superiors, the verb is generally employed in the third person plural. Thus, a servant, in speaking of his master, would say, اگر جناب عالی قبول فرمایند صاحب خانه بیرون رفته اند * جهان پناه بسیار خوار هستند* اگر امیر قدم رنجه نمایند*

215. محذوف=**The Omission of a Verb.**

When two or more sentences having the same predicate are connected by the conjunction و, the verb is not repeated in the next sentence; this omission of the verb is called محذوف (حذف *omitted*) = Ellipsis.

نہ روز آرام دارم و نہ شب خواب

عابد طعام لذیذ خوردن گرفت و کسوت لطیف پوشیدن و فواکہ شیرین چشیدن* بخت بلندت یاوری کرد و اقبال رہبری* خدا خالق زمین و آسمان است و رازق شاہ و گدا* ہمہ کسوا عقل خود بہ کمال نماید و روی خود بہ جمال*

Note.—Sometimes the subject, and sometimes the subject together with its verb, is omitted from a sentence without affecting the sense; this omission is known by the term مُقدر = Ellipsis, as, "ابتدا می کنم" ;بنام جہاندار و جان آفرین is omitted from the beginning of this sentence.

چنان پہن خوان کرم گسترد—کہ سیمرغ در قاف قسمت خورد

In this sentence "پروردگار" is مُقدر = Ellipsis.

216. Different kinds of مفعول

I. مفعول فیہ = The accusative of "time"; as آن شخص سہ روز بر دکان بقال نشست*

اگر صد سال گبر آتش فروزد :امروز بکش چو میتوان کشت دو بامداد گر آید کسی بخدمت شاہ ;تمام شب نیارمید

II. مفعول مُطلق = The cognate accusative. Some verbs take a noun of *kindred meaning* for their object, and it is called the *cognate object*; as,

بکوشید کوشیدن مردوار * ہمہ گفتنیہا بدو باز گفت

مُطربان سرود مي سرایند * ابر باران مي بارد

بچشیدم چشیدني * او خواست کہ دمي در دمد *

III. مفعول بہ = The object of a transitive verb; as, مرد شیر را کشت ;باغبان خر را زد,

Note.—It may be either the *direct object* — مفعول اول or the *indirect object* = مفعول ثاني; as, این کتابرا به سهراب بده پادشاه وزیررا خلعت بخشید * استاد شاگردرا انعام داد

Classification of Sentences = اقسام جملہ

جملہ **A Sentence** is a thought expressed in words.

217. Sentences are of three kinds, *Simple* = مُفرد, *Complex* مُرکب, and *Compound* = مُرکب.

جملۀ مفرد **A Simple Sentence** contains *only one subject* and one *finite verb*.

سهراب کتاب میخواند * نوشیروان می آید *

جملہ مرکب = **A Complex Sentence** not only contains a principal subject and its verb, but has other *subordinate sentences*, which have subjects and verbs of their own; as,

طفلي که جور آموزگار نبیند جفا بیند از روزگار
پسري که سبق نمیخواند در امتحان کامیاب نمیشود

218. جملۀ مرکب = **A Compound Sentence** contains two or more complete sentences or propositions, connected by *conjunctions*; as,

سهراب آمد ونزد فریدون نشست و هردو باهم کتاب خواندند

219. جملۀ مفرد is subdivided into—

I. جملۀ اسمیہ = The *noun sentence* is that in which the predicate must be always a noun; as,

سهراب وکیل است * نوشیران مُعلم بود *
رستم طبیب نیست * طوطي پرنده است *

II. جملۀ فعلیہ = The *verbal sentence* is that in which the predicate must be always a verb; as, پادشاه ظفر یافت; زاهدی بباغ رفت

Subdivisions of جملۂ فعلیہ

220. جملۂ فعلیہ is subdivided into—

I. جملۂ خبریہ = The *Affirmative* or *Assertive sentence* may be either اسمیہ or فعلیہ as,

پادشاہ پاسبان درویش است ; آن حاکم ظالم است
پادشاہ بر تخت نشست * استاد شاگردانرا درس میدہد *

II. جملۂ انشائیہ = The *Interrogative sentence*; as,

چرا فلانہ را زدی ; امروز چہ خوردی ; کدام شخص حاضر بود

Note.—It also includes Imperative sentences ; as,

نگہ کن برین گنبد زرنگار ; میاموز جز علم گر عاقلی

III. جملۂ دعائیہ = The *Optative sentence* ; as,

چون رستم زور آور باد — چون نوشیروان عادل باد *
جہان آفرین بر تو رحمت کناد ; دلت روشن و وقت مجموع باد

IV. جملۂ ندائیہ = The *Exclamatory sentence*; as,

کریما ببخشای بر حال ما * پروردگارا توانگر توئی
دلا در وفا باش ثابت قدم * ای قناعت توانگرم گردان

V. جملہ شرطیہ = The *Conditional sentence*;

اگر چرخ گردد بکام بخیل * اگر درین زمان حاتم بودی

Subdivisions of جملۂ مرکب

221. جملۂ مرکب = The Complex Sentence is subdivided into a *principal* sentence = جملۂ اصلی and a *subordinate* sentence = جملۂ متابع

The varieties of subordinate sentences are—

I. جملۂ موصولہ or جملۂ وصفیہ = The *relative clause* or the *adjective sentence* ; as,

پادشاہی کہ طرح ظلم فگند — پای دیوار ملک خویش بکند
درختی کہ اکنون گرفتست پای — بنیروی شخصی بر آید زجای

II. جملۂ ظرفیہ = The *adverbial sentence.*

ہرگاہ بمدرسہ میروی کتاب با خود ببری •

ہرجا کہ میروی دیانتدار و راستگو شوی •

جملہ مرکب = Compound Sentences.

1. جملہ معطوفہ = The *co-ordinate sentences*; as,

پادشاہ در جنگ شکست یافت و ہزیمت را غنیمت شناخت

قاضی جلاد را طلبید و فرمود کہ روبروی من اورا بکش

II. جملہ نتیجہ = The *consequent clause*; as,

اگررنج نبری گنج نیابی ؛ اگردروغ خواہی گفت سزا خواہی یافت

III. جملہ سببیہ = The *causal sentence*; as, جفا مکن کہ جفا رسم یار نیست • دروغ مگو کہ دروغ گفتن خطاست

IV. جملہ معترضہ = The *parenthetical sentence*; as,

آنچہ خداوند (دام ملکہ) فرمود عین صواب است

وزیر گفت (دولت و اقبال خداوندی باقی باد) ہمگنانرا راضی کردم * در چندین سالی مختفی (دور از دوستان) نعمتی بی کران داشت

Fifth Parsing Model.

شخصی مکتوبی می نوشت و رازہای پنہان دران درج می کرد

شخصی — اسم عام مذکر واحد حالت فاعلی متعلق بفعل "می نوشت"

مکتوبی — اسم عام غیر ذی روح واحد حالت مفعولی متعلق بفعل "می نوشت"

مي نوشت — فعل متعدي ماضي استمراری واحد غایب متعلق بفاعل "شخصي"

و — حرف عطف

رازها — اسم عام غیرذی روح جمع حالت مفعولي متعلق بفعل "درج مي کرد"

پنهان — صفت منسوب بموصوف "رازها"

در — حرف جر

آن — اسم اشاره بعید غیر ذي روح واحد حالت جری

درج مي کرد — فعل متعدي مُرکب ماضي استمراری واحد غایب متعلق بفاعل "شخصي"

Sixth Parsing Model.

یکی در پهلویش نشسته بر آن نظر می انداخت

یکي — اسم عدد مُذکر واحد حالت فاعلي متعلق به فعل "مي انداخت"

در — حرف جر

پهلو — اسم عام غیر ذی روح واحد حالت جری

ش — اسم ضمیر متصل مُذکر واحد غایب حالت اضافت

نشسته — اسم مفعول

بر — حرف جر

آن — اسم اشاره بعید غیر ذی روح واحد حالت جری

نظر — اسم عام غیرذی روح واحد حالت مفعولي متعلق بفعل "مي انداخت"

مي انداخت — فعل متعدی ماضي استمراري واحد غایب متعلق بفاعل "یکي"

Examples of Analysis.

I. شخصي مکتوبي مينوشت — و رازهاى پنهان دران درج ميکرد — و يکي در پهلويش نشسته بر آن نظر مي انداخت — آن شخص نوشت که مردکي نادان در مکتوب من نگاه مي کرد — ازين سبب ديگر رازهاى خود ننوشتم *

خبر Predicate.	مفعول Object.	مُبتدا Subject.	اقسام جمله Kind of sentence.	جمله Sentence.
مي نوشت	مکتوبي	شخصي	خبريه	شخصي مکتوبي مي نوشت
درآن درج ميکرد	رازهاى پنهان	شخصي	معطوفه	و رازهاى پنهان در آن درج ميکرد
برآن مي انداخت	نظر	يکي در پهلويش نشسته	معطوفه	و يکي در پهلويش نشسته بر آن نظر مي انداخت
نوشت	که مردکي نادان در مکتوب من نگاه ميکرد	آن شخص	خبريه	آن شخص نوشت که مردکي نادان در مکتوب من نگاه مي کرد
در مکتوب من نگاه ميکرد	"	مردکي نادان	خبريه	که مردکي نادان در مکتوب من نگاه مي کرد

خبر Predicate.	مفعول Object.	مُبتدا Subject.	اقسام جُمله Kind of sentence.	جُمله Sentence.
ازین سبب ننوشتم	دیگر رازهاي خود	من (understood)	مسببیه	ازین سبب دیگر رازهاي خود ننوشتم

II. روزي نوشیروان عادل بشکار بیرون آمد-دهقاني پیر را دید که درختي مي نشاند—پادشاه گفت اي پیر طمع داري که برِ آن بخوري-پیر گفت کسان کشتند و ماخوردیم-ما نیز بکاریم تا دیگران بخورند*

خبر Predicate.	مفعول Object.	مُبتدا Subject.	اقسام جُمله Kind of sentence.	جُمله Sentence.
بشکار بیرون آمد	....	نوشیروان عادل	خبریه	روزي نوشیروان عادل بشکار بیرون آمد
دید	دهقاني پیر را که درختي مي نشاند	او (understood)	خبریه	دهقاني پیر را دید که درختي مي نشاند
مي نشاند	درختي	که	موصوله	که درختي مي نشاند

پادشاه گفت ای پیر طمع داری که برِ آن بخوری	خبریه	پادشاه	ای پیر طمع داری که برِ آن بخوری	گفت
ای پیر طمع داری..................	ندائیه	(ای پیر) تو	طمع	داری
که برِ آن بخوری..................	خبریه	تو (understood)	برِ آن	بخوری
پیر گفت کسان کشتند و ما خوردیم ما نیز بکاریم تا دیگران بخورند	خبریه	پیر	کسانِ کشتند و ما خوردیم ما نیز بکاریم تا دیگران بخورند	گفت
کسانِ کشتند..................	خبریه	کسان	....	کشتند
و ما خوردیم..................	معطوفه	ما	....	خوردیم
ما نیز بکاریم..................	خبریه	ما	....	بکاریم
تا دیگران بخورند..................	نتیجه	دیگران	....	بخورند

Questions on Syntax.

I. What do you understand by the term نحو? **(204)**

II. What is a جمله? What are its principal parts? Name them in Persian. **(206, 207)**

III. How are Subject, Predicate and Copula called in Persian? **(207, 208, 209)**

IV. Give short sentences to explain the difference between رابط اثبات and رابط نفي. **(210)**

V. What are the general rules for the arrangement of words in a sentence? *i. e.*, mention the rules which we are guided by in constructing Persian sentences. (**211**).

VI. State clearly the rules of Persian Syntax with regard to the complement of a verb. (**214**).

VII. Give examples of—

(*a*) The nominative put after the verb;

(*b*) The object emphatically placed first;

(*c*) The verb standing first in a sentence.

VIII. How do we, in Persian, report the speech of another? What sort of construction is generally used? **(211, VI).**

IX. Show, with examples, what parts of speech are used as the subject and the object of a verb. **(212, 213).**

X. When does the object precede the verb? Give examples. **(211, I, N. B.)**

XI. The subject usually precedes the verb. Does it ever follow the verb? Give examples. **(211, I, N. B.)**

XII. Show, in short sentences, that the infinitive may be used as, (1) the subject, (2) the object of a verb **(212, 213.)**

XIII. Mention some sentences in which the whole clause is used as, (1) the subject, (2) the object of a verb. **(212, 213.)**

XIV. Correct any errors of arrangement in the following sentences :— دو توانگر برادران به سفر رفتند
ده توانا مرد کمان اوزازه نکردندي * درويشي روزی
بر دکان بقالی رفت در شهري * بر کنار دريا ديدم
پارسائی را که زخم پلنگ داشت * انبار پنبه بدزدی
رفت درشهری * دوعزيز ياران روزی به باغ رفتند *

XV. Give with examples the rules for the concord of a verb with its subject in number and person. (214)

XVI. Give examples of a subject in the singular, taking a verb in the plural and *vice versa*. (214 III, V, IX)

XVII. When may the plural suffix of a noun be omitted?

XVIII. "ده شريکان" و "ده شريک" which is correct? Why? (214, V.)

XIX. When may the verb be omitted in Persian? (215)

XX. Point out with examples the grammatical difference between محذوف and مُقدر. (215)

XXI. Name and explain the different kinds of مفعول (216.)

XXII. Explain with examples مفعول فيه and مفعول مطلق (216.)

XXIII. Name the different kinds of sentences in Persian with their English equivalents. (219-221)

XXIV. What do you understand by جمله — جمله مُفرد جمله متابع and جمله اصليه - مُرکب. (217, 221)

XXV. Distinguish between جمله اسميه and جمله فعليه (219)

XXVI Explain with examples — (1) Adjective, (2) Adverbial, (3) Conditional, (4) Consequent clauses.

XXVII. Name the sub-divisions of جمله فعليه (220)

XXVIII. How many kinds of جمله مُرکب are there in Persian? Name them and give examples. (221)

XXIX. Correct or justify the syntax in the following sentences, giving in each case your reason, *i.e.* the rule that is in question.

در چمن گل و ریحان و لاله تازه شدند*
تمام انجیرها خورده شدند* اقاویل علما بسیار اند* حکما
در بارگاه کسری بمصلحتی سخن همی گفت* پدر بخندید
ارکان دولت بپسندید و برادر بجان رنجیده شدند* خلقی
برسماط او گرد آمده اند* چون سه چهار ماه بدین منوال
گذشتند* انگور و انجیر و آلو و بادام و پسته و خرما همه
در ایران یافته مي شوند* آهو و شیر و روباه و پلنگ
به بیابان رسید* من و دوستي هردو باهم سیر کردند*
تو واو هردو درباغ تفرج کردند*

XXX. What grammatical rules of Persian syntax are violated in the following sentences?

حکما می گوید که فواید سفر بسیار اند* فضل و هنر ضایع
اند تا نه نمایند* حدود ایران تغیرات بسیار یافته اند*
من و اهل‌بیت من از قحط باز رهند*

XXXI. Parse and analyse fully in Persian :—

شخصی در نیم شب بربام خانهٔ خود ایستاده صدا میزد که
همسایگان مدد کنید که دزدان بخانهٔ من آمده اند*
همسایگان می دویدند— چون از دزدان اثری نمی دیدند
باز می رفتند و آن شخص می خندید*

CHAPTER XV.

The Significations of Letters.

222—معانی ا

(1) الف تحسین کلام — (حسن beauty, کلام word). It is used at the end of past and present tenses, and nouns and infinitives to beautify an expression without affecting the sense; as, گفتا, he said; نمایدا he shows; بسترا, a bed; کردنا, doing.

گفتا من گلی ناچیز بودم ; گفتا نیک مردی کن ای پسر

(2) الف دعا or تمنا — (دعا prayer, تمنا wish). It is used to express benediction or desire in the first and third person singular of the aorist; as, میرام O! that I may die! رساد, God grant he may arrive!

جهان آفرین بر تو رحمت کناد ∴ خداوند بر او رحمت رساناد

(3) الف رابط or اتصال —(ربط or وصل, he joined). —It is used between two nouns of the same signification, and it has the force of the preposition به as, دمادم = دم به دم, every moment; دوشا دوش = دوش به دوش, side by side; سراسر entirely.

بزرگی سراسر بگفتار نیست ∴ پیاپی بدنبال صیدی براند

(4) الف عطف — It occurs between two words of different meanings, and in force it is equivalent to the conjunction و; as, سراپا = سروپا, from head to foot, totally; تکاپو = تک و پو; running and searching.

بعد از شبا روزی دیگر بر کنار افتاد

(5) الف فاعلیت — It is added to an imperative to form a noun of agency; as, بینا, a beholder; گویا, a speaker; شنوا, a hearer; جویا, a seeker.

توانا بود هرکه دانا بود ∴ که دارای خلق است و دانای راز

(6) الف مبالغه — It is added to adjectives to denote excess or exaggeration; as, خوشا, very glad.

بسا نامدارا و بسا کامگار ∴ خوشا آندل که دارد تمنای دوست

(7) الف ندبه — It expresses grief; as, دردا, حسرتا, دریغا, alas!

دریغا ای فلک با من چه کردی ∴ دردا که راز شان خواهد شد آشکار

(8) الف مصدر — It is added to adjectives to form abstract nouns; as, فراخا, spaciousness; درازا length; پهنا, breadth, ژرفا depth.

درویشی برهنه بر سرما خفته بود

(9) الف ندا — It is added to a noun to form the vocative case; as, ! پروردگارا, O God!

دلا در وفا باش ثابت قدم ; بابلا مژدهٔ بهار بیار

(10) الف زاید (superfluous) — It is prefixed to the particles بر, با and بی, and to some nouns without affecting the sense; as, ابر = بر, upon; ابا = با; with; ابی=بی, without; اسکندر=سکندر, Alexander, اشکم = شکم, the belly; اشتر = شتر, a camel.

ابی حکم شرع آب خوردن خطا است

(11) الف اماله—This alif is sometimes changed into ی in poetry for the sake of rhyme. This change is called اماله (bending); thus, رکاب is

changed into رکیب ;حساب is changed into حسیب;

زهی ملک دوران سرد رنشیب ∴ پدر رفت وپای پسر دررکیب

به قدرت نگه دار بالا و شیب ∴ خداوند دیوان روز حسیب

Exercise.

Name and explain the ا in the following :—

الها قادرا پروردگارا ∴ کریما منعما آمرزگارا

خدا شمارا خیرو عافیت دهاد ; توانای حقایق و بینای دقایق

همی تاخت اندر فراز و نشیب ∴ همی زد بگرز و بتیغ و رکیب

که رادا دلیرا شها نوذرا ∴ گوا تاجدارا مها داورا

ستایش کنم ایزد پاکرا ∴ که گویا و بینا کند خاکرا

خسروا داد گرا شیردلا بحرکفا ;دردا که طبیب صبر می فرماید

ای خوشا چشمی که آن گریان اوست ; خوشا و خرما وقت حبیبان

بگفتا حکایت کن ای نیک بخت ;دمادم شراب الم در کشند

223—معانی ب

(1) بائ زاید—It is used as a redundant particle with nouns, followed by the prepositions در and اندر, بر, and with verbs, before the past, aorist and imperative; as, بدریا در منافع بیشمار است .

بروی زمین برفشان نهاند ;بگو ای برادر بلطف و خوشی

NOTE.—When the particle ب is prefixed to the imperative it is pronounced with the vowel *zamma*, if the first letter has *zamma* for its vowel; as, بُگذر ,بُکن ,بُگو. In the case of other vowels it takes *kasra*; as, بِمیر ,بِخر ,بِگیر ,بِزن

(2) بائ ظرفیت (ظرف a vessel).—It denotes place and means, "در" "in" or within"; as بگوش اوگفتم

کودکان بمدرسه می روند ;بدنبال خصم شتافتند

(3) سببي or بای علت—It denotes motive or cause; as, بدیدن اورفتم ;آبادي ملک به انصاف است

(4) بای علویت (علي upon).—It signifies بر "upon;" as, بررویش نظر کردم ;جانم به لب رسید

(5) معیت or بای مصاحبت (صحبت, company, مع, with).—It denotes association; as,
جهان ای برادر نماند بکس ;پادشاه به شاهزاده بشکار رفت

(6) باي مفعول—It is prefixed to a noun or pronoun to form the dative case;as, بدو شاه سپرد تخت وتاج
بهرمزچنین گفت نوشیروان

(7) باي الصاق (لصق he joined)—It signifies "with," or "by;" as, بخواری چومفلس خورد گوشمال;
بلطف و سخاوت جهانگیرباش ;بکرم معذور داری

(8) آلت or باي استعانت—(عون, assistance; آلت, instrument).—It denotes instrumentality: as,
قاضي فلاعرا به تازیانه زد ;جلاد اورا به شمشیر بکشت

(9) بای قربت (قرب, he was near).—It signifies "near" or "before;" as, بدرخت گل رسیدم
پنبه فروشان شکایت بپاد شاه بردند ;زن گریان بقاضي رفت

(10) باي قسمیر—It expresses an "oath;" as, بخدا ہرگز دروغ نمیگویم ;بجان من که فراموش نیستی

(11) بای ابتدایر (بدا he began). — It indicates "commencement;" as, اول دفتر بنام ایزد دانا
بنام جهاندار و جان آفرین ;بنام خداوند جان و خرد

(12) باي انتهايہ (نهي, it ended).—It signifies "تا" "end;" ز مشرق بہ مغرب ; ز عرش تابہ فرش

(13) اتصال or باي رابط (ربط or وصل he joined).—It occurs between two nouns of the same meaning and signifies "by;" "to;" as, روبرو face to face; قدم بقدم step by step; سوبہ سو side by side.

(14) باي تشبيہ (شبہ, like).—It denotes "likeness;" باقبال تو در عالم نيست : بحسن صورت او درجهان نيست

(15) باي موافقت (وفق he agreed).—It signifies "according to;" as,

اگرچرخ گردد بکام بخيل ; برتخت شاهي نشيند بمراد

(16) مبادلہ or باي تعويض (عوض or بدل, he changed).—It expresses exchange; as,

اين اسپ بهزار دينار خريدم ; بدرد سرنمي ارزد

Exercise.

Name and explain the ب in the following:—

بخدا کہ گربميرم ∴ کہ دل از تو برنگيرم

بدانش بزرگ و بهمت بلند ∴ ببازو دليرو بدل هوشمند

گرفتيم عالم بمردي و زور ∴ وليکن نبرديم با خود بگور

ملک بفرمود تا غلام را بدريا انداختند ; گفت عالم بگوش

جان بشنو—اگر آب حيات فروشند بآبرو دانا نخرد

توانگري بدلست نہ بمال ∴ بزرگي بعقل ست نہ بہ سال

224.—معاني ت

(1) تاي اضافت—It represents the possessive pronoun تو, "thy;" as, کتابت کجا است ; اسپت گريخت

(2) تاي مفعول—It represents the dative or accusative case; as, پادشاه اسپت بخشید ;دیروز دیدمت

225—معاني چ

(1) چیم استفهام (فهم, he understood).—The interrogative pronoun "what;" as, چه مي گوئي

چه تدبیر سازم چه چاره کنم ;امروز چه خوردي

(2) چیم استفهام نفي —Interrogative in form but negative in meaning: as, از معدهٔ خالي چه قوت آید

از پشه چه قوت آید وز خر چه عقل
آنرا که حساب پاک است از محاسبه چه باک

(3) چیم مساوات (سوي, it was equal).—It denotes "similarity" or "equality;" as, چه مردان لشکر چه خیل زنان

تشنه را در دهان چه دُر چه صدف
چه بر تخت مردن چه برروي خاک

(4) چیم مبالغه (بلغ, he exaggerated).—It denotes "exaggeration"; as, چه خوش گفت بازرگان اسیر

How beautiful! چه زیبا; How well! چه خوش

(5) چیم تعظیم (عظم, he was great).—It expresses a feeling of "reverence" or "sublimity;" as, قاآني چه شاعر است ;نوشیروان چه شهنشاه عادل بود

(6) چیم تحقیر (حقر, he despised).—It denotes "contempt;" as چه برخیزد از دست و کردار من
من چه کسم که بر تخت نشینم

(7) چیم تحسر — It signifies "grief;" as,
دریغا ای فلک با من چه کردی : دردا این چه ستم است

(8) چیم تصغیر (صغر, he was small).—It is generally added to inanimate objects to form the diminutive; as باغیچه, a small garden; قالیچه a small carpet; کوچه, a lane; مورچه, a little ant.

(9) چیم سببی or علت — It is used to show "cause;" as, پند پدر بشنو چه او خیر خواه تو است
عاقل را باید که دروغ نمیگوید چه بر دروغ گو کسی اعتماد ندارد

Exercise.

Name and explain the چ in the following :—

چه روبه به پیشش چه درنده شیر ; چه مردی به پیشش چه سیصد دلیر ; بدختر چه خوش گفت بانوی ده
چه دشمن برین خوان یغما چه دوست ; بقای پادشاهی در چیست ; نکو گوئی گر دیر گوی چه غم ; من چه کسم که نامش برزبان آرم ; چه خوش وقتي و خرم روزگار
از معدهٔ خالي چه قوت آید ; از پاي بسته چه سیر آید

معاني ز

This is the contracted form of the preposition از, and it is generally used in poetry.

(1) زاي مادیه — It denotes the material of which a thing is made; as, شمشیر نیک ز آهن بد چون کند کسي
خاتم ز طلا می سازند ; ز پنبه پارچه می سازند

(2) زای ابتدایہ—It shows "commencement"; as, زِ عرش تا بفرش ; زِ مشرق به مغرب

(3) زاي تفضيل—It is used with the comparative degree and signifies "than;" as, دست کرم به زِ بازوی زور, جور استاد به زِ مهر پدر

(4) زاي علت—It expresses cause; as, پادشاه زِ لشکر کند سروري

معاني ش

(1) شين اضافت—It represents the possessive pronouns "his, her, &c."; as, مادرش ; کتاب او=کتابش, مادر او= خدایا امیدش برآر : اسپ او=اسپش,.

(2) شين مفعول—It represents the dative or accusative case; as, پادشاه خلعتش بخشید

(3) شين مصدري—It is added to an imperative to form a verbal noun; as, بخشش, charity; کوشش. endeavour; آسایش, rest; دهش gift.

226.—معاني ک

It has the following significations:—

(1) کاف استفهام (فهم he understood).—The interrogative pronoun "who" is used only for persons; as, ادب از که آموختي ; نیک بخت کیست

(2) کاف استفهام نفي—Interrogative in form, but negative in meaning; as, که داند کودن از نیست هست زِ فرمان داور که داند گریخت ; کرا جاودان بودن امید هست

(3) کاف موصول (وصل he joined).—The relative pronoun "that" or "which" is used for persons and things; as, این همان سنگ است که تو بر سر من زدی

پادشاهی که طرح ظلم فگند ∴ پای دیوار ملک خویش بکند

(4) کاف تردید (رد he turned).—It signifies "or;" as, گلستان خوانم که بستان ; جمشید رفت که رستم

(5) کاف تشبیه or تسویه (شبه it resembled).—It denotes "comparison" or equality;" as,

نیست در جنگ سلحدار که او ∴ نیست در جهان دغاباز که او

(6) کاف تفسیر or بیانی (فسر he inquired).—Conjunction, meaning "that"; as,

پادشاه پرسید که حکمت چه بود

پدر مرا نصیحت کرد که شهوت آتش است

(7) کاف عطف—It signifies "and," "while;" as,

بسا اسپ تیزرو که بماند ∴ که خر لنگ جان بمنزل برد

بسا چاره دان کو بسختی بمرد ∴ که بیچارگان گوی سلامت ببرد

(8) کاف علت — It denotes "cause;" as,

جفا مکن که جفا رسم یار نیست

دروغ مگو که دروغ گفتن خطا است

(9) کاف مبالغه (بلغ he exaggerated).— It signifies "nay;" as,

نه من به هیچ وجه ازو کمترم ∴ که به علم و هنر ازو برترم

نام حق بر زبان همیرانم ∴ که بدل وجان همی خوانم

(10) کاف مفاجات (فجا it fell suddenly).— It expresses "suddenness;" as,

بودیم بیخبر که سپاه عدو رسید
پادشاهي در خواب بود که سواری از در در آمد

(11) کاف تصغیر (صغر he was small).—It is added to names of persons or things to form the diminutive; as, اسپک, a little horse; رودک, a rivulet, دخترک.

(12) کاف تفضیل (فضل he excelled).—It is used with the comparative degree and signifies "than;" as, معزولی به که مشغولي ;کوتاه خردمند به که نادان بلند

(13) کاف شرطیه (شرط a condition.)—It is used for the conditional particle اگر "if;" as,

شحنهٔ معزول از نابکاري چه کند که توبه نکند
چه شود که سوي دوست بلطف نگاه کنی

(14) کاف تحقیر (حقر he despised).—It denotes contempt; as, ما که باشیم که در بزم تو داخل شویم;
او کیست که با صاحب خود دوستي کند

Exercise.

Name and explain the ک in the following :—

نه من کردم از دست جورت نفرین که خلقي ;بوز نه درین گفتگو بود که درودگرباز آمد ;که از دست قهرش امان یافتی
چه کند کشتهٔ عشقت که نگوید غم دل ∴
نه قندی که مردم بصورت خورند ∴ که ارباب معنی به کاغذ برند
سواری که بنمود در جنگ پشت ∴ نه خود را که نام آوران را بکشت
مردک سنگدل چنان بگزید که خون از او چکید
گدارا چوحاصل شود نان شام ∴ چنان خوش خسپد که سلطان شام

227.—معاني م

It has the following significations:—

(1) ميم اضافت—It represents the possessive pronoun "my"; as, كتابم كجاست ; اسبم گريخت

(2) ميم مفعول—It represents the dative or accusative case; as, اجل ناگهم در ربود ,
پادشاه خلعتم بخشيد ; اي قناعت توانگرم گردان

(3) ميم متكلم—(كلم, he spoke).—It is used as a verbal suffix for the first person singular; as, گفتم, I said; مي خورم, I eat; مي نمودم, I was showing.

(4) ميم اثبات فعل—(ثبت, fixed).—Affirmative. When it is suffixed to a noun or an adjective, it is used as the contracted form of ام; as, شاگردم, I am a pupil; بيمارم, I am sick; سلطانم, I am a king.

(5) ميم تعين تعداد or صفاتي (عدد, number; صفت adjective.)—It is suffixed to the cardinal numerals to form the ordinal numerals; as, باب هفتم—
حكايت بيستم—روز چهارم—سال ششم

(6) ميم نهي—It is prefixed to the imperative to form the negative imperative; as, مخور ; مرو ; مكن.

(7) ميم تانيث (انثي a female).—It is added to some Turkish nouns to form the feminine gender; as, بيگم a lady; خانم a princess.

(8) میم ظرفیت (ظرف, a vessel.)—It is prefixed to a word to form a noun of place; as, مدرسه, a college; مسجد a mosque; مقتل, a slaughter-house. This م is always movable by فتح ـَ.

(9) میم آلت — It is prefixed to a word to form a noun of instrumentality; as, مفتاح a key; منقار, a beak; مقراض, scissors; میزان, a balance. This م is always movable by کسر ـِ.

(10) میم فاعلیت.—It is prefixed to a word to form the noun of agency; as, مُصاحب, a companion; مُدرس, a tutor; مُحب, a friend; مُطرب, a musician. This م is always movable by ضمه ـُ.

معاني ن

(1) نون نفی.—It is used with verbs as a negative particle; as, نکرد; نگفت, نه کوشید

(2) نون نفي اثبات — It is used as a negative particle that requires an affirmative answer; as, نه پیش از تو بیش از تو الد و ختم اند; نه شمشیر دوران آخت است نه شرطست وقتي که روزي خوري ∴ که نام خداوند روزي بري

228.—معاني و

(1) واو عطف — It is used as a copulative conjunction. It signifies "and"; as, قلم و کاغذ بیار این بگفت و پدر را وداع کرد و همت خواست و روان شد

(2) واو تصغیر (صغر he was small).—Diminutive; as, دخترو, a little girl; پسرو, a little boy.

(3) واوتردید (رد be turned).—It signifies "or"; as, گل همین پنج روزو شش باشد; کلمه اسم است و فعل و حرف

(4) واوتسویه (سو like).—It shows "equality"; as یک پیری و صد بیماري ; یک تندرستی و هزار نعمت

معانی ہ

هاي مختفي is used in the following ways:—

(1) هاي فاعليت — It is added to the aorist third person plural to form the "noun of agency"; as, پرستندهٔ آفرینندہ باش .·. در ایوان طاعت نشینندہ باش

(2) هاي لياقت — It is suffixed to nouns in the plural number to form adjectives showing "likeness or resemblance"; as, جشن خسروانہ ; جامۂ درویشانہ ; کلاہ شاہانہ ; ضیافت امیرانہ.

(3) هاي نسبت—It is used at the end of a second part of a compound noun to show relation which it bears to the first; as, شاہنامہ, اکبرنامہ, سکندر نامہ

(4) هاي مقداريہ—It is added to a noun to form an adjective implying space of time, as, یکروزہ, one day old; صدسالہ, hundred years old. چہل سالہ

(5) هاي مفعول—It is added to the past tense to form the "past participle"; as, کردہ, گفتہ, دیدہ.

(6) هاي زايد—It is used at the end of a word as a redundant particle; as, پای=پایہ, foundation, دنب = دنبہ, a tail, انبان = انبانہ, a leathern bag.

(7) هاي فعليت—It is added to the imperative of a verb to form a verbal noun; as, خنده laughing; لرزه, trembling; انديشه, consideration.

(8) هاي عطف — It has the same force as the conjunction و and signifies "and"; as,

استاد آمده نشست و سبق داده باز رفت

خمر خورده عربده كرده كسي را كشته بگريخت

(9) هاي تانيث — It is added to Arabic nouns to form the "feminine gender"; as, صاحبه, a lady; ملكه, a queen: والده, a mother; سلطانه a queen.

229.—معاني ي

(*a*) When ي is added to nouns, it has the following significations :—

(1) وحدت or ياي تنكير (نكر it was indefinite, وحد one).—It expresses the indefinite article "a" or "an"; as,

حيواني از دريا سربر آورد; شخصي پيش اميري رفت

(2) ياي تعريف (عرف he knew).—When ي is followed by كاف موصول, it expresses the definite article "the"; as, درختي كه اكنون گرفتست پاى

طفلي كه جور آموزگار ∴ نه بينه جفا بيند از روزگار

(3) ياى نسبت—It is added to names of countries to show relation; as, زبان پارسي ;مرد يمني

غلام عجمي ;قصب مصري ;زنان بغدادي

(4) اسمی or یای مصدری — It is added to substantives as well as adjectives to form abstract nouns; it denotes the state or profession indicated by the noun; as, گدائی, beggary; پادشاہی, sovereignty; جاہلی, ignorance; معزولی, dismissal; نیکی, goodness; درویشی, poverty.

(5) یای متکلم — It is equivalent to the conjunctive personal pronoun of the first person singular; as, مخدومی=مخدوم من, my master; خداوندی, ربی, my lord; مشفقی my kind friend.

(6) یای اضافت — It is used with nouns ending in ا or و as the sign of the genitive case; as, موی سر, the hair of the head; پای لنگ, a lame foot; وفای دوست, fidelity of a friend; گدای کور a blind beggar; روی زیبا, a beautiful face.

مگردان زکوی وفا روی دل .·. که در روی جانان نباشی خجل

(7) یای فاعلی — It is added to nouns to denote the doer of an action; as, شکاری, a hunter; جنگی, a warrior; شرابی, a drunkard; حلوائی, a confectioner; خونی, a murderer; نحوی و صرفی, a grammarian.

(8) یای مفعولی — It is added to nouns to express the force of the "perfect participle"; as, سندی, established by authority; دستخطی, signed; لعنتی, cursed.

(9) یای اشارت (شار , he pointed).—It is used to intimate an event or circumstance; as, وقتی کہ دو زاغ را یک جا نشستہ بینی مرا خبر کن ; در حالتی کہ ملکرا پروای او نبود حالش بگفتند [برفت
حالی کہ من این سخن بگفتم عنان طاقت از دست درویش

(10) یای مبالغہ—It denotes "excess or universality"; as, خلقی بررو بتعصب گرد آمدند ;خلقی, the whole nation; عشق آفتی است ;آفتی, excessive calamity; علامی, most exceedingly wise.

(b) When ی is added to verbs, it has the following significations:—

(1) یای لیاقت—It is added to the infinitives to denote fitness; as, آمدنی, income; خوردنی, fit to be eaten, provisions; دیدنی, fit to be seen; ستودنی, laudable; کردنی, fit to be done, practicable; کشتنی, deserving of being killed; سوختنی, fit to be burnt; خواندنی, worth reading.

(2) یای خطاب—It is used as a verbal suffix for the second person singular in all tenses; as, میکنی, thou art doing; خواہی یافت, thou wilt obtain.

(3) یای استمراری—It is added to the past tense to form the Past Habitual Tense; it conveys the idea of continued action; as,

ماهیگیری ماهیان دریا گرفتی و در بازار فروختی
پادشاہی در رعایت مملکت سستی کردی و لشکر بسختی داشتی

4. یای متمنّي—It is added to the past tense to form the Optative Past; as, کاش گفتندي, would they had said; کاش رفتمي, would to God I had gone.

Exercise.

Name and explain the ي in the following :—

شمع گر با تو زند دموي نازک بدني ∴
کشتني سوختني باشد و گردن زدني ∴

فرق شاهي و بندگي برخاست ∴ خلقي برسماط او گرد آمده‌اند ; باري که موافق نباشد باري را نشاید

تنگ دستان را سیم و زر دادي و مسافران را سفرة نهادي

مگر خوردي فراموش کردي که درشتي میکني

راستي موجب رضاي خداست

دو درویش خراساني ملازم صحبت یکدیگر سفر کردندي

درختي که اکنون گرفتست پاي ∴ بنیروي شخصي برآید زجاي

پادشاهي با غلامي عجمي در کشتي نشست

Questions.

(1) Enumerate and explain all the uses of ي-ک-چ-ب-ا.

(2) ا *alif* in the middle of a word is of three kinds. Name them and give examples. (222)

(3) Name, define and illustrate the different kinds of ا *alif* used at the end of adjectives and verbs. (222)

(4) Define and illustrate :—

ا-ب-ة-ي-(زاید) ∴ ا-ب (رابط) ∴ ا-ک-و-ة (عطف)
ا-ش-ي (مصدر) ∴ ا-ة-ي (فاعلیت) ∴ ا-چ-ک-ي (مبالغه)
ب-م (ظرفیت) ∴ ب-چ-ک (علت) ∴ ب (ابتدا and استعانت)
ب-م-ت-ش-ة-ي (مفعول) ∴ ت-م-ش-ي (اضافت)

ب-ک-ی (تشبیه) ∴ چ-ک (استفهام and استفهام نفی)
چ-و (مساوات) ∴ چ-ک-و (تصغیر) ∴ م-ی (متکلم)
ک-و (تردید) ∴ ه-م (تانیث) ∴ ه-ي (لیاقت and نسبت)

(5) Name the different kinds of ي used with verbs and give examples. (229)

CHAPTER XVI.

The Numerical Order of the Alphabet.

حساب جمل

230. The twenty-eight letters of the Arabic alphabet have each a numeric value, as shown in the following table:—

kaliman.	*hutti.*	*hawwaz.*	*abjad.*
كلمن	حُطّي	هوّز	ابجد
50, 40, 30, 20	10, 9, 8	7, 6, 5	4, 3, 2, 1

zazagh.	*sakhaz.*	*kurshat.*	*sa'afas.*
ضظغ	ثخذ	قرشت	سعفص

1000, 900, 800, 700, 600, 500, 400, 300, 200, 100, 90, 80, 70, 60

The numerical values are counted from *one* to *ten*, then from *ten* to *hundred* by tens, and from *hundred* to *thousand* by hundreds.

N.B.—This arrangement is also called the *Abjad* system from the first word of the numerical order.

Note.—The letter ح is called حاى حُطّي and the letter ز is called زاي هوّز, because they begin the words حُطّي and هوّز in the *Abjad* system.

Note.—*Numbers* are also formed by *letters* according to this method; for example—

يا=11; يب=12; يج=13; يد=14; يه=15; يو=16; يز=17; يح=18; يط=19; ک=20; کا=21; کب=22; کج=23; کد=24; که=25; کو=26; کز=27; کح=28; کط=29; ل=30, etc.

231. This numeric system is used in forming chronograms (*inscriptions in which certain dates are expressed by numerical letters*) denoting dates of historical events. These are expressed by a short sentence, such that the numerical values of all the letters, when added together, amount to the year (of the Hijra) in which the event took place. Thus, Sultan Babar was born on the *sixth* of the *Muharram* month. It is strange that the numerical value of شش محرم gives the year in which this prince was born; 888 A. H.

Note—ہجرة = flight or departure, *i. e.*, the day on which Muhammad departed from Mecca to Medina. It was on Friday the 15th of July, 622 A. D.

N.B.—The four Persian letters, *viz.*, پ—چ—ژ—گ have the same value as their cognate letters, ب—ج—ز—ک.

Note.—In order to find the *Christian* date corresponding to any *Hijri* year, apply the following rule :—

Rule I.—From the given number of *Mussalman* years deduct three per cent., and to the remainder add the number 621·54; the sum is the period of the *Chirstian* era. For example, Sultan Baber died in 937 A. H. From this number deduct three per cent., *i. e.*, 28, and the remainder is 909. To this number add 621, and the sum is 1530 A. D.

Note.—In order to find the *Mahomedan* year corresponding to any *Christian* date, apply the following rule :—

Rule II.—From the given number of *Christian* years, deduct the number 621·54, and to the remainder add three per cent. of the same; as, for instance, Baber died in 1530 A. D. From this number deduct 621, and the remainder is 909. To this last number add three per cent, of the same *i. e.*, 28, and the sum is 937 A. H.

Questions.

I. Name the twenty-eight letters of the Arabic alphabet in order of their numerical values.

II. Mention those letters of حساب جهل whose numeric values are 500, 600, 700, 800, 900, and 1,000.

III. How is the numeric order of letters otherwise called?

IV. Give the numerical values, according to the *Abjad* system, of — ق — ک — گ — ژ — ز — چ — ج —
پ — ب — ة — خ.

V. What is meant by the term هجرة? Mention the event connected with it.

VI. Give and illustrate rules for finding out the corresponding *Christian* year from any *Hijri* year and *vice versa*.

Exercise.

Find out the dates of the deaths of—

I. اکبر *from* فوت اکبر شاه

II. امیر خسرو *from* طوطی شیرین مقال

III. اہلی *from* پادشاہ شعرا بود اہلی

IV. بابر *from* بہشت روزی باد

V. تیمور لنگ *from* وداع شہر یاری

VI. جامی *from* کاشف سر آلہ

VII. جہانگیر *from* جہان از جہانگیر رفت

VIII. حافظ *from* خاک مصلی

IX. حیدر *from* جان بالا گہاك برفت

X. سعدی *from* خاص

XI. فردوسی *from* میوۂ فردوس

XII. مراد *from* از گلشن اقبال نہالی شدہ گم

XIII. ہمایون *from* { ہمایون بود وارث ملک وی
ہمایون پادشاہ از بام افتاد }

CHAPTER XVII.

Arabic Forms and Measures.

232. In modern Persian more than half the substantives and adjectives in use are pure Arabic. In almost every page of even the most popular Persian books, such as the *Gulistan* and the *Bustan* of Sa'adi, the *Akhlak-i-Muhsini* and the *Anwar-i-Suhili* of Kashifi, whole phrases and sentences from the Arabic are introduced. It is, therefore, absolutely necessary to point out and explain the more prominent peculiarities of such Arabic words as are of frequent occurrence in the Persian language.

N.B.—Sir Charles Wilkins says, "Arabic words introduced into the Persian language, might be counted by thousands. The two languages, Persian and Arabic, are so copious and are so extensively cultivated that the best Persian writers may and do employ Arabic words at their own discretion without limit or reserve."

233. The radical words of the Arabic language generally consist of three letters, and the Arabian grammarians consider the third person singular of the past tense of every verb as the ROOT or BASIS of such verb; as, كتب, he wrote; نظر, he looked.

These roots are expanded by means of certain letters, either prefixed or inserted somewhere between the beginning and the end, so as to produce certain forms, bearing a relation to the original root; as, انتظار — منظور — انظار — ناظر (*root* نظر). کاتب — کتاب — مکتوب — مکتب (*root* کتب).

234. The letters employed for the development and expansion of the triliteral roots of the Arabic language are called Servile Letters (حروف زايد) and they are seven in number, *viz.*, ت, س, م, ن, و, and ي.

The radical letters (حروف اصلي) are twenty-one in number, and they are so called because they are always found in the roots or primitive forms of Arabic words.

Rules for the Insertion of Servile Letters.

235. Rule I. The serviles ا and ت may occur either at the beginning, or in the middle, or at the end of a word; as, اقبال, fortune; اكرام, respect; مرحبا, welcome; تعليم, instruction; استفسار, inquiry; حقيقت = truth.

Rule II. The servile س is always used as the second letter of a word, and it is preceded either by ا or م, and followed by ت; as, استقبال, reception; استبصار, foresight; مستفيد, a gainer; مستوجب, worthy.

Rule III. The servile م is always used at the beginning; as, مفتاح a key; مدرسه, a college; مُذهب.

Rule IV. The serviles ن and ى are employed either in the interior, or at the end; as, انفعال, shame; عصيان, sin; شريف, noble; حاجي, a pilgrim.

Rule V. The و is employed in the middle of a word; as, مظلوم, oppressed; معلوم, known; محروم.

Rule for finding the Root.

236. If we strip every Arabic word of its servile letters, we at once come to the Root. Thus, in the words انفعال = shame, استغفار = forgiveness, and معرفت = knowledge, we at once see that the *roots* are فعل, غفر and عرف, respectively.

Note.—In finding roots of Arabic words with a تّ, one ت should be considered as servile, and the other ت, should be changed into radical و; as, اتّفاق = accident (root وفق *it happened*); اتّكال = confidence (وكل = *he entrusted*); اتّصال = union (وصل = *he united*).

The servile ت which comes after ز and ض is changed into د and ط respectively; as, ازدواج (*rt.* زوج) ازدحام (*rt.* زحم) اضطراب (*rt.* ضرب) اضطرار (*rt.* ضرر).

N.B.—It must be observed, however, that the seven serviles may be employed as radical letters (حروف اصلي) of the triliteral root; as, تعليم (علم he taught) instruction; منظر (نظر he looked) scene; مكتب (كتب he wrote) a school; منطق (نطق, he spoke) oration.

Note.—A little practice, however, will enable the student to get over difficulties of this sort.

The term Form is adopted to denote the more outward appearance of the primary root. The various modifications or changes which a form may undergo by the application of the short vowels, are called *Measures* of such form.

The Arabs have adopted the triliteral root فعل, with a view to exemplify the various forms and measures of their words.

237. The following forms and measures, all springing from the triliteral root, comprehend such only as will be found most useful to Persian students.

First Form. فاعل—This form has two measures, *viz.* 1st فاعل, which is the Noun of Agency in Arabic, and may be either used as a substantive or an adjective in Persian; thus حاکم = a governor; غالب = a conqueror; شاعر = a poet; قادر = powerful; حاذق = skilful. 2nd, فاعَل; thus خاتَم = a ring; قالَب = a mould.

Second Form. مفعول—This form has only one measure, *viz.*, مَفْعُول. It is the passive participle in Arabic and it may be used as a substantive in Persian, thus مَکْتُوب (*written*) a letter or a book; مَخْلُوق (*created*) a creature; مَعْلُوم (known) science; مَعْشُوق (loved) a mistress.

Third Form. افعل — This form has only one measure, *viz.*, اَفْعَل, which is an adjective of the comparative or superlative degree; as, اکبر = اعظم = greater or greatest; احسن = more or most beautiful; اشرف = more or most glorious; اجمل = more or most beautiful.

Fourth Form. افعال — This form has two measures, *viz.*, 1st, اَفْعال, which is one of the Arabic plurals of the most frequent occurrence in Persian; thus, قول, pl اقوال = words; سبب, pl. اسباب = causes; طرف, pl. اطراف = sides; طفل, pl. اِطفال = children. 2nd, اِفعال, as, اخراج, expulsion; اِخلاص, sincerity; اِقرار, = agreement.

Fifth Form. فعلا — This form has one measure, *viz.*, فُعَلا, a very frequent form of one of the Arabic plurals, as وکیل, pl. وُکَلا = agents; ندیم, pl. نُدَما = courtiers; وزیر,

pl. وُزرا = ministers; امیر, pl. اُمرا = noblemen; فقیر pl. فُقرا = poor men; غریب pl. غُربا = strangers.

Sixth Form. مفعل — This form has one measure, *viz.*, مَفعَل which is the "*noun of place*," because it denotes the "*place where*," the action indicated by the root is performed; thus مَکتَب (*lit.*, place of writing), a school; مَجلِس (*lit.*, place of sitting), an assembly; مَنزِل (*lit.*, place of alighting) an inn or a stage; مَشرِق (the place of rising) the east; مَغرِب (the place of setting) the west.

Seventh Form. مفعال — This form has only one measure, *viz.*, مِفعال, which is a "*noun of instrument*," as, مِفتاح = a key; مِقراض = a pair of scissors; مِنقار = a beak; مِیزان = a balance.

Eighth Form. فعال — This form has two measures, *viz.*, 1st. فَعّال. As a substantive it indicates the trade or profession of a person; صرّاف = a banker; بقّال = a green-grocer; جلّاد = an executioner; خیّاط = a tailor; نجّار = a carpenter; حمّال = a porter; قصّاب = a butcher; عطّار = a perfumer; نقّاش = a painter; 2nd فُعّال, which is the measure of one of the Arabic plurals; as, جاهل, pl. جُهّال = fools; عامل pl. عُمّال = officers; عاشق, pl. عُشّاق = lovers.

Ninth Form. فعول — This form has one measure, فعول, a very frequent form of one of the Arabic plurals, as

ملک pl. مُلوک = kings ; حرف pl. حروف ; علم pl. علوم = sciences ; نفس pl. نفوس ; رسم pl. رسوم = customs.

Tenth Form. فعیل — (*subs. or adj.*) رحیل = a journey; دلیل = a proof ; حسین = beautiful ; کریم = generous ; رحیم = merciful.

N.B.—It should be remembered that no single root in the language has ever furnished all the forms and measures assigned by grammarians to the root فعل.

Arabic Prefixes.

I. ال—" the " ; as, الدولت = (*Addaulat*) the kingdom ; الشمس = (*Ashshams*) the sun.

II. بو — " *a father* " ; *possessed of* ; as, بوالعجب = wonderful ; بوالہوس = lustful ; بوجہل = ignorant.

III. ذو—" *possessed of* " ; as, ذوجلال, glorious ; ذوفنون, learned; ذوجاہ, dignified ; ذوالقدر ; powerful.

IV. ذی — " *possessed of* " ; as, ذی روح, animate ; ذی قیمت, precious ; ذی ہوش sensible.

علی — " *in, on, to, near* " ; as علی الصباح = in the morning ; علی الخصوص = especially ; علی العموم = generally.

VI. فی — " *in, of, to, by with* " ; as, فی الجملہ = in short ; فی الحال = instantly ; فی الحقیقت = really.

VII. لا — " *without* " ; as. لاوارث = heirless ; لاجواب = answerless ; لاشک = undoubtedly ; لاعلاج = helpless.

VIII. ما—" *whatsoever* " ; as, ماحضر = whatever is ready; ما لا کلام = inexpressible ; مالزم = that which is necessary ; ماجرا = (*whatever happens*) accident ; ما باقی (*whatever remains*), the remainder.

Questions.

I. How do you find the root of a word ? (236)

II. Why are the Servile Letters so called ? (234)

III. Give the principal rules for the insertion of Servile Letters. What letters are so called ? (235)

IV. Are the Serviles ever used as Radical letters ? If so, how ? Give examples. (236 **Note**)

V. Why is وفق the root of the word اتفاق ? How do you account for it ? (236 **Note**)

VI. How do you find the root of Arabic words with a ت ? Give examples. (236 **Note**)

VII. How many Radical letters are there ? Why are they so called ? (234)

VIII. Form words on the measures of فاعل, افعال and مفعول from the triliteral roots نظر , خلق , قبل , and عرف . (237)

IX. Give some words of the same nature as افعل , مفعل, مفعال , and فعال . (237)

X. Mention some Arabic plurals formed on the measures of إفعال , فعلا . (237)

XI. Name and give examples of Arabic Prefixes.

XII. Explain the following words, giving the meanings of the prefixes :—بوالعجب — لاشک — مالاکلام — ذوفنون— ذی روح — ماجرا — ذوالقدر — ذیہوش — فی الحال —

XIII. Give the Persian words for Servile letters and Radical letters. (234)

XIV. Of the 28 letters of the Arabic Alphabet, 7 are Serviles and 21 are Radical letters. Enumerate and name them. (234)

XV. Servile letters are sometimes used as Radical letters. Give examples. (236 **Note**)

CHAPTER XVIII.

Numerals.

238. اسم عدد — Words denoting number: it is divided into the following classes:—

I. عدد مطلق or ذاتي — **Cardinal Numerals**; as, یک , دہ , بیست , شصت , صد , ہزار , &c.

In construction they precede the substantive to which they belong, and the substantive preserves the singular number; as, دہ درویش — صد اسپ — ہزار مرد.

Note—Sometimes they follow the substantive, and in that case the letter ي is added to the noun; as, سالي دو بوین بر آمد ; روزی دو بلا و محنت کشید

N.B.—Multiplicatives are expressed by adding تا or گانہ to the cardinals; as, یگانہ = یکتا single; دوگانہ = دوتا double; سہ گانہ = سہ تا, triple.

II. عدد وصفي or معین — **Ordinal Numerals.** These are formed by adding the termination ـُم to the cardinal numbers; as, پنجم, بیستم , چہلم , &c.

These are placed after the substantives to which they belong; as, روز چہارم — باب ہشتم — حکایت شصتم.

Note—This م is called میم تعداد = م of *number*.

Note—When more words than one are required to express the ordinal number, the ـُم is added to the last only, as بیست و ہفتم the twenty-seventh.

N. B.—The word نخستین expresses the first of the ordinals, as, دشمن نخستین ; نخستین اسقاد. The Arabic word اول is also frequently used, as, باب اول, the first chapter.

کُسور—Fractions.

239. In Persian Fractions are expressed by prefixing the denominator to the numerator; as $\frac{1}{3}$, ۱/۳, one-third, سہ یک; $\frac{1}{4}$, ۱/۴, one-fourth, چہار یک; $\frac{1}{8}$, ۱/۸, one-eighth, ہشت یک; $\frac{1}{10}$, ۱/۱۰, one-tenth, دہ یک; two-thirds سہ دو; three-fourth, چہار سہ.

240. In the following table the leading Cardinal numbers, together with the corresponding Arabian and European figures, are given.

The **Numerals** are written and read from left to right; thus, the year 1916 A. D. is written ۱۹۱۶

یک	۱	1	دوازدہ	۱۲	12	سی و یک	۳۱	31
دو	۲	2	سیزدہ	۱۳	13	چہل	۴۰	40
سہ	۳	3	چہاردہ	۱۴	14	پنجاہ	۵۰	50
چہار	۴	4	پانزدہ	۱۵	15	شصت	۶۰	60
پنج	۵	5	شانزدہ	۱۶	16	ہفتاد	۷۰	70
شش	۶	6	ہفدہ	۱۷	17	ہشتاد	۸۰	80
ہفت	۷	7	ہجدہ, ہشدہ	۱۸	18	نود	۹۰	90
ہشت	۸	8	نوزدہ	۱۹	19	صد	۱۰۰	100
نہ	۹	9	بیست	۲۰	20	صد و یک	۱۰۱	101
دہ	۱۰	10	بیست و یک	۲۱	21	دو صد	۲۰۰	200
یازدہ	۱۱	11	سی	۳۰	30	سہ صد	۳۰۰	300

چہارصد	۴۰۰	400	نہ صد	۹۰۰	900
پنج صد, پانصد	۵۰۰	500	ہزار	۱۰۰۰	1,000
ششصد	۶۰۰	600	دہ ہزار	۱۰۰۰۰	10,000
ہفتصد	۷۰۰	700	لک	۱۰۰۰۰۰	100,000
ہشتصد	۸۰۰	800	کرور	۱۰۰۰۰۰۰۰	10,000,000

Note—All the other numbers occurring between the tens are formed simply by adding the smaller number to the decade by means of the conjunction و; thus, بیست و دو, 22; شصت و شش, 66; یک صد و پنجاه و پنج 155, &c.

241. The following are the names of the days of the week:—

یک شنبه=Sunday. پنج شنبه=Thursday.
دو شنبه=Monday. جمعه or آدینه=Friday.
سه شنبه=Tuesday. شنبه=Saturday.
چهار شنبه=Wednesday.

Questions.

I. What are the sub-divisions of اسم عدد? (238)

II. Distinguish between عدد مطلق and عدد معین.

III. How are Ordinal Numerals expressed? Give examples.

IV. How are Cardinal and Ordinal Numerals used with nouns to which they belong? Give examples.

V. What two ways are there of expressing multiplicatives? Give examples. (238 Note)

VI. Mention the first three Persian Ordinal Numerals.

VII. What do you understand by عدد وصفي and عدد ذاتي? (238)

VIII. How are Fractions expressed in Persian? Give examples. (239)

IX. Name the first *ten Cardinal Numerals* in Persian.

X. Give Persian words for 10, 20, 30, 40, 50, 60, 70, 80, 90 and 100.

CHAPTER XIX.

صنايع بدايع=Figures of Speech.

243. صنايع بدايع (*pl.* of صنعت=*art*; and بديعت=*new; strange*) (lit. *rare and wonderful works of art*) Figures of Speech.

244. صنايع=**Figures** are divided into:

I. صنايع لفظي=Figures of *words*.

II. صنايع معنوی=Figures of *thought*.

245. The following sub-divisions of صنايع لفظی are frequently used in Persian:—

I.	تجنيس تام	II.	تجنيس ناقص
III.	تجنيس زايد	IV.	تجنيس مزيل
V.	تجنيس مضارع	VI.	تجنيس مكرر
VII.	تجنيس مركب	VIII.	تجنيس خط
IX.	تشبيهی	X.	استعاره
XI.	طرد و عكس	XII.	ردالعجزعلی الصدر
XIII.	قطارالبعيرين		

I. تجنيس تام = Perfect Homonym (*homos* = same; *onoma*=name) is a Figure of Speech in which two or more words similar in spelling and pronunciation are used with different meanings; thus:—

* چرا يزد ترا اين همه كام داد—چرا برنيارى سرانجام داد
2 1

1. داد=gave. 2 داد=justice.

مشو تا توان از سخاوت بری — که گوی بهي از سخاوت بري*

2 1

1. برى=far. 2. بري=thou wilt carry.

گدارا چون حاصل شودنان شام — چنان خوش خسپد كه سلطان شام

2 1

1. شام = evening. 2. شام = Syria.

تا توانی مدد از كف به بهار اي ساقي!

لب جام و لب جوي و لب يار اى ساقي!

3 2 1

1. لب = a brim. 2 لب = bank. 3. لب = lip.

II تجنيس ناقص = Imperfect *or* Defective Homonym is a figure of speech in which words of the same spelling but of different pronunciation and meaning are used; thus

بگفتا من گل ناچيز بودم — وليكن مدتى با گل نشستم

2 1

1. گل = a clod of earth. 2. گُل = a rose.

گروزير از خدا بترسيدي — همچنان كز مَلِک مَلَک بودی*

2 1

1. مَلِک = a king. 2. مَلَک = an angel.

III تجنيس زايد = (lit. *increased Homonym.*) It is a figure of speech in which two words almost similar in spelling and sound are used with different meanings, but one of them has a letter more than the other in the beginning; thus,

شرف هرکس به كمال است نه به مال*

2 1

1. کمال = perfection. 2. مال = wealth.

اند کي جمال به از بسیاری مال *

1. جمال beauty. 2. مال = wealth.

قدم باید اندر طریقت نه دم *

1. قدم (a step) an action. 2. دم (breath) a word.

IV. تجنیس مذیل is a figure of speech in which two words almost similar in spelling and sound are used, but one of them has a letter more than the other at the end; thus:

آئین ماست سینه چو آئینه داشتن *

1. آئین = custom. 2. آئینه = mirror.

شکم بند دست است وز نجیر پای۔شکم بندہ نادر پرستد خدای

1. بند = a chain. 2. بندہ = a slave.

V. تجنیس مُضارع is a figure in which two words similar in sound, but differing in initial letters, are used with different meanings, as,

اجل بگسلاندش طناب امل — وفاتش فروبست دست عمل *

1. امل = hope. 2. عمل = action.

VI. تجنیس مکرر (lit. *repeated Homonym*). It is a figure in which two words similar in spelling and sound, but differing in meaning are used immediately one after the other; as,

اگرچه هست گلقوا چو من هزار هزار

مرا بدست نباید چو تو نگار نگار

1. هزار = thousand. 2. هزار = nightingale.

1. نگار = mistress. 2. نگار = beautiful.

VII. تجنیس مُرکب (lit. *the Compound Homonym*). It is a figure of speech in which two compound words similar in spelling and pronunciation are used with different meanings. Sometimes one of them is used in its simple sense and the other in the compound sense; thus,

چه مردي کند در صف کارزار (1) — که دستش تهی باشد و کار زار (2) *

1. کارزار = a battle-field. 2. کار زار = straitened [circumstances.

یکی دختري داشت کز دلبری (1) — پري را برخ کرد از دل بري (2) *

1. دلبری = enchantment. 2. دل بری = separate [from her heart.

رفتم بر یار و گفتمش دلدارم (1) — داغي زغم عشق تو بر دل دارم (2)

1. دلدارم = I am a lover. 2. دل دارم = I have [(on my) heart.

VIII. تجنیس خط is that when the linear forms of the words are the same, but different significations, depending upon either the diacritical points or vowel marks or both are used; thus, باج tribute; تاج a crown.

گفت از جاهت اندیشه مي کردم اکنون که در چاهت دیدم

فرصت غنیمت دانستم * جاه = rank; چاه = a pit

IX. تشبيهي (شبه=*it resembled*)=**Simile.** A simile is the *comparison* between two objects of *different kinds* or *species*. This *comparison* is expressed by the word چون = *like*, as, رستم چون شير جنگيد

رعيت چو بيخ اند و سلطان درخت-درخت اي پسر باشد از بيخ سخت •
نصيحت كه خالي بود از غرض-چو داروی تلخ است دفع مرض

Note.—In the aforesaid examples the thing compared is called مُشبہ and the thing compared to is called مُشبہ بہ and چون is called حرف تشبيهی = particle of comparison.

X. إستعارہ (عور=*he borrowed*) = **Metaphor**. It is a *simile* without the sign of comparison چون=*like*. It is a figure by which one object is designated by the name of another object to which it bears some resemblance; thus, رستم شير است

N.B.—حرف تشبيهی *viz.*, چون *is not used.*

رعيت درخت است اگر پروري — به كام دل دوستان برخوری •
خبرداری ای استخوان قفس! — كه جان تو مرغ ست و نامش نفس •
دو ابرو كمان و دو گيسو كمند — بهالا بگردار سرو بلند •

XI. طرد و عكس (lit. طرد=*driving away*; عكس=*placing the last first*)=*Inversion*. It is a figure in which the words used in the beginning of the first hemistich are repeated at the end of the second hemistich and the words occurring at the end of the first hemistich are repeated in the beginning of the second hemistich; thus,

دلبر جانان من برد دل و جان من - برد دل و جان من دلبر جانان من
زلب جانان من زنده شود جان من - زنده شود جان من از لب جانان من
سرو گلستان من قامت دلجوي تست - قامت دلجوي تست سرو گلستان من

XII. رد العجز علي الصدر (lit. رد = *rejection*, ال = *the*; عجز = *the second hemistich*; علي = *from*; صدر = *the first hemistich.*) = **Antistrophe.** (lit. *The repetition of words in an inverse order.*) It is a figure in which the first word of the first hemistich is the last word of the second hemistich; thus,

شمار غم او ندانم از آنکه — بيرون شد غم او ز حد شمار *
سخن را سراست اي خردمند و بن - ميار و رسخن در ميان سخن *

Note.—Sometimes the last word of the first hemistich is repeated at the end of the second hemistich; thus,

ساقي بيار بادة كه آمد زمان گل
تا بشكنيم توبه ديگر در ميان گل •

XIII. قطار البعيرين (قطار = a string; ال = the; بعير = a camel; lit. *two camels tied together with a string*). It is figure in which the last word of the first hemistich is the first word of the second hemistich; thus,

دل زمن بستد بشوخي دلبري •
دلبري شيرين لبي جان پروري

نگه دار مارا زراه خطا — خطا در گذار و صوابم نما *

XIV. مقلوب (lit. inverted) an anagram.

(*a*) مقلوب كل is that when some words, in prose and poetry, are anagrams of one another; as, کاخ and خاک ; روز and زور

(*b*) مقلوب بعض (lit. partly inverted). When the letters used in a word are transposed to form another; as کمر and مکر; میان and نیام

(*c*) مقلوب مستوي (Palindrome) is a figure in which a sentence may be read backwards and forwards with the same signification; as,

مرادي دارم — بر آید یارب

246. The important varieties of صنایع معنوی are:—

I. إستدارک II. تضاد

III. سوال و جواب IV. مبالغہ

V. لف و نشر VI. مراعات نظیر

I. إستدارک (lit. *Emendation*) is a figure in which a poet first describes a person or a thing and again changes or rejects the same in order to intensify it; thus.

گر گویمت کہ سروی — سرو اینچنین نباشد*

گر گویمت کہ ماہی — مہ بر زمین نباشد*

تو گفتی کہ الماس مرجان فشاند

چہ مرجان کہ در کین ہمی جان فشاند*

II. تضاد (ضدّ = *it was opposite*) = **Antithesis.** It is a figure by which words and ideas are contrasted, *i. e.*, a figure in which contrary terms are used; as,

درشتي و نرمي بهم در به است
چون رگزن که جراح و مرهم نه است*

پشت من بشکن و پیمان مشکن—خون من میخور و زنهار مخور*

جهانرا بلندی و پستي توئی—ندانم چه هرچه هستی توئي*

III. سوال و جواب = A dialogue. It is a figure which contains questions and answers; thus,

گفتم اي سلطان خوبان رحم کن بر این غریب
گفت در دنبال دل ره گم کند مسکین غریب*

گفتمش بنشین زماني—گفت معذورم بدار*

گفتم که خطا کردی و تدبیر نه این بود
گفتا چه توان کرد که تقدیر چنین بود

گفتم که خداداد مرادت بوصالش
گفتا که مرادم بوصالش نه همین بود*

IV. مبالغه (بلغ = *he exaggerated*) = **Hyperbole.** (lit. *excess* or *exaggeration*). It is a figure by which more is expressed than is literally true; thus,

چو بنمودي بوقت خشم دندان—شدي از هیبتش چون آب سندان*

شود کوه آهن چو دریای آب—اگر بشنود نام افراسیاب*

ز گرز تو خورشید گریان شود—ز تیغ تو ناهید بریان شود*

V. لف و نشر (lit. لفّ = *he joined*, نشر = *he spread*). It is a figure in which a number of words are used together which are to be distributed to each of the words mentioned in the next line; thus,

بروز نبرد آن یل ارجمند—بشمشیر و خنجر بگرز و کمند
برید و درید و شکست و به بست—یلانرا سر و سینه پای و دست

VI. مراعات نظیر (analogy) is a figure in which a poet uses all the correlative terms; as,

نگار من که بمکتب نرفت و خط ننوشت
بغمزهٔ مسئله آموز صد مدرس شد

Questions.

I.—Name the different kinds of تجنیس generally used in Persian (245)

II.—How do you distinguish between تجنیس تام and تجنیس مذیل and تجنیس زاید — تجنیس ناقص

III.—Explain and illustrate with examples:—(245)
تجنیس مرکب — تجنیس مکرر — تجنیس مضارع

IV.—What are Persian technical terms for *Homonym*, *Simile*, *Metaphor*, *Antistrophe*, *Antithesis*, and *Hyperbole*?

V.—Define and illustrate:— ردالعجز علي الصدر —
استعارة — تشبیهي — قطار البعیرین — مبالغه — تضاد
— استدراک — طرد و عکس — لف و نشر.

VI.—What do you understand by the terms:—
صنایع معنوی — صنایع بدایع — صنایع لفظي.

VII.—Name that figure—

(*a*) Which contains contrary terms.

(*b*) Which contains questions and answers.

(*c*) Which denotes exaggeration.

VIII.—State with examples the distinction between

(*a*) تشبیهي and استعارة

(*b*) تجنیس تام and تجنیس مکرر

Exercise.

Explain the following sentences and mention the *figures of speech* used in them:—

(۱)—کوفته را نان تهي کوفته است*

(۲)—کي کار گر باشد سنان خار برخارا؟

(۳)—یارب! چه شد؟ کان تُرک من تَرک مُحبان کرده است

(۴)—طمع کرده بودم که کرمان خورم
که ناگه بخوردند کرمان سرم

(۵)—رخش رستم چون باد میدوید

(٦)—پادشاه تختم را بر تخت اختیار کرد

(۷)—دمی پیش عالِم به از عَالم است

(۸)—طراران آن گوسفند را دیده دیدهٔ طمع بگشادند

(۹)—به احسان توی حاتم—برفعت توی کسرا

(۱۰)—گفتم غم تو دارم گفتا غمت سر آید
گفتم که ماه من شو گفتا اگر بر آید

(۱۱)—جوان چون پیل مست در میدان در آمد به صدمتی
که اگر کوه روئین بودی از جای برکندی

(۱۲)—شهنشاه عادلرا رعیت لشکر است

(۱۳)—زیک شاخیم اگر شیرین اگر تلخ
زیک بزمیم اگر هشیار اگر مست

(۱۴)—گفتم صنما گر بمیرم چه کنی؟
گفتا که بیک عشوه ترا زنده کنم

(۱۵)—سلطان شبانست و عامی گله

CHAPTER XX.

Derivations and Derivatives.

آبرو—(آب, lustre ; رو , face) *lit.* lustre of the face, dignity, honour. [the shining sun.

آفتاب — (آف , the sun ; تاب , from تافتن , to shine) ;

اتصال—(وصل , closely united) وصال , conjunction. متصل , conjunctive. موصول , joined.

اجابت — (جاب , he answered) acceptance. جواب , an answer. مجیب , an answerer. مستجاب , answered.

اجتماع — (جمع , he assembled) a concourse. جماعت , an assembly. جامع , a collector. مجموع , collected. مجمع , a place of assembly.

احتباس—(حبس , he confined) imprisonment. حابس , a detainer. محبوس , imprisoned. محبس , a prison.

احتراث—(حرث , he tilled) tillage. حارث , a farmer. حراثت , agriculture. محروث , tilled. محرث , a plough.

احتراس—(حرس , he preserved) guarding, حراست , custody. حارس , a guardian. محروس , guarded.

احتراص—(حرص , he coveted) avarice. حریص , greedy. محروص , greedily desired.

احتساب—(حسب , he computed) محاسبت , calculation. حساب , arithmetic. محاسب , an examiner of accounts. مُحتسب , the superintendent of the police, who examines weights and measures.

احتمال—(حمل he carried a load) patience. حمال, a porter. حامل, pregnant. تحمل, patience.

اختصار—(خصر, he abridged) abridgment. مختصر abridged.

اختلاف—(خلف, he differed) disagreement. خلاف, opposition. مخالف, contrary. مخالف op-posite. مخالفت opposition.

اخلاص—(خلص, he purified) friendship. خالص, pure. مخلص, sincere.

ارتفاع—(رفع, he raised) elevation, height, revenue.

ارتفاق—(رفق, he associated with) مرافقت, friendship; رفيق, a friend.

ارجمند—(ارج, value; مند, full of) valuable; rare.

اردشير—from cuneiform *arta-khshtra*, Zend *asha-khshtra*, *i. e.*, a righteous king.

ازدحام—(زحم, he pressed) pressure of a crowd. زحمت, trouble. مزاحمت, hindrance.

ازدواج—(زوج, he coupled) marriage. زوجه, wife.

استبصار—(بصر, he perceived) intelligence. بصارت, بصيرت, foresight.

استحقار—(حقر, he despised) contempt. حقارت, disgust. حقير, contemptible.

استخلاص—(خلص, he was free) خلاصي, freedom. تخليص, deliverance.

استره—From ستردن to shave; a razor.

استعانت—(عون, he helped). معاونت, assistance.

استعجاب—(عجب, he surprised) astonishment. تعجب, amazement. متعجب, amazed.

استعمال—(عمل, he worked) application. عامل, an officer. معمول, customary. معاملت, business.

استغفار—(غفر, he pardoned) forgiveness. مغفرت forgiveness. غافر, غفور, forgiving.

استفسار—(فسر, he inquired) inquiry. تفسیر, explanation.

استماع—(سمع, he listened) hearing. مسمع, ear, سامع, مستمع, a hearer. مسموع, heard.

اشتغال—(شغل, he employed) occupation. مُشتغل, مشغول, busy.

اشتقاق—(شق, he derived) derivation. مُشتق. derivative.

اشتہا—(شہو, he desired) appetite. شہوت, lust.

اشتیاق—(شوق, desired) an eager desire. مشتاق, anxious.

اضطراب—(ضرب, he struck) confusion. مُضطرب, confounded.

اطلاع—(طلع, he knew) information. مُطلع, informed.

اعتبار—(عبر, he believed) confidence. مُعتبر, trustworthy.

اعتدال—(عدل, he was just) moderation. مُعتدل moderate. معدلت, justice. عادل, just.

اعتراف—(عرف, he knew) confession. معرفت, acquaintance. معروف, known.

اعتقاد—(عقد, he believed) confidence. مُعتقد, a faithful friend. عقیدت faith.

اعتماد—(عمد, he trusted) confidence. مُعتمد confidential.

افتقار—(فقر, he was poor) poverty; فقیر a poor man; مُفتقر, reduced to poverty.

افتکار—(فکر, he thought) meditation. مُتفکر thoughtful.

اقبال—(قبل, approached) good fortune. مُقبل, fortunate. مُستقبل, future.

اقرب—(قرب, he was near) nearest. اقارب, relations. قریب, a kinsman.

اکبر—(کبر, he was great) greatest. کبیر, great. تکبر, pride. مُستکبر, proud.

امتناع—(منع he prevented) abstaining. مانع, forbidder. مُمتنع, prohibited ممنوع.

امتحان—(محن, he tested) examination; ممتحن, examiner.

انتظار—(نظر he looked) expectation مُنتظر, expectant. منظر, aspect. منظور; ناظر

انتظام—(نظم, he arranged) order. مُنتظم, arranged.

انتقام—(نقم, he punished), revenge, avenger, منتقم.

انجمن—From zend *hanjamana,* from the root *hanjam,* to meet together; an assembly.

انصاف—(نصف, he divided) justice. مُنصف, a magistrate. [مُنعم, beneficent.

انعام—(نعم, he bestowed) a gift. نعمت, beneficence;

انقلاب—(قلب, he changed) revolution. مقلوب inverted.

انکار—(نکر, he denied) refusal. مُنکر, forbidden.

انوشہ—From Zend *an*=not; Zend aosho=old Per. ہوش death; not dying; blessed.

ایران—From Zend airya, Sanskrit arya, respectable, of noble birth. The country of a respectable, dignified nation, *i. e*, the Aryans.

بازار—(باز, back; آر fr. آوردن, to bring); 2nd (ابا broth; زار, place) a market.

بزاز—(بز, linen) a cloth merchant; a draper.

بشارت—(بشر, he rejoiced) joyful tidings, بشیر, a messenger of good news.

بیعانہ—(بیع, he sold) the money given in advance; earnest-money, بایع, a seller.

پاانداز—(پا, foot; انداز fr. انداختن, to throw) a carpet spread at the entrance of a room on which the feet are cleaned.

پاپوش—(پا, foot; پوش, cover) a shoe.

پاکباز—(پاک, pure; باز fr. باختن to play) a fair dealer.

پیشکش—(پیش, before, کش fr. کشیدن, to draw) something worth carrying, *i. e.*, a magnificent present.

پیغمبر—(پیغم, a message; بر fr. بردن, to carry) a messenger; a prophet.

پینہ‌دوز—(پینہ, a patch; دوز fr. دوختن, to sew) a patcher; a cobbler.

تاخیر—(اخر, he postponed) delay. مُتاخر, delayed.

تازیانہ—(تاز, fr. تاختن, to drive) a whip.

تبدیل—(بدل, he changed) alteration. مُبدل, changed. مبادلت, exchange.

تجارت—(تجر, he traded) commerce. تاجر, a merchant.

تجاہل—(جہل he was ignorant) indiffernce. جاہلیت, ignorance. جاہل, ignorant; مجہول.

تحصیل—(حصل, he gained) acquisition. محصول, revenue. حاصل, profit.

تدریج—(درج he advanced) degree. درجہ rank.

تصنیف—(صنف he composed) literary composition. مُصنف, a compiler, an author.

تعجیل—(عجل, he made haste) haste. عاجل, swift. مستعجل, one who hastens.

تعجب—(عجب, he was astonished) amazement. مُتعجب, astonished, amazed.

تعظیم—(عظم, he honoured) respect, عظمت, greatness, مُعظم, respectable. عظیم, glorious.

تعلق—(علق, he depended) dependence, connection. مُتعلق, a dependent.

تعلیم—(علم he knew) instruction. مُعلم, a teacher. عالم, learned. معلوم, known.

تفصيل—(فصل, he separated) distinction; منفصل, disjunctive.

تفسير—(فسر, he explained) interpretation, مُفسر.

تقاضا—(قضي, he dunned) demand.

تقدير—(قدر, he arranged or determined) fate. مقدور, predestined, decreed.

تمليک — (ملک, he possessed) possession. مالک, a master. مملوک, possessed, a slave.

تناول—(نول, he carried off) eating. نوالہ, a morsel.

تندرو—(تند, swift; رو fr. رفتن to go) a quick goer. 2nd (تند, fierce; رو face) passionate.

توقف—(وقف, he stopped) delay. موقوف postponed.

تولد—(ولد he brought forth) birth. والد father. مولود, son. متولد, born.

تهنيت—(هنا, he congratulated) congratulation.

جراحت — (جرح he wounded) a wound. جراح, a surgeon. مجروح wounded.

جماعت—(جمع collected) a crowd, جمعيت. tranquillity. مجموع assembled.

چوگان—(a short form of چولگان, چول bent) a stick with one end bent, used in a game at ball (hockey).

حبيب—(حب he loved) a friend; مُحب a lover; محبت affection; محبوب beloved.

حرکت — (حرک he moved) motion; disturbance. مُتحرک moved; movable.

حکايت—(حکي he related) a story. حاکي a historian.

حکومت — (حکم he commanded) dominion. حاکم a governor. محکوم ordered.

خارپشت — (خار thorn, پشت back) a porcupine.

خانسامان—(خان a lord, سامان household articles) a house steward. [existent ; God.

خدای—(خود self, آي fr. آمدن to come) self-

خرچنگ—(خر large, چنگ claw) a crab. [dervish.

خرقه پوش—(خرقه a religious habit, پوش cover) a

خرگاه—(خر large, گاه place) a spacious place, a pavilion, a tent. [corn, the harvest.

خرمن—(خر large, من a heap or a pile) a heap of

خرمهره—(خر large, مهره a shell) glass-beads.

خلقت—(خلق he created) creation. خالق the creator. مخلوق created.

خمار—(خمر he drank wine) headache after drinking. مخمور intoxicated.

خورده بين—(خورده minute, بين fr. ديدن to see) a microscope.

خورشيد—(خور the sun, شيد bright) the sun.

دارالادب—(دار, a house, ال the, ادب learning) a seat of learning, University.

دارالبقا—(دار, house, ال the, بقا eternity) house of eternity, the other world.

دارالحرب—(دار, ال , حرب war) an enemy's country, a hostile country.

دارالحكومت—(دار, ال, حكومت authority) capital.

دارالسلطنت—(دار, ال, سلطنت power) metropolis.

دارالشفا—(دار, ال, شفا cure) a hospital.

دارالضرب—(دار, ال, ضرب struck or coined money), the mint. world.

دارالفنا—(دار, ال, فنا frailty) the frail house, the

دارالقرار—(دار, ال, قرار tranquillity) the other world. [justice.

دارالقضا—(دار, ال, قضا judgment) tribunal of

دارالکتب—(دار, ال, کتب books) a library.

دارالمرض—(دار, ال, مرض disease) a hospital.

درویش—(در, a door, ویز=ویش fr. آویختن to hang), 2nd (در a pearl, ویش like) a dervish.

دستور— Pehlvi dastobar (from دست, the hand), one who leads by the hand; a spiritual guide.

دُشمن—From دُش Zend *dush*, bad and منیدن (old, Per.) to think; an evil thinker; an enemy.

دوربین—(دور far, بین fr. دیدن to see) a telescope.

دهقان—(ده a village, قان = خان a prince) the headman or chief of a village; 2nd (ده a village, قان pertaining to) a peasant.

دیباچه—(دیبا brocade) a preface (so called because it is generally written in an ornate style).

ذوالقدر—(ذو, possessed of, ال the, قدر, power) powerful. [ship) kinsman.

ذوالقربی—(ذو, possessed of, ال the, قربی relation-

ذوالقرنین—(ذو, قرنین two horns) having two horns (of the world), implying that he conquered the world from east to west; a title of Alexander the Great.

رحلت—(رحل he travelled) journey, departure. مرحله an inn for travellers.

رستاخیز—From رستا, Zend *irista*=the dead, and خیز from خاستن to rise; resurrection.

رعایت—(رعی he protected) favour. رعیت, subject. راعی a shepherd. مراعات, regard.

رکاب — (رکب he mounted) a stirrup, مرکب a horse.

زادبوم—From زادن to give birth, and برم, Zend *bumi*, Sanskrit *bhumi*, a place; a native place.

زراعت—(زرع he sowed) agriculture. مزرع a field. مُزارع, a husbandman. مزروع sown.

زردوز—(زر gold. دوز fr. دوختن to sew) an embroiderer.

زمستان—(زم Zend, zim Sanskrit Hima, cold and ستان place; cold season; winter.

سال گرہ—(سال a year, گرہ a knot) Birthday (on the anniversary of which a knot was annually added on a string kept for this purpose).

سپنج—(سہ three, پنج five) a place where one halts for a few days, *i.e.*, the world.

سپہسالار—(سپہ an army, سالار a general) commander-in-chief.

سخن چین—(سخن a word, چین fr. چیدن to gather) an informer, a tale-bearer.

سدرمق—(سد an obstruction, رمق the last breath) a bare subsistence, just enough to keep body and soul together.

سرباز—(سر head, باز fr. باختن to play) risking one's own head; brave; a soldier.

سرزنش—(سر, زن fr. زدن to strike) reproach.

سرکش—(سر, کش fr. کشیدن to draw) proud.

سرمایہ—(سر source, مایہ wealth) capital.

سکنجبین—(for سکنگبین, fr. سک = سرکہ vinegar, انگبین honey) a mixture of vinegar and honey; Oxymel. [a champion, warrior.

سلحشور—(سلح arms, شور he tried) trained to arms;

سنگ پشت — (سنگ stone, پشت back) a tortoise.
سیاه گوش — (سیاه black, گوش ear) lynx.
سیراب — (سیر full of, آب water) fresh, juicy.
سیماب — (سیم silver; آب water) mercury.
شاباش — (for شاد باش, fr. شاد happy, باد be) Bravo!, Excellent! well done!
شبنم — (شب, نم moisture), night-moisture; dew.
شراکت — (شرک became partners), partnership. شریک, a partner. مُشترک shared, common.
شطرنج — (صد رنج fr. صد hundred, رنج care), *lit.* (a hundred cares), 2ndly (ششرنگ fr. شش six, رنگ kind), *lit.* (six ranks, viz., فیل, elephant; فرزین, queen; شاہ, king; پیادہ, pawn; فرس knight; رخ, castle); chess.
شفاعت — (شفع he interceded), recommendation. شفیع an intercessor, an advocate.
شمشیر — (شم claw, شیر a lion), a sword, scimitar.
شور بوم — (شور brackish, بوم land), barren ground.
شہادت — (شہد he testified), evidence. شاہد a witness.
شہرت — (شہر, published), renown. مشہور famous.
صاحب قران — (صاحب lord, قران conjunction), *lit.* Lord of the happy conjunction (of two stars or planets) a fortunate and invincible hero. A title of Timur.
صوفی — (صاف pure, clean) wise, pions or religious; 2nd صوف = wool, in allusion to the coarse woollen garments usually worn by Sûfis.
صحبت — (صحب he associated together), society, مصاحب a friend; مصاحبت intimacy.
صیاد — (صید he hunted), a hunter, a fowler.
ضحاک — Zend *azhi dahâka,* Pehlvi *ajdahâk,* the

stinging snake; this is an Arabicised word from Persian, اژدرہا — اژدہا a dragon.

طباخ — (طبخ he cooked), طابخ a cook; مطبوخ cooked. مطبخ a kitchen.

طبیب — (طب, he made up medicine), a physician; طبابت the medical art.

طوفان — (طوف went round), storm, tempest.

طہارت — (طہر he cleaned), cleanness, ablution.

عابد — (عبد he adored), an adorer; عبادت worship; مُعبد a worshipper; معبود worshipped.

عبارت — (عبر he explained), style; تعبیر interpretation; عابر an interpreter.

عابر — (عبر he crossed), a passenger; عبور passage; مَعبر a ford; معبر a ferry-boat.

عمارت — (عمر he repaired, inhabited), an edifice; معمار an architect; معمور inhabited.

غالب — (غلب he conquered), a conqueror; مغلوب conquered; غلبہ victory.

غنیمت — (غنم he carried off booty), plunder, spoil.

غیبدان — (غیب hidden, دان fr. دانستن to know), Omniscient.

فراش — (فرش he spread) one who spreads the carpet or cushions; a chamberlain.

فرومایہ — (فرو low. مایہ origin), mean.

فصاحت — (فصح he employed elegant language), eloquence; فصیح eloquent.

فضیلت — (فضل he excelled), virtue, learning; فاضل excellent, learned.

فیلسوف — (the Arabicised form of the Greek word *philo-sophia*, "I love wisdom"); hence

فیلاسوف (فیلا a lover, سوف wisdom), a philosopher.

قایم مقام—(قایم perpetual, مقام position), *locum-tenens,* deputy, successor.

قزاگند—(قز raw silk, آگند filled) a garment quilted with silk and worn in battle; a coat of mail.

قشلاق—(قش, winter; لاق = لاخ, place); winter-quarters.

قلمتراش—(قلم a pen, تراش to cut), a penknife.

قلم رو—(قلم, pen; رو, go); the jurisdiction within which the orders written by a ruler go; an empire.

کاتب—(کتب he wrote), a writer; کتاب a book; مکتوب written; مَکتب a school.

کاغذباد—(کاغذ paper, باد wind), a paper-kite.

کتخدا—for کد خدا; کد (Zend kata a house, خدا master), master of the house; a rich or great man.

کجباز—(کج crooked, باز fr. باختن to play), an unfair player; fraudulent.

کج بین—کج چشم—(کج crooked, بین fr. دیدن to see, چشم eye), squint-eyed.

کراہت—(کرہ he loathed) disgust; مکروہ detestable.

کژدم—(کژ crooked, دم a tail), a scorpion.

کلوخ انداز—(کلوخ a clod of earth, انداز fr. انداختن to throw), a slinger.

کلوخ کرب—(کلوخ, کوب fr. کوفتن to break), a clod crusher; a mallet for breaking clods.

کہربا—(کہ straw, grass; ربا fr. ربودن to carry), *lit.* attracting straw; amber.

گران گوش—(گران heavy, گوش ear), deaf.

گران مایه — (گران, مایه origin) of noble birth; precious.

گربز — (for گرگبز, گرگ a wolf, بز a lamb), a wolf in the guise of a lamb; a cheat.

گرداب - (گرد it turned round آب water), a whirlpool.

گرد باد —(گرد it turned round, باد wind), a whirlwind.

گریبان —(گری the neck, بان keeper), a collar.

گلقند - گلشکر —(گل a rose, شکر , قند sugar), conserve of roses.

گورخر — (گور a desert خر an ass), a wild ass; the onager.

گوشمال — (گوش the ear, مال fr. مالیدن to rub), chastisement, especially that of schoolmasters upon boys by rubbing their ears.

گوشوار —(گوش the ear, وار worthy), *lit.* an ornament befitting the ear, *i.e.*, an ear-ring.

مالا کلام — (ما whatever, لا not, کلام speech), unspeakable, inexpressible.

مبالغت —(بلغ he endeavoured) diligence, exertion; exaggeration.

متابعت —(تبع he followed), obedience; تابع a follower; مُتابع obedient.

مُجادلت —(جدل he contented), contention, dispute; جدال strife, battle.

مجلس —(جلس he sat down), assembly; جلیس a chum; جلسہ a meeting; جلوس accession to the throne.

مَحبس —(حبس he imprisoned), a prison; حابس a detainer; محبوس confined.

محروم —(حرم prohibited), excluded (from favour), frustrated, disappointed.

محمود — (حمد he praised), praiseworthy; محمود praised; حمید laudable.

مخالفت — (خلف he opposed), opposition; مخالف opposite; an enemy.

مدرسہ — (درس he read), college, a public school; مُدرس a schoolmaster.

مراسلت — (رسل he wrote a letter), correspondence; رسالہ a letter. مُترسل, a letter-writer.

مرزبان — (مرز a limit, land; بان a keeper, a governor on the borders of a hostile country; a landed proprietor.

مُزدور — (مُزد salary, ور possessor), a hired labourer. [boxer, pugilist.

مُشت زن — (مُشت the fist, زن fr. زدن to strike), a.

مُصارعت — (صرع he wrestled), wrestling, a contest.

مُصنف —(صنف he composed), a compiler, an author.

مطبوع — (طبع printed), printed, impressed; 2ndly (طبع nature), natural, agreeable.

مُطرب — (طرب he danced for joy), a musician.

مطلع — (طلع he arose), the place of rising, the east.

معدوم — (عدم lost), non-existent; عدمیت non-existence; منعدم extinct.

معزولي — (عزل removed from office), dismissal; عزلت retirement from office.

معصوم — (عصم he defended), innocent, chaste; معصومی innocence.

مفتاح — (فتح he opened), a key; مفتوح opened.

مُکالمت — (کلم he spoke), conversation; مُتکلم a speaker.

مکیدہ — (کید he deceived), deceit, stratagem.

مُلازمت.(لزم he served), مُلازمی service; مُلازم servant.

مُلاطفت — (لطف he showed favour), kindness; courtesy; لطیف kind.

ملامت — (لوم he blamed), reproach; لایم a censurer.

مُنادي — (ندا he proclaimed), proclamation.

مُنازعت — (نزع he contended), contest, strife.

مُناسبت — (نسب he resembled or related), resemblance, relation; مُناسب fit, suitable; نسبت relation.

مُناصحت — (نصح he advised), admonition; نصیحت advice; ناصح adviser.

مُناظره—(نظر he disputed), contest, strife.

مُناکحت—(نکح he married), nuptial; نکاح marriage.

منت شناس — (منت favour or obligation, شناس from شناختن to recognise), one who appreciates favours, or recognizes obligations; grateful.

مُنجم—(نجم he predicted by the aspect of the stars); نجومی an astronomer, astrologer.

منزل—(نزل he descended or alighted), dwelling-house, halting-place.

منصب — (نصب he fixed or appointed), office, post; منصوب appointed, established.

منصور — (نصر he helped), triumphant, victorious; نصرت victory.

موروث — (ورث he inherited), hereditary; وارث an heir; میراث inheritance.

میرزا — (میر lord, زا fr. زادن to be born), the son of a lord, a gentleman.

ناخدا—(ناو=نا Sanskrit nâu, L. Navis, a ship, خدا master), a captain.

ناقص عقل—(ناقص deficient, عقل understanding), deficient in understanding; dull.

ندامت — (ندم he repented), repentance, regret.

نقاش — (نقش he painted), a painter ; نقشہ a map.

نگارخانہ — (نگار a picture, خانہ a house), a picture-gallery.

نگونبخت—(نگون inverted. بخت luck), unlucky.

نیشکر—(نی cane, شکر sugar), sugarcane. [moral.

نیکوروش—(نیکو good, روش manner), well-behaved,

واعظ—(وعظ he preached), a preacher, موعظت, sermon, admonition. [a pensioner.

وظیفہ خور—(وظیفہ a pension, خور fr. خوردن to eat),

ولي عهد—(ولي a prince, lord, عهد reign), heir-apparent, acknowledged successor.

ہمایون—from ہما, phœnix, and یون a suffix; ہما is considered to be a bird of good omen; hence fortunate, auspicious.

ہواپرست—(ہوا lust, پرست fr. پرستیدن to worship) a worshipper of lust, sensualist.

ہواخواہ—(ہوا pleasure خواہ fr. خواستن to desire) a well-wisher.

CHAPTER XXI.

Moral Maxims and Poetical Quotations.

A bird in the hand is worth two in the bush=
گنجشک در دست به که باز در هوا

An ass is always imposed upon=
خرالرا کس در عروس نخواند مگر آن زمان که آب و
هیزم نماند

After death the doctor=
بعد از مردن سهراب نوش دارو

A rolling stone gathers no moss=
برسنگ گردان نروید نبات

A prudent enemy is better than a foolish friend=
دشمن دانا به از دوست نادان

A burnt child dreads the fire=
کسي که از شیر سوخته شد دوغ را پف کرده می خورد

A word to the wise is sufficient=
عاقل را اشارت بس است

A friend in need is a friend indeed=
دوست آن باشد که گیرد دست دوست
در پریشان حالي و درماندگي

A drowning man catches at a straw=
وقت ضرورت چو نماند گریز — دست بگیرد سر شمشیر تیز

All is not gold that glitters=هر درخشنده طلا نیست
فریبي شکلی دیگر و آساس چیزي دیگر

A constant guest is never welcome=
مهمان عزیز است مگر تا سه روز

Avarice is the root of all evils=

بدوزد شره دیدهٔ هوشمند — در آرد طمع مُرغ و ماهی ببند
مرد قانع بزرگوار بود — طامع البته خوار و زار بود

Appearances are always delusive=

آنکه چون پسته دیدمش همه مغز
پوست بر پوست بود همچون پیاز

A new broom sweeps clean =

ملازم نو تیزرو — کوزهٔ نو آبرا دو روز سرد دارد

A man is liable to err=

گه باشد که از حکیم روشن رای برنیاید درست تدبیری

A lie has no legs =

آنرا که حساب پاک است از محاسبه چه باک

An ass is an ass though he be clad in silk and scarlet=خر ار جل اطلس پوشد خر است

A man is known by the company he keeps=

هر که با بدان نشیند نیکوی نبیند

As you sow so shall you reap=چندانکه بکاری بدروی

A penny saved is a penny gained=

پولی که سلامت داشت میسر شد

A bad workman quarrels with his tools=

قلم بدست و مُرکب بدست کاغذ بد
گناه هر سه چه باشد که دست کاتب بد

هر که کشتیگیر نیست فنش بسیار است

A man's nature does not change.

ریسمان سوخته لیکن کجیش بیرون نرفته — دُم سگ راست نشود

All cannot go to Corinth=اره کشیدن کار بوزنه نیست

A stitch in time saves nine=

درختی که اکنون گرفتست پای — بنیروی شخصی برآید زجای
سر چشمه شاید گرفتن بمیل — چو پرشد نشاید گذشتن بپیل

Better late than never=دیر آید درست آید

Birds of a feather flock together=

کند همجنس با همجنس پرواز—کبوتر با کبوتر باز با باز

Black stones will never turn white=

زنگی بگرما به سفید نگردد * باسیه دل چه سود گفتن وعظ؟
نصیحت کن چندان که خواهی—نتوان شستن از زنگی سیاهی

Beauty unadorned is adorned the most=

یک طلعت زیبا به از هزار خلعت دیبا
حاجت مشاطه نیست روی دلارا مرا
مُشک آنست که خود ببوید نه که عطار بگوید

You cannot burn the candle at both ends=

ابلهی کو روز روشن شمع کافوری نهد
زود بیني کش بشب روغن نباشد در چراغ

Be slow and sure= هرکاری نیکو شود لیکن بصبر

Charity begins at home=اول خویش بعد درویش

Cut your coat according to your cloth=

جامه به اندازهٔ تن باید دوخت * خرج به اندازهٔ دخل کن

Continual dropping wears away adamant, and little strokes fell great oaks=

اندک اندک خیلی شود و قطره قطره سیلی گردد

Coming events cast their shadows beforehand.

سالی که نیکوست، از بهارش پیداست

Diamond cuts diamond=

سنگ سنگرا می شکند ;شراب خورده را شراب دوا است

Delay is dangerous= آفتست در تاخیر

Do as you would be done by=

مپسند بکس آنچه بخود نپسندی
هرچه درباب خویش نه پسندی در حق دیگران روا نداری

سلوک آنچنان کن بخلق جهان }
که خواهی که باتو کنند آنچنان }

Evil company corrupts good manners=
صحبت مُفسدان و بدفعلان مردم نیکورا تباه کند
هرکه با دیگ همنشین گردد جامهٔ خویش را سیاه کند

Evil to him who evil thinks=کردهٔ خویش آید پیش
اگرخاری بکاری خاری بدروی ; چاه کن را چاه درپیش است

Every dog has his day =هرکسی پنج روز نوبت اوست

Empty vessels make most sound=
در ظرف خالی صدا زیاد میپیچد

Every sore has its salve=
= هردردی را درمانی مقرر کرده است

Fools rush in where angels fear to tread =
احمقان در پي آن میروند که عاقلان از آن پرهیزمیکنند

Friends are plenty when the purse is full =
هرکجا چشمهٔ بود شیرین— مردم و مرغ و مور گرد آیند

Fair is not fair, but that which pleases =
هرعیب که سلطان پسندد هنراست

Fair faces need no paint = Good wine needs no bush = مُشک آنست که خود ببوید نه که عطار بگوید
حاجت مشاطه نیست روی دلارامرا
به آب و رنگ و خال و خط چه حاجت روی زیبا را

Health is wealth =
هزار نعمت و یک تندرستی—گنج بیقیاس است تندرستي

Health is not valued till sickness comes =
قدرعافیت کسي داند که بمصیبتی گرفتار آید

Haste is waste = تعجیل کار شیاطین است
مستعجل بسر در آید

He jests at scars that never felt a wound =
تندرستانرا نباشد درد ریش

He is a dog in the manger=نه خود خورد نه کسي راده‌د

Hunger is the best sauce=کوفته را نان تهی کوفته است

It's distance lends enchantment to the view=
آواز دهل از دور خوش می نماید
In Rome do as the Romans do=هرملکی را هر رسمی
جای گل گل باش و جای خار خار
Idleness is the source of misery=
خر خفته جو نمی خورد * باز افتاده را چه قوت بود
I talk of chalk, you talk of cheese=
سوال از آسمان جواب از ریسمان
It is not the cowl that makes the frair=
It is not the hood that makes the monk=
در عمل کوش هرچه خواهی پوش
درویش صفت باش و کلاه تتری دار
Jack of all trades.
پیش ناظم ناثر و پیش ناثر ناظم
و پیش هردو هیچ و پیش هیچ هردو
Knowledge is power=توانا بود هرکه دانا بود
King Stork for king Log=
شد غلامی که آب جو آرد — آب جو آمد و غلامرا ببرد
Let bygones be bygones=
تیر که از کمان رفت نیاید به شست
Love's labour's lost=کفچه زدم کفچه زدم حلوا کو؟
Look before you leap=
اول اندیشه و آنگه گفتار— پای پیش آمدست پس دیوار
Look not a gift horse in the mouth=
مفت را چه باید گفت؟
Little learning is a dangerous thing=
نیم حکیم خطرجان
More wasps are caught by honey than by vinegar.
به شیرین زبانی و لطف و خوشی—توانی که پیلی به موی کشی
تیزی و تندی نیاید بکار—بنرمی بر آید زسوراخ مار

وقتی بہ لطفگوی و مدارا و مردمی
باشد کہ در کمند قبول آوری دلی

Might is right=دست زور بالا * ستم آمد داد برخاست
Many a penny makes a pound=
اندک اندک شود بهم بسیار — دانہ دانہ است غلہ در انبار
Much ado about nothing=
کوہ کندن و موش بر آوردن
Misfortunes seldom come singly=
ہر جا کہ سنگ آید بالای لنگ آید
Make hay while the sun shines=فرصت را غنیمت شمار
تنور تا گرم است نان بپز * چون میدان فراخ است گوی بزن
Man proposes, God disposes=
ہرچہ خدا خواست ہمان می شود
Make the best of a bad bargain=
سنگی را کہ نتوان برداشت باید بوسید و گذاشت
Money makes the mare go=واکن کیسہ بخور ہریسہ
No pains no gains=No sweat no sweet=
تا دانہ نیفشانی نروید ; تا بردہ رنج گنج میسر نشود
نوش بینیش حاصل نمیشود ; گل راحت بی خار محنت نروید
No rose without a thorn=ہرجا کہ گل است خار است
ہر بہاری را خزان در پی است
No smoke without fire=
تا نباشد چیزکی مردم نگویند چیزہا
One flower makes no garland=ازیک گل بہار نمی شود
One man's meat is another's poison=
یکی را نوش دیگری را نیش
معشوق من است آنکہ نزدیک تو زشت است
Out of sight out of mind=
ہر کہ از دیدہ دور از دل دور
One vacancy, a hundred applicants=
یک موش و صد گربہ * یک انگور و صد زنبور ; یک آہو و صد سگ

Out of the frying pan into the fire=
از قفص بر آمده در چاه اُفتادن

Patience and perseverance overcome mountains.
صبر گرچه تلخ است لیکن بر شیرین دارد
کارها به صبر بر آید

Prosperity gains friends and adversity tries them.
اقبال دوستانرا جمع میکند و ادبار ایشانرا می آزماید

Pride goes before destruction =
تکبر عزازیل را خوار کرد

Practice makes a man perfect=
شاگرد رفته رفته به استاد رسد

Procrastination is the thief of time=
کار امروز را به فردا نباید گذاشت

Pearls before swine= خر چه داند بهاي قند و نبات
آئینه داشتن در مجلس کوران

Penny-wise and pound-foolish=
درمی نگاه داشتن و دینارها خرچ کردن حماقت است

Prevention is better than cure=
علاج واقعه پیش از وقوع باید کرد

Praise is pleasing to fools =
احمق را ستایش خویش خوش می آید

Risk not, gain not=
تا جان در خطر نه نهی بر دشمن ظفر نیابی

غوّاص گر اندیشه کند کام نهنگ
هرگز نیارد دُرِّ گرانمایه بچنگ

Robbing Peter to pay Paul.
از ریش کندن و بر بروت بستن
از دامن بریدن و بر شانه پیوند کردن

Speak of the devil and he will appear.
نام سگ گیری چوب در دست گیري

Stretch your legs according to your coverlet.
به اندازهٔ گلیم پا دراز کن * پا از گلیم خویش پیشتر نباید کرد

Spare the rod and spoil the child=
جور اُستاد به ز مهر پدر
هر آن طفل کو جور آموزگار—نبیند جفا بیند از روزگار
گر نبودی چوب تر—فرمان نبردی گاو و خر

Strike the iron while it is hot=فرصت را غنیمت شمار
چو میدان فراخ است گوی بزن

Silence gives consent = خاموشي علامت رضا است

Set a thief to catch a thief = دزد دزد را میشناسد

Sufficient for the day is the evil thereof =
غم فردا امروز نباید خورد

To carry coals to Newcastle = گل به بوستان بردن
لقمان حکیم را حکمت آموختن * آب بدریا انداختن

To kill two birds with one stone. بیک تیر دو نشانه زدن

To count chickens ere they are hatched.

To sell the bear's skin before the bear is taken.
آهوی نا گرفته پوست فروختن

Too many cooks spoil the soup =
قابله چون دو شود سر بچه کج شود

The sleeping fox catches no poultry =
خر خفته جو نمیخورد

Two of a trade seldom agree.
بود همپیشه با همپیشه دشمن

The race is not always to the swift =
The battle is not always to the strong =
صیاد نه هر بار شکاري ببرد— باشد که روزي پلنگش بدرد
بسا اسپ تیزرو بماند—که خر لنگ جان بمنزل برد

To shut the stable after the steed is stolen =
بعد از مُردن سهراب نوش دارو

The wearer knows where the shoe pinches=
تندرستانرا نباشد درد ریش * تن آسوده نداند که دل خسته چه باشد

The boughs that bear most hang lowest=
تواضع کند هوشمند گزین — نهد شاخ پر میوه سر بر زمین

Tit for tat.

سخت زنی سخت خوری
در کسی مزن بانگشت تا نزند در ترا بمشت

There is no armour against fate=
تیر تقدیر از سپر تدبیر رد نمی گردد

The kettle calls the pot black=
خود فضیحت دیگر را نصیحت

The jaundiced see everything about them yellow=
تشنگانرا نماید اندر خواب — همه عالم بچشم چشمهٔ آب

Union is strength= پشه چو پر شد بزند پیلرا

What is bred in the bone will never wear out of the flesh=
عاقبت گرگزاده گرگ شود — گرچه با آدمی بزرگ شود
خوی بد در طبیعتی که نشست — نرود جز بوقت مرگ از دست

When the cat is away the mice will play=
استاد معلم چو بود کم آزار — خرسک بازند کودکان در بازار

Wisdom alone is age = بزرگی بعقل است نه بسال

Where there is a will there is a way=
دل نخواسته عذر بسیار

CHAPTER XXII.

Idioms explained and illustrated.

آب در دیده گردانیدن (*lit.* to roll water in one's eyes) *i.e.*, to shed tears; to weep.

پادشاه از شنیدن خبر مرگ پسر خود آب در دیده گردانید

آب از دیده پاک کردن (*lit.* to wipe off one's tears) *i. e.*, to dismiss uneasiness of mind.

گهش میزند تا شود دردناک—گهش میکند آبش از دیده پاک

آب نمودن و تشنه داشتن (*lit.* to show water and keep thirsty) *i.e.*, to torment by exciting hopes which are never realised; to *tantalize*.

Note.—A Phrygian king named *Tantalus* was punished in the lower world by being placed in the midst of a lake whose waters reached his chin, but receded whenever he attempted to allay his thirst, while over his head hung branches laden with fruits, which likewise receded whenever he stretched out his hand to grasp them.

آب در غربال داشتن (*lit.* to keep water in a sieve).
آب در سبد کردن (*lit.* to keep water in a basket).
آب به ریسمان بستن (*lit.* to bind water with a string), *i.e.*, to strive in vain; to make a fruitless attempt.

نصیحت همه عالم به گوش مرد نادان چو آب در سبد است
و در غربال

آب در هاون سودن (or) کوفتن (*lit.* to bray *or* pound water in a mortar) *i.e.*, to be uselessly employed; to act foolishly.

تخم بدی کاشتن و چشم نیکی داشتن مثل آب در هاون سودن است

آستین برچشم گذاشتن (*lit.* to place one's sleeve on one's eyes) *i.e.*, to weep secretly; to hide one's tears.

چون آن شخص احوال آن فقیر بیچاره شنید آستین بر چشم خود گذاشت

آستین بردهان داشتن (or) نهادن (*lit.* to put one's sleeve on one's mouth; to cover one's mouth) to laugh in the sleeve; *i.e.*, to laugh secretly.

پادشاه از شنیدن سخن مسخره آستین بردهان نهاد

آهن سرد کوفتن (*lit.* to beat cold iron) *i.e.*, to make a fruitless attempt; to try in vain.

کاهلی ورزیدن و در امتحان کامیاب شدن اُمید داشتن همچو آهن سرد کوفتن است

اجل گریبان حیاتش گرفت (*lit* death seized the collar of his life) *i.e.*, he died.

پیش از آنکه اجل گریبان حیات پادشاه گرفت او پسر خود را طلبید و وصیت کرد

از بر مادهٔ شیر دوشیدن (*lit.* to draw milk from the breast of a lioness) *i.e.*, to accomplish some wonderful feat.

با رستم گرد جنگیدن و از بر مادهٔ شیر دوشیدن یکسان بود

از پهلوی کسی شکم پر کردن (*lit* to fill one's belly with the ribs of others) *i.e.*, to live at the expense of others.

آن شخص از پهلوي دوست خود شکم پر میکند

از ریگ روغن کشیدن (*lit.* to extract oil from sand) *i.e.*, to try in vain.

از نی بوریا شکر خوردن (*lit.* to eat sugar from mat-reeds) *i.e.*, to try in vain.

اسپ برروي دریا تاختن (*lit.* to urge a steed upon the surface of the sea) *i.e.*, to strive in vain.

از فرومایه اُمید نیکی داشتن مثل اسپ بر روی دریا تاختن و از ریگ روغن کشیدن و از نی بوریا شکر خوردن است

انگشت به دندان گزیدن (*lit.* to bite the finger with the teeth) *i.e.*, to be amazed; to grieve.

پادشاه از دیدن این حال انگشت به دندان گزید

انگشت نما شدن (*lit.* to be pointed at with the finger) *i.e.*, to be notorious.

آن شخص به دزدی انگشت نمای جهان شده است

انقلابات روزگار دیدن (*lit.* to see the changes of time) *i.e.*, to experience the vicissitudes of life.

در آن شهر شخصی بود انقلابات روزگار دیده

باب لاینصرف خواندن (*lit.* to read the chapter "*not to spend*") *i.e.*, to be parsimonious.

آن دوست باب لاینصرف نه خوانده است

با اسلاف خود پیوستن (*lit* to be joined with one's own ancestors) *i.e.*, to die.

جد من به اسلاف خویش پیوست

باد در کف (or مُشت) داشتن (*lit.* to keep wind in the first) *i.e.*, to be penniless, poor.

آن بیچاره جز از باد چیزی در کف نمیدارد

باہم شیر و شکر بودن (*lit.* to be milk and sugar together; to be thoroughly mixed) to be hand and glove with a person, *i.e.*, to be on very friendly terms; to be very intimate.

آن دو پسر باہم شیر و شکر شده اند

بر شیر نر زین نہادن (*lit.* to put a saddle on *or* to saddle the male lion) to bell the cat, *i.e.*, to risk one's life for the sake of others.

Note.—"To bell the cat." The allusion is to the fable of the cunning old mouse, who suggested that they should hang a bell on the cat's neck to give notice to all mice of her approach. "Excellent," said a shrewd young mouse, "but who is to undertake the job?"

بر ابرو گره زدن (*lit.* to bring forth a knot on one's eyebrow) *i.e.*, to look angry, to frown.

به زندان قاضی گرفتار به — که در خانه بینی بر ابرو گره

بساط زندگانی نوردیدن (*lit.* to roll up the carpet of life) *i.e.*, to die.

آن پادشاه بساط زندگانی نوردید

به رحمت ایزدی پیوستن (*lit.* to be joined to divine mercy) *i.e.*, to die.

آن پیر مرد به رحمت ایزدی پیوست

به بال دیگر پریدن (*lit.* to fly in borrowed feathers) *i.e.*, to succeed by the assistance of others.

آنانکه به بال دیگر پرواز میکنند آخر کامیاب نمیشوند

پشم در کلاه داشتن (*lit.* to keep a feather in one's cap) *i.e.*, to possess a mark of distinction, or rank.

این ظفر پشم دیگر است در کلاه آن سردار

تغیرات لیل و نهار مشاهده کردن (*lit.* to see the

revolutions of night and day) *i.e.*, to experience the vicissitudes of life.

تلخ و شیرین ایام چشیدن (*lit.* to taste the bitters and sweets of life.) *i.e.*, to go through the ups and downs of life.

در ولایت حلب پادشاهي بود تلخ و شیرین ایام چشیده و تغیرات لیل و نهار مُشاهده کرده

تیشهٔ برپای خود زدن (*lit.* to strike an axe on one's legs) *i.e.*, to mar one's own affair.

آن شخص تیشه برپای خود میزند

جامهٔ زنان پوشیدن (*lit.* to wear the garments of women) *i.e.*, to prove cowards.

پادشاه گفت اي مردان! بکوشید تا جامهٔ زنان نپوشید

جان به حق تسلیم کردن (*lit.* to surrender the soul to God) *i.e.*, to give up the ghost; to die.

برادر من جان به حق تسلیم کرد

جو فروش و گندم نما (*lit.* one who sells barley and shows wheat) *i.e.*, an impostor, a cheat.

بزارید وقتی زني پیش شوي—که دیگر مخر نان زبقال کوي
ببازار گندم فروشان گراي—که این جو فروش است وگندم نماي

چشم و گوش شدن (*lit.* to be all eye and ear) *i.e.*, to give strict attention to.

برپند پدر و نصیحت اُستاد چشم و گوش باش

چین بر ابرو افگندن (*lit.* to bring forth a wrinkle on one's eyebrow) *i.e.*, to frown.

چون صاحب این سخن شنید چین بر ابرو افگند

خاک با خون سرشتن (*lit.* to mix blood with dust) *i.e.*, to make a general massacre.

لشکر پادشاه بر آن شهر حمله برد و خاک با خون سرشت

خون دل به ناخن آوردن (*lit.* to tear the breast with the nails) *i.e.,* to cry bitterly.

چون خبر مرگ شاهزاده به گوش پادشاه رسید
او خون دل به ناخن بر آورد

در پوستین کسی أفتادن (*lit.* to pick a hole in one's coat) *i.e.,* to find out some cause of blame; to tell one's faults; to speak ill of.

ترا هر که گوید فلان کس بدست
چنین دان که در پوستین خودست

در راحت بر خود بستن (*lit.* to shut the door of rest) *i.e.,* to renounce all rest and comfort.

آن شخص در کار خود چنان اشتغال میدارد که در راحت بر خود بسته است

در زیر لب خنده کردن = to laugh in the sleeve, *i.e.,* to laugh secretly so as not to be observed.

چون وزیر سخن آن مسخره شنید در زیرلب خنده کرد

در معني سفتن (*lit.* to perforate the pearls of speech) *i.e.,* to speak fluently.

وزیر بدین منوال دُرّ معنی بسفت که پادشاه از او خوشنود شد

درمیان دریا گرد خواستن (*lit.* to seek for dust in the midst of the ocean) *i.e.,* to form a foolish idea; to try in vain.

تخم بدي کاشتن و چشم نیکي داشتن چو درمیان دریا گرد خواستن است

دست از جان شستن (*lit.* to wash one's hands of life) *i.e.,* to despair of life; to give up hope of life.

هرکه دست از جان بشوید هرچه در دل آید بگوید

دست بر دست زدن = to smite one's hands together in grief; to repent.

آن شخص دست بر دست میزند که دریغ! نشنیدم نصیحت دانشمند

دعوت ایزدی را اجابت گفتن (*lit.* to accept the invitation of God) *i.e.*, to die.

چون پادشاه دعوت ایزدی را اجابت گفت شاهزاده را بر سریر سلطنت نشاندند

دفتر عهد و پیمان را برطاق نسیان نهادن (*lit.* to place the book of promise and compact upon the shelf of forgetfulness) *i.e.*, to break one's promise.

آن شخص دفتر پیمانرا برطاق نسیان نهاد

در حبالۀ نکاح در آوردن (*lit.* to bring into the snare of marriage) *i.e.*, to marry.

در سلک ازدواج کشیدن (*lit.* to draw into the string of marriage) *i.e.*, to marry.

پادشاه دخترخود را با پسر وزیر در سلک ازدواج کشید

رخت هستی به صحرای نیستی بردن (*lit.* to carry the goods of existence to the field of non-existence) *i.e.*, to die.

دیشب آن پادشاه رخت هستی به صحرای نیستی برد

ریش خراشیدن و نمک پاشیدن (*lit.* to irritate the wound and sprinkle salt thereon) *i.e.*, to add bitterness to taunt; to add insult (to injury).

پس دران حالت مصلحت ندیدم ریش درویش خراشیدن و نمک پاشیدن

روباه بازی کردن (*lit.* to play the fox) *i.e.*, to act with wiliness; to deceive.

روباه بازی کردن کار خردمندان نیست

روی درهم کشیدن (*lit.* to contract the face into wrinkles) *i.e.*, to frown.

چون استاد این سخن بشنید روی درهم کشید و او را سیاست کرد

زیر قلم آوردن (*lit.* to bring beneath the sway of one's pen) *i.e.*, to control; to govern.

در آورد مملکتی بزیر قلم — کز وبر وجودی نیامد الم

راه گریز پیمودن (*lit.* to measure the road of flight) to take to the heels, *i.e.*, to flee.

سپر انداختن (*lit.* to throw away the shield) *i.e.*, to lay down one's arms; to surrender.

لشکر دشمن سپر بینداختند و راه گریز پیمودند

سراز بالین تهی کردن (*lit.* to put aside every thought of pillow *or* rest) *i.e.*, to work incessantly.

آن شخص در کار خود چنان مشتغل شده است که سراز بالین تهی کرده است

سر از پا نشناختن (*lit.* not to know one's head from one's feet) *i. e.*, to be greatly perplexed; to be utterly confused.

آن شخص در دام حرص چندین مبتلا گشته است که سراز پا شناختن نمیتواند

سربه جیب تفکر فرو بردن = سربه گریبان بردن (*lit.* to carry down one's head into the collar of meditation) *i.e.*, to be deeply absorbed in thought.

پادشاه سربه جیب تفکر فرو برد و بعد از تامل بسیار سر بر آورد

سرخویش گرفتن = to follow one's own course; to attend to one's own business.

اگر پابندی رضا پیش گیر — وگر یک سواره سر خویش گیر

سرد و گرم دنیا (or) روزگار آزمودن (*lit.* to see

warmth and cold of the world) *i.e.*, to experience the ups and downs of fortune; to go through the vicissitudes of life.

پیر مردی جهاندیده سرد و گرم دنیا آزموده بود

سیاه و سفید فرق کردن (*lit.* to distinguish black from white) *i.e.*, to read a book.

آن شخص چنان بیعلم و بیخبر است که سیاه و سفید فرق کردن نمیتواند

شال کهنه داشتن (*lit.* to wear an old shawl) *i.e.*, to be very poor.

آن بیچاره شال کهنه و کثیف میدارد

عقد نکاح بستن (*lit.* to tie a marriage knot) *i.e.*, to marry.

ملک مصر عقد نکاح دختر خود با پسر پادشاه شام بسته است

قالب از جان تهی کردن (*lit.* to empty the body) *i.e.*, to give up the ghost; to die.

پدر پیر او قالب از جان تهی کرد

کارد به استخوان رسید (*lit.* the knife has reached the bone) *i.e.*, he is reduced to the last extremity.

در زمان باستان دهقانی بود که کارش به آخر رسیده و کارد به استخوان

کشتی برخشکی راندن (*lit.* to drive a vessel upon the ground) *i.e.*, to make a fruitless attempt; to strive in vain.

وزیر گفت ای پادشاه! این کار مثل اسپ بر دریا تاختن است و کشتی برخشکی راندن

مار بدست دیگر گرفتن (*lit.* to seize the snake with the hand of another) *i.e.*, to employ another in any perilous business.

مثل دو مغز بادام صحبت داشتن (*lit.* to be as closely united as two kernels of an almond) *i.e.*, to be hand and glove; to be very intimate.

من و او چون دو مغز بادام صحبت میداریم

مراحل زندگانی طی نمودن (*lit.* to pass all the stages of life) *i.e.*, to die.

پیر مردی را دیدم که مدت عمرش سپری شده بود و مراحل زندگانی طی نموده

نقش بر آب زدن (or) کشیدن (*lit.* to draw figures on the water) to build castles in the air, *i.e.*, to be engaged in unprofitable pursuits.

از ستمگاران امید لطف و رحم داشتن همچو نقش بر آب زدن است

متاع هستی بر باد فنا سپردن = نقد حیات بر باد فنا دادن (*lit.* to give the coin (or) property of life to the wind of destruction) *i.e.*, to die.

ودیعت حیات سپردن (*lit.* to entrust (to God) the deposit of life) *i.e.*, to resign one's life=to die.

CHAPTER XXIII.

Arabic Plurals.

The Arabs have adopted several modes of forming artificial Plurals.

Of these, some, which are of very common occurrence in Persian, are given here.

Rule I.—The plural of some triliteral nouns is formed by prefixing an ا *alif*, and inserting an ا *alif* between the last two letters.

Sing. Meaning.	Plural.	Sing. Meaning.	Plural.
اجل, death.	آجال	رُکن, pillar.	ارکان
ادب, respect.	آداب	رطل, pound.	ارطال
ازل, eternity.	آزال	روح, soul.	ارواح
اثر, effect.	آثار	سبب, cause.	اسباب
اُفق, region.	آفاق	سفر, journey.	اسفار
الم, pain.	آلام	سمع, ear.	اسماع
امل, desire.	آمال	شجر, tree.	اشجار
بیت, couplet.	ابیات	شخص, person.	اشخاص
ثمر, fruit.	اثمار	شعر, verse.	اشعار
جنس, thing.	اجناس	شکل, figure.	اشکال
جسم, body.	اجسام	صدف, shell.	اصداف
حُکم, order.	احکام	صنم, idol.	اصنام
خبر, information.	اخبار	صنف, kind.	اصناف
خُلق, nature.	اخلاق	صوت, voice.	اصوات
خیر, safety.	اخیار	طرف, side.	اطراف
دور, revolution.	ادوار	طور, way.	اطوار

Sing. Meaning.	Plural.	Sing. Meaning.	Plural.
طفل, child.	اطفال	کنف, side.	اکناف
عدد, number.	اعداد	لطف, favour.	الطاف
عذر, excuse.	اعذار	لفظ, word.	الفاظ
علم, flag.	اعلام	لقب, title.	القاب
عمر, life.	اعمار	لوح, plank.	الواح
عمل, action.	اعمال	لون, colour.	الوان
عون, assistance.	اعوان	مرض, disease.	امراض
عید, festival.	اعیاد	مثل, instance.	امثال
عین, nobleman.	اعیان	مصر, city.	امصار
غیر, stranger.	اغیار	ملک, property.	املاک
فضل, excellence.	افضال	موج, wave.	امواج
فعل, action.	افعال	نجس, dirtything	انجاس
فکر, thought.	افکار	نظر, sight.	انظار
فلک, sky.	افلاک	نور, light.	انوار
فوج, army.	افواج	نوع, kind.	انواع
فوه, mouth.	افواه	نهر, river.	انهار
فهم, wisdom.	افهام	وبش, vagabond.	اوباش
فیل, elephant.	افیال	ورد, rose.	اوراد
قدح, cup.	اقداح	ورق, leaf.	اوراق
قدم, step.	اقدام	وزن, weight.	اوزان
قسم, kind.	اقسام	وصف, quality.	اوصاف
قول, word.	اقوال	وصل, joint.	اوصال
قوم, tribe.	اقوام	وطن, native country	اوطان
کتف, shoulder.	اکتاف	وقت, time.	اوقات

Rule II.—The plural of some triliteral nouns is formed by inserting the letter و between the last two letters, and marking the first letter with ـُ "*pesh.*"

Sing.	Meaning.	Plural.	Sing.	Meaning.	Plural.
اصل	origin.	أُصول	بحر	sea.	بُحور
امر	business.	أُمور	بيت	house.	بُيوت
جلد	volume.	جُلود	عرق	vein.	عُروق
جمع	crowd.	جُموع	علم	knowledge.	عُلوم
جيب	pocket.	جُيوب	عهد	promise.	عُهود
جيش	army.	جُيوش	عيب	vice.	عُيوب
حرب	war.	حُروب	عين	eye.	عُيون
حرف	letter.	حُروف	فصل	season.	فُصول
رسم	custom.	رُسوم	فلس	coin.	فُلوس
سطر	line.	سُطور	قصر	palace.	قُصور
سقف	roof.	سُقوف	قيد	chain.	قُيود
شرح	explanation.	شُروح	كسر	fraction.	كُسور
شرط	condition	شُروط	مَلک	king.	مُلوک
شمس	sun.	شُموس	نذر	gift.	نُذور
شمع	candle.	شُموع	نفس	soul.	نُفوس
شهر	month.	شُهور	نقد	money.	نُقود
ضرب	blow.	ضُروب	نقش	picture.	نُقوش
طير	bird.	طُيور	نقل	copy.	نُقول
ظرف	vessel.	ظُروف	نعت	praise.	نُعوت
			وحش	wild beast	وُحوش

Rule III.—The plural of those triliteral nouns whose second letter is ا *alif*, is formed by prefixing an ا *alif*, and inserting the letter و between the first two letters.

Sing.	Meaning.	Plural.	Sing.	Meaning.	Plural.
باب	, chapter.	ابواب	غار	, cave.	اغوار
جار	, neighbour.	اجوار	قاع	, plain.	اقواع
جام	, cup.	اجوام	کاخ	, palace.	اکواخ
حال	, state.	احوال	مال	, property.	اموال
خال	, uncle.	اخوال	نار	, fire.	انوار
عام	, year.	اعوام	نال	, gift.	انوال
عون	, aid.	اعوان			

Rule IV.—Triliteral words ending in ی form their plurals by prefixing and suffixing an ا *alif* to the singular.

Sing.	Meaning.	Plural.	Sing.	Meaning.	Plural.
تقی	, pious man.	اتقیا	غنی	, rich man.	اغنیا
زکی	, virtuous man.	ازکیا	قوی	, strong man.	اقویا
سخی	, liberal man.	اسخیا	نبی	, prophet.	انبیا
شقی	, miserable man	اشقیا	ولی	, saint.	اولیا
صفی	, sincere man.	اصفیا			

Rule V.—Quadriliteral words, whose third letter is ی, form their plurals by dropping ی, suffixing an ا *alif* and marking the first letter with ـُ *pesh*.

Sing.	Meaning.	Plural.	Sing.	Meaning.	Plural.
امیر	, nobleman.	اُمرا	رقیب	, guardian.	رُقبا
امین	, secretary.	اُمنا	سفیر	, broker.	سُفرا
ادیب	, learned.	اُدبا	سفیہ	, fool.	سُفہا
بصیر	, intelligent.	بُصرا	شریف	, nobleman.	شُرفا
خلیف	, successor.	خُلفا	عظیم	, grandee.	عُظما
رفیق	, companion.	رُفقا	غریب	, stranger.	غُربا

Sing. Meaning	Plural.	Sing. Meaning.	Plural.
بليغ, eloquent.	بُلَغا	فقيه, lawyer.	فُقها
جليس, comrade.	جُلسا	قديم, ancient.	قُدما
حكيم, doctor.	حُكما	نديم, courtier.	نُدما
صديق, true man.	صُدقا	نقيب, a leader.	نُقبا
فصيح, eloquent.	فُصحا	وزير, minister.	وُزرا
فقير, poor man.	فُقرا	وكيل, deputy.	وُكلا

Rule VI.—Some Quadriliteral words form their plurals by inserting an ا *alif* between the second and the third letter.

Sing. Meaning.	Plural.	Sing. Meaning.	Plural.
بربط, lute.	برابط	موقف, station.	مواقف
بندر, sea-port.	بنادر	موقع, accident.	مواقع
دفتر, book.	دفاتر	مزرع, farm.	مزارع
دعوى, claim.	دعاوى	منفذ, passage.	منافذ
سبيل, way.	سبايل	معدن, mine.	معادن
ضمير, mind.	ضماير	مشعل, torch.	مشاعل
طريق, path.	طرايق	مرهم, plaster.	مراهم
عجيب, strange.	عجايب	مذهب, religion.	مذاهب
عسكر, army.	عساكر	جوهر, jewel.	جواهر
عنصر, element.	عناصر	خندق, ditch.	خنادق
غريب, strange.	غرايب	مديح, praise.	مدايح
فتوى, decree.	فتاوى	مجلس, assembly.	مجالس
قبيح, base.	قبايح	موكب, army.	مواكب
كوكب, star.	كواكب	موضع, place.	مواضع
محرم, unlawful.	محارم	منظر, aspect.	مناظر
محفل, assembly.	محافل	منصب, office.	مناصب
معبد, temple.	معابد	منزل, stage.	منازل
		منبر, pulpit.	منابر

Sing.	Meaning.	Plural.	Sing.	Meaning.	Plural.
مقصد	object.	مقاصد	مسجد	mosque.	مساجد
مطلع	east.	مطالع	مذبح	altar.	مذابح
مطلب	demand.	مطالب	مدخل	entrance.	مداخل
مطبخ	kitchen.	مطابخ	مخرج	expense.	مخارج
مصدر	source.	مصادر	معنی	meaning.	معانی
مصحف	book.	مُصاحف	نسیم	breeze.	نسایم
مشرب	reservoir.	مشارب	نفیس	precious.	نفایس
مسکن	abode.	مساکن			

Rule. VII.—Some Quadriliteral words, whose second letter is ا *alif* form their plurals by inserting the letter و between the first two letters.

Sing.	Meaning.	Plural.	Sing.	Meaning.	Plural.
باطن	interior.	بواطن	رابط	connection.	روابط
تابع	follower.	توابع	راحل	caravan.	رواحل
جامع	mosque.	جوامع	ساحل	shore.	سواحل
جانب	side.	جوانب	کاغذ	paper.	کواغذ
حاصل	profit.	حواصل	مانع	obstacle.	موانع
خاطر	mind.	خواطر	نادر	curiosity.	نوادر
خاتم	ring.	خواتم			

Rule. VIII.—Some Quadriliteral words, whose second letter is ا *alif* form their plurals by transposing the second and third letters, marking the first letter with ـُ "*pesh*" and the second letter with ـّ "*tashdid.*"

Sing.	Meaning.	Plural.	Sing.	Meaning.	Plural.
جاہل	fool.	جُہّال	حاجب	porter.	حُجّاب
حاکم	governor.	حُکّام	خادم	servant.	خُدّام
حاضر	present.	حُضّار	زاہد	hermit.	زُہّاد

Sing. Meaning.	Plural.	Sing. Meaning.	Plural.
ساکن, inhabitant.	سُکّان	کاتب , writer.	کُتّاب
طالب , beggar.	طُلّاب	کافر , infidel.	کُفّار
عاشق , lover.	عُشّاق	عامل , officer.	عُمّال
عابد, worshipper.	عُبّاد	مالک , owner.	مُلّاک

Rule IX.—Some Quadriliteral words, whose second letter is ا, form their plurals by removing the ا *alif* to the end, and marking the first letter with ـُ.

Sing. Meaning.	Plural.	Sing. Meaning.	Plural.
شاعر , poet.	شُعرا	عالم, learned man	عُلما
صالح, pious man.	صُلحا	فاضل , excellent.	فُضلا
عاقل , wise man.	عُقلا		

Rule X.—Some Quadriliteral words, whose third letter is ا *alif*, form their plurals by removing that ا to the beginning and adding the letter ة at the end.

Sing. Meaning.	Plural.	Sing. Meaning.	Plural.
جواب , answer.	اجوبه	شراب , wine.	اشربه
جهاز , ship.	اجهزه	طعام , food.	اطعمه
دماغ , brain.	ادمغه	قماش , cloth.	اقمشه
زمام , bridle.	ازمّه	لسان , tongue.	السنه
زمان , time.	ازمنه	مکان , place.	امکنه
سوال , question.	اسوله	متاع, property.	امتعه
سلاح , weapon.	اسلحه	نکاح, marriage.	انکحه

Rule XI.—Some Quadriliteral words ending in ة or ث, form their plurals by dropping the last letter.

Sing.	Meaning.	Plural.	Sing.	Meaning.	Plural.
تحفه	present.	تُحف	صورت	form.	صُور
حکمت	skill.	حکم	فرصت	opportunity.	فُرص
حیله	fraud.	حیل	قیمت	price.	قیم
خُطبه	sermon.	خُطب	قریه	village.	قُری
خیمه	tent.	خیم	نُقطه	dot.	نُقط
دولت	state.	دول	نُکته	witty point.	نُکت
سیرت	quality.	سیر	نوبت	turn.	نوب

Rule XII.—Adjectives of the comparative degree form their plurals by inserting an ا *alif* between the second and the third letter.

Sing.	Meaning.	Plural.	Sing.	Meaning.	Plural.
اکبر	greater.	اکابر	اعلی	higher.	اعالی
افضل	more excellent.	افاضل	اقرب	nearer.	اقارب
اصغر	smaller.	اصاغر	اکرم	more charitable.	اکارم
اعظم	greater.	اعاظم			

Rule XIII.—Substantives of five letters, whose fourth letter is any one of the long vowels ا , و or ی , form their plurals by inserting an ا *alif* between the second and the third letter, and changing the fourth letter into ی . If the fourth letter be ي itself, no change takes place.

Sing.	Meaning.	Plural.	Sing.	Meaning.	Plural.
ابریق	jug.	اباریق	تدبیر	contrivance.	تدابیر
اُستاد	teacher.	اساتید	تصویر	picture.	تصاویر
اقلیم	country.	اقالیم	درویش	dervish.	دراویش
برہان	proof.	براہین	دہقان	peasant.	دہاقین
بندوق	musket.	بنادیق	سلطان	emperor.	سلاطین

Sing. Meaning.	Plural.	Sing. Meaning.	Plural.
شیطان , devil.	شیاطین	مسکین, poor man.	مساکین
صندوق, box.	صنادیق	مضمون, meaning.	مضامین
فردوس, a garden.	فرادیس	مفتاح , key.	مفاتیح
فرمان , order.	فرامین	مقدار, quantity.	مقادیر
قندیل , lamp.	قنادیل	مقراض, scissors.	مقاریض
تقدیر , fate.	تقادیر		
تکلیف , trouble.	تکالیف	مکتوب , a letter.	مکاتیب
تلمیذ , disciple.	تلامیذ	منقار , a beak.	مناقیر
مخلوق, creature.	مخالیق	میدان , field.	میادین

Rule XIV.—Some Substantives of five letters, whose second letter is ا *alif*, form their plurals by inserting و between the first two letters and changing the fourth letter into ی .

Sing. Meaning.	Plural.	Sing. Meaning.	Plural.
تاریخ, history.	تواریخ	خاتون , lady.	خواتین
تابوت, coffin.	توابیت	خاقان , emperor.	خواقین
جاسوس , spy.	جواسیس	قانون , rule.	قوانین
جاموس , buffalo.	جوامیس		

Rule XV.—Substantives or Adjectives of five letters, whose last letter is ت or ۃ, form their plurals by omitting the final ت or ۃ and inserting an ا *alif* between the second and third letter.

Sing. Meaning.	Plural.	Sing. Meaning.	Plural.
بہیمہ , beast.	بہایم	ذخیرہ , store.	ذخایر
جزیرہ , island.	جزایر	سفینہ , ship.	سفاین
حقیقت , truth.	حقایق	شریطہ, condition.	شرایط
خزینہ , treasure.	خزاین	طبیعت, nature.	طبایع
دقیقہ , minute.	دقایق	غنیمت , booty.	غنایم
ذمیمہ , misdeed.	ذمایم	فریضہ , duty.	فرایض

Sing. Meaning.	Plural.	Sing. Meaning.	Plural.
قبيله, family.	قبايل	مرحله, stage.	مراحل
لطيفه, jest.	لطايف	مرتبه, dignity.	مراتب
مقبره, grave-yard.	مقابر	مدرسه, school.	مدارس
منفعت, profit.	منافع	نصيحت, advice.	نصايح
مصلحت, advice.	مصالح	نتيجه, result.	نتايج

Rule XVI.—Some Substantives of five letters, whose second letter is ا *alif* and last letter ه, form their plurals by omitting the final ه and inserting the letter و between the first two letters.

Sing. Meaning.	Plural.	Sing. Meaning.	Plural.
جارحه, limb.	جوارح	فايده, profit.	فوايد
حادثه, accident.	حوادث	فاكهه, fruit.	فواكه
دايره, circle.	دواير	قاعده, rule.	قواعد
طايفه, tribe.	طوايف	قافله, caravan.	قوافل
عارضه, accident.	عوارض	ناحيه, vicinity.	نواحی
عاطفه, favour.	عواطف	ناهيه, prohibition.	نواهی

N.B.—Besides these, there are several other modes of forming Arabic plurals; but there are so many irregularities and exceptions, that it is impossible to reduce them to any general rule. In some cases we cannot determine what kind of Arabic plural any individual word may form, consequently we must be guided entirely by usage.

Broken or Irregular Plurals جمع التكسير

Sing. Meaning.	Plural.	Sing. Meaning.	Plural.
آفت, calamity.	آفات	اول, beginning.	اوايل
آلت, machine.	آلات	آخر, end.	اواخر
آيت, verse.	آيات	حديث, tradition.	احاديث
اخ, brother.	اخوان	حاجت, need.	حوايج
انسان, man.	أناس	حاجی, pilgrim.	حُجّاج
امام, priest.	ايمه	حبيب, friend.	احباب

Sing.	Meaning.	Plural.	Sing.	Meaning.	Plural.
حصه	share.	حصص	ضد	opponent.	اضداد
حب	particle.	حبوب	طبیب	physician.	اطبا
حد	limit.	حدود	ظن	opinion.	ظنون
حق	right.	حقوق	عم	paternal uncle	اعمام
خصلت	habit.	خصایل	عدو	enemy.	اعدا
خلق	people.	خلایق	عضو	limb.	اعضا
خان	lord.	خوانین	عادت	habit.	عادات
دینار	dinar.	دنانیر	غازی	warrior.	غزات
دیوان	court.	دواوین	غم	grief,	غموم
در	pearl.	درر	غصه	anger.	غصص
دمل	boil.	دمامیل	فیلسوف	philosopher.	فلاسفه
دار	house.	دیار	فن	science.	فنون
دوا	medicine.	ادویه	قصه	fable.	قصص
دعا	prayer.	ادعیه	قیصر	emperor.	قیاصره
رعیت	subject.	رعایا	قضیه	dispute.	قضایا
رب	master.	ارباب	قاضی	judge.	قضات
رئیس	chief.	روسای	کتاب	book.	کتب
ساقی	cup-bearer.	سقات	لولو	pearl.	لآلی
سر	secret.	اسرار	منت	obligation.	منن
سن	tooth.	اسنان	وصیت	will.	وصایا
ساعت	hour.	ساعات	ولایت	country.	ولایا
سید	lord.	سادات	هم	care.	هموم
شر	wicked thing.	شرور	یتیم	orphan.	ایتام or یتامی
شیخ	holy man.	مشایخ	یوم	day.	ایام
صف	rank.	صفوف			
صحرا	desert.	صحاری			

CHAPTER XXIV.

Antonyms = الفاظ اضداد

Words having opposite meanings.

Words.	Meanings.	Contrary Terms.	Meanings.
ابتدا	beginning.	انتہا	end.
اسفل	lower.	اعلی	upper.
اقرار	confession.	انکار	denial.
اندک	a little.	بسیار	much.
اوج	summit.	قعر	bottom.
آسان	easy.	دشوار	difficult.
آشنا	friend.	بیگانہ	stranger.
آشکار	public.	نہان	private.
ارزان	cheap.	گران	dear.
اقبال	prosperity.	ادبار	adversity.
امین	honest.	خاین	dishonest.
اول	first.	آخر	last.
آباد	populous.	ویران	depopulated.
آفرین	blessing.	نفرین	curse.
امیدوار	hopeful.	ناامید	hopeless.
ایمان	belief.	کفر	unbelief.
برنا	young.	بزرگ	old.
بقا	permanency.	فنا	frailty.
بلی	yes.	نہ	not.
برخی	a little.	خیلی	much.
بزرگ	great.	کوچک	small.

Words.	Meanings.	Contrary Terms.	Meanings.
بالا	above	فرو	below.
بحر	sea.	بر	land.
باطن	interior.	ظاهر	exterior.
بلند	sublime, high.	پست	humble, low.
برتر	superior.	کمتر	inferior.
برهنه	naked.	پوشیده	covered.
بیش	much.	کم	little.
بینا	seeing.	نابینا	blind.
بیدار	awake.	خفته	asleep.
بام	morning.	شام	evening.
بینوا	poor.	مالدار	rich.
بیگناه	innocent.	گنهگار	sinful.
بهرهمند	fortunate.	بی بهره	unfortunate.
پر	full.	تهي-خالی	empty.
پاک	pure.	ناپاک-پلید	impure.
پیدا	manifest.	پنهان	concealed.
پیر	old.	جوان	young.
پیش	before.	پس	behind.
تندرست	healthy.	ناتوان	weak.
تازه	fresh.	پژمرده	withered.
تنگی	poverty.	فراخی	prosperity.
توانگر	rich.	مفلس	poor.
تکبر	pride.	تواضع	humility.
تهنیت	congratulation.	تعزیت	condolence.
تیز	sharp.	کند	blunt.
ثواب	reward.	عقاب	punishment.
جمع	plural.	واحد	singular.
جوان	young.	پیر	old.

Words.	Meanings.	Contrary Terms.	Meanings.
جنت	paradise.	جهنم	hell.
جنگ	war.	صلح	peace.
جبلی	natural.	عارضی	accidental.
چالاک	active.	سُست	lazy.
حقشناس	grateful.	ناسپاس	ungrateful.
حقیقت	truth.	باطل	falsehood.
حلال	lawful.	حرام	unlawful.
حیات	existence.	وفات	death.
حاضر	present.	غیب	absent.
حق	truth.	باطل	falsehood.
خیرخواه	well-wisher.	بداندیش	malevolent.
خطا	sin.	صواب	righteousness.
خاص	proper.	عام	common.
خاکسار	humble.	گردنکش	proud.
خیر	good.	شرّ	bad, evil.
خشک	dry.	تر	wet.
خورد	young.	بزرگ	old.
خسیس	worthless.	نفیس	precious.
خام	raw.	رسیده پُختہ	} ripe.
دراز	long.	کوتاه	short.
دوزخ	hell.	بهشت	heaven.
دانا	learned.	نادان	ignorant.
دخل	receipt.	خرج	disbursement.
دخول	income.	خروج	expense.
داد	justice.	بیداد	injustice.
درو	far.	نزدیک	near.

Words.	Meanings.	Contrary Terms.	Meanings.
دوست	friend.	دشمن	enemy.
دیانت	honesty.	خیانت	dishonesty.
ذاتی	natural.	عارضی	accidental.
روشن	bright.	تاریک	dark.
راحت	happiness.	رنج	affliction.
راست	right.	چپ	left.
راستی	truth.	کذب دروغ	falsehood.
زبردست	superior.	زیردست	inferior.
زیبا	beautiful.	زشت	ugly.
زنده	alive.	مُرده	dead.
زود	quick, sooner.	دیر	slow, later.
سائل	questioner.	مجیب	answerer.
سرفراز	eminent.	خاکسار	humble.
سخی	liberal.	بخیل	parsimonious.
سختی	severity.	نرمی	mildness.
سود	gain.	زیان	loss.
سوار	horseman.	پیاده	footman.
سهل	easy.	مُشکل	difficult.
سحر	morning.	مسا	evening.
سبک	light.	گران	heavy.
سرّا	prosperity.	ضرّا	adversity.
شادمان	delightful.	غمگین	sorrowful.
شیرین	sweet.	تلخ	bitter.
شجاعت	courage.	جبانیت	cowardice.
شب	night.	روز	day.
شریف	high.	وضیع	low.
شیردل	brave.	بزدل	coward.

Words.	Meanings.	Contrary Terms.	Meanings.
صبوری	patience.	تعجیل	haste.
صبح	morning.	شام	evening.
صدق	truth.	کذب	lie.
ضعیف	weak.	قوي	strong.
طلوع	rising.	غروب	setting.
طرب	joy.	غم	sorrow.
طامع	avaricious.	قانع	contented.
طول	length.	عرض	breadth.
سودمند	profitable.	خطرناک	dangerous.
ظالم	oppressive.	عادل	just.
ظفر	victory.	شکست	defeat.
عزیز	dear.	خوار	wretched.
عالم	learned.	جاهل	ignorant.
عیب	defect.	هنر	merit.
عابد	pious.	عاصي	sinful.
عاقل	wise.	غافل	ignorant.
عنا	adversity.	غنا	prosperity.
عزّت	honour.	ذلّت	insult.
عالی	high.	دون	low.
غازي	brave.	بُزدل	coward.
غنی	rich.	فقیر	poor.
فتح	victory.	شکست	defeat.
فلاح	prosperity.	شامت	adversity.
فراز	above.	نشیب	below.
فربه	fat.	لاغر	lean.
قریب	near.	بعید	far.
قوي	strong.	ضعیف	weak.

Words.	Meanings.	Contrary Terms.	Meanings.
قناعت	contentment.	طمع	avarice.
قوّت	strength.	ضعف	weakness.
کبیر	great.	صغیر	small.
کوچک	small.	کلان	great.
کثرت	many.	وحدت	single.
کم	small.	مه	great.
گرم	hot.	سرد	cold.
لیل	night.	نهار	day.
مُمکن	possible.	مُحال	impossible.
موجود	existing.	معدوم	non-existent.
مُتدین	honest.	خاین	dishonest.
مُقبل	fortunate.	مُدبر	unfortunate.
مُستحسن	laudable.	مُستقبح	contemptible.
مُظفّر، منصور	victorious.	مغلوب	vanquished.
موافق	agreeable.	مخالف	contrary.
معروف	known.	مجهول	unknown.
مهمان	guest.	میزبان	host.
مدح	praise.	هجو	curse.
مذکّر	male.	مونّث	female.
نو	new.	کُهن	old.
نامراد	disappointed.	کامگار	successful.
نیک	good.	بد	bad.
نثر	prose.	نظم	poetry.
نرم	smooth.	درشت	rough.
نعم	yes.	لا	no.
نور	light.	ظلمت	darkness.

Words.	Meanings.	Contrary Terms.	Meanings.
نیک محضر	good-natured.	بد خو	ill-tempered.
نیک خُلق	good-natured.	بد خُلق	ill-tempered.
نادان	foolish.	عاقل	wise.
نیکبخت	fortunate.	بدبخت	unfortunate.
نفع	profit.	نقصان or ضرر	loss.
نهان	private.	آشکار	public.
نیکی	virtue.	بدی	vice.
وجود	existence.	عدم	non-existence.
وفا	fidelity.	دغا	treachery.
وفادار	faithful.	بیوفا — دغاباز	faithless.
وصل	union.	هجران	separation.
هستی	existence.	نیستی	non-existence.
یکسان	similar.	مختلف	dissimilar.
یمین	right.	یسار	left.
یمن	prosperity.	شامت	adversity.

SYNONYMS = مُرادف

Words having the same meaning.

الفاظ هم معنی

Military Terms.

Admiral, میربحر, امیرالبحر
Ambassador, سفیر, ایلچی
Ammunition, اسباب جنگ, آلات رزم, اسلحه
Armour, زره, جوشن
Arsenal, سلاح خانه, توپخانه
Artillery, توپخانه, آتشخانه
Ball, گلوله, قره

Banner, لوا , رایت, عَلم
Barrack, سپاہی خانہ, لشکرگاہ
Battalion, فوج , پلٹن
Battery, تعبیہ توپ , مورچہ
Bullet, گلولہ , فندق
Camp, أردو , لشکرگاہ
Campaign, صحرا, میدان
Cannon, مدفع , توپ
Castle, حصن , حصار , قلعہ
Cavalier, فارس , ترکسوار
Cavalry, قشون سوارہ , خیل
Colonel, سرخیل , سالار
Commander-in-Chief, سردار , سپہ سالار
Dagger, دشنہ , خنجر
Foot-soldier, پیک , پیادہ
General, سردار , سپہ سالار
Infantry, اراجیل , پیادگان
Magazine, سلاح خانہ
March, رحلت , کوچ
Musketeer, بندوقچی, تفنگچی
Peace, آشتی , صُلح
Quarter, پناہ , امان
Recruit, تازہ عسکری سپاہی نو
Siege, قلعہ بندی , محاصرہ
Soldier, سپاہی , سرباز, لشکری , عسکری
Treaty, قول و قرار و عہدنامہ

Arts and Sciences=علوم و فنون

Alchemy, الکیمیا
Algebra, الجبرا
Anatomy, علم تشریح
Architecture, معماری
Arithmetic, علم حساب
Astrology, تنجیم, علم نجوم
Astronomy, علم ہیئت
Botany, علم نبات
Chemistry, کیمیا
Geology, علم طبقات زمین
Geography, تخطیط بلاد, علمِ جغرافیہ
Geometry, علم مساحت
Grammar, صرف و نحو
History, روایت , تواریخ
Logic, علم منطق
Mathematics, علم ریاضی
Mechanics, علم منجنیق
Philosophy, علمِ حکمت
Philology, علم لُغات
Physiognomy, علمِ فراست
Phonography, علمِ صوت
Zoology, علمِ حیوانات

Planets = سیارگان

Jupiter, اورمز , مشتری	Saturn, زُحل , کیوان
Mercury, دبیر, تیر, عطارد,	Venus, زهره , ناہید
Mars, باقو, بهرام , مریخ	

HOMONYMS, الفاظ ہم تلفظ

Words spelt and pronounced alike, but differing in meaning.

بار , a load; time; a fruit; rain.
باز , a hawk; again; open.
بر , breast; a fruit; on.
بوم , an owl; a country.
بیت, a house; a couplet.
حق, God; truth; claim.
داد , justice; gave.
دار , a house; gallows.
در, a door; in; tear (imp.)
ده , a village; ten; give.
سر, the head; thought; end; a leader.
عین, a lord; the eye.
کام, desire; palate.
کنار, a shore; embrace.
گور, a tomb; a desert.
لب, the lip; bank, edge.
ماه , the moon; a month.

PARONYMS, الفاظ ہم آواز

Words similar in sound, but differing in spelling and meaning.

افتکار , thinking; افتقار , poverty.
ثواب, recompense: صواب , righteousness.
حارس , keeper; حارص , greedy.
حور, nymph; ہور the sun.
حیات, life; ہیات , face,
سلاح , weapon; صلاح , advice.
شق, a crevice; شک doubt.
قید , chain; کید , deceit.
ذیق , pleasure; نیک good.

Words differing in pronunciation and meaning according to the nature of the primitive Vowels.

بَرد, cold ; بُرد he carried.
بَز , linen ; بُز , a goat.
جَو , barley; جُو , a river.
خَلق, people; خُلق, nature.
دَم , breath ; دُم , a tail.
شَکر , sugar : شُکر thanks.
قَسم , oath ; قِسم , kind.

گَرد , dust ; گِرد , circuit ; گُرد , a hero.
گِل , mud ; گُل , a rose.
مَهر , a dowry : مِهر , the sun ; مُهر , a seal.
مَلَک , an angel ; مُلک , a country; مِلک , property; مَلِک , a king.

Matriculation Examination.
1868.

I. (a) How many Arabic letters are there in the Persian Alphabet? (12) [27]

(b) Explain the terms مکتوبی and ملفوظی—مسروری

(c) When does the letter *nun* become غنّہ? (20)

II. Give some examples explanatory of the forms معروف , مجہول , لازمی and متعدی. (134, 135, 136, 137.)

III. How many varieties of the Past Tense are there in Persian? Name them, and give an example of each. (157)

IV. (a) What is the meaning of the alif in the word کاہلوی?

(b) What name have the Grammarians given to this alif? (222)

V. (a) Give the Aorist tenses of : فرستادن – گسیختن – کافتن – شنفتن – پیختن – انگاشتن – مانستن – کاستن (153, 154)

VI. Decline بلبل - گل - دانا - خانم (90)

VII. How do the Persians express *thee* and *thine*, *who* and *which*, *whosoever* and *whatsoever* ? (124, 126)

VIII. Give an example of a noun in the plural, taking a verb in the singular. (214—III.)

IX. Mention the Mood and Tense from which all other Tenses are formed. (Ans.—Imperative Mood and Past Tense.)

X. What do you mean by *Izafat* ? When is it used? (80)

1869.

I. Conjugate کاشتن in the following forms :—
First person singular of the Past Tense. (151)
Third person plural of the Aorist. (154)
Second person singular of the Future Tense. (153)
Present Participle. (173)

II. How is the accusative case of the following nouns formed? رو — پا — گلزار — ماہی — شاہی (78)

III. When is ب prefixed to such words, as گیر—گو— زن? Is it to be accented according to the same vowels? (223 *Note.*)

IV. What is the difference between موصوف and صفت ? Explain fully. (92, 93)

V. How is the Passive Voice formed in Persian? (138)

VI. Correct the following Persian sentence :—

من دیروز گل سبزرنگ در باغ دیدم کہ گاہی ندیدہ بود

(Ans.) دیروز من در باغ گل سبزرنگ دیدم کہ ہرگز ندیدہ بودم

VII. Give the plural forms of کشتہ — نوشتہ — چوب — چشم — میوہ — کارخانہ. (61)

VIII. How is the Superlative Degree formed in Persian and Arabic ? (100, 101)

1870.

I. How many letters are there in Persian ? Which of them are Arabic ? (3, 12) [لبالب (222)

II. What is the meaning of the alif in the words سراسر —

III. Give the Aorist of the following verbs :— گسلیدن — خستن — جستن — جُستن — استادن — داشتن and خستن. (183, 154)

IV. What is the difference between the forms of the imperative of these verbs — رَستن — رُستن ? (188)

V. Correct the following sentence :—

افواج پادشاهان باهم دیگر جنگهای سخت کرده است
اکنون مصالحت می کردند

(Ans.) افواج پادشاهان باهم دیگر جنگهای سخت کرده اند
اکنون مصالحت می کنند

VI. How do the Persians express '*me*,' '*my*,' '*which*,' and "*what*" ? (125, 126)

1871.

I. What does بان mean in دربان ? Give other examples of a similar nature. (187)

II. How many forms of ماضی are there in the Persian language ? Give their examples. (157-168)

III. What is the difference between the prefixes م and ن when they are used with verbs ? Give meanings of the prefixes بی and نا (145 and 104)

IV. What parts of speech are عاقل , غافل ? (Ans.) (صفت.)

V. What sense has the affix ی when it is used with nouns and verbs ? (229)

VI. How many kinds of *Izafat* are there in Persian ? Give the rules and illustrate them by examples. (83 to 89)

VII. Give examples of حاصل مصدر, اسم حالیه (173, 184)

VIII. State the terminations of abstract nouns in Persian, together with examples. (46)

IX. How many حروف زاید are there in Persian? Name them. (201)

X. Give synonyms of احسان and قرار.

1872.

I. From what language are most of the terms of Persian Grammar taken? Ans. (Arabic.)

II. (*a*) How many parts of speech are there in Persian according to the Oriental system? (41)

(*b*) Under what heads will the various Parts of Speech of European Grammar fall according to the Oriental system? (41)

III. (*a*) Give examples of امر حاضر, امر دعایی (175, 176)

(*b*) What is the meaning of the میم نہی.? (177)

IV. Give examples of the different kinds of الف (222)

V. Write Infinitives of the following Imperatives: (183)

افت ـ هل ـ روب ـ گسل ـ افراز ـ آشوب ـ سنب ـ نویس ـ گرد

VI. Put the following words in the singular number: (61)

میوجات — نوشتجات — کارخانجات

VII. In what manner are the masculine and feminine expressed in Persian with reference to animals? (54)

1873.

I. Describe the marks called حرکات ثلاثه. (15)

II. Give the diminutive of دختر — مرد. (48)

III. Give the technical and literal meanings of the words مخاطب, متکلم and غائب. (113)

IV. Translate the following distich; point out the *Izafats* and mention their names:—

الهی غنچهٔ امید بگشا (86) گل از روضهٔ جاوید بنما (85)

V. Give the second person singular of the Imperative of the verbs:—کاشتن — رستن — خاستن — ریستن — انباشتن — فریفتن — هشتن — سودن — جنگیدن — سنجیدن (183)

VI. Give the ماضي شرطیه of رفتن, the ماضي مشکی of گفتن, and the زمان مضارع of بوئیدن, all in the third person singular only. (166, 163, 154)

1874.

I. Give the Arabic plurals of:— سطر — کتاب — دفینه — علم — قطره — امر — منقار — خاقان — طبیب.

II. How is the Imperative formed in Persian? State the changes it undergoes, and give examples. (183)

III. Give words which will contain the following affixes, with their meanings:—(49, 105, 106, 187)

سار — زار — لاخ — ناک — گین — گر — آنه

IV. Analyse these words, give their Etymology and meanings:—

معلوم — مقابل — منجم — مشتق — مشترک — مفتاح — تندرو — پاکباز — شمشیر — استعمال — (Chap. XX.)

V. Mark out the Arabic words in the following passage:—

از تاجری که مال وافر داشت زر بسیار بظلم وتعدي گرفته بیچاره را بکشت و امرای معتبر را نیز که باوي بودند بقتل رسانیده در آن ولایت دم از استقلال زد

1875.

I. (*a*) What are pronominal affixes? How are they used with nouns and verbs? Give examples. (117-120)

(*b*) Give the full pronouns for the pronominal affixes in the following words:— بردمش — دادمت — گفتیم (120)

II. (*a*) State shortly the various modes of forming the plural number in Persian, exemplifying each. (61)

(*b*) Give the plurals of پای — نوشته — بیدا — دفتر — حکیم — فضیلت.

III. (*a*) How are the passive verbs formed in Persian?

(*b*) Conjugate the perfect tense, passive voice. **(138)**

IV. Give the rules of the Relative Pronouns. **(122, 123)**

V. Give imperatives of the following verbs:— انگیختن — کردن — نوردیدن — نگاشتن — سوختن. **(133)**

VI. Give adjectives from برکت — عقل — سعادت — عزت.

VII. Give the Etymology of دوربین — سکنگبین — دهقان منزل — مفتاح — معاملات. (Chap. XX).

VIII. Explain fully:—

دعوت حقرا اجابت گفتن — تلخ و شیرین ایام چشیدن

1876.

I. (*a*) Write down the Aorist forms of the following infinitives with their meanings:— گسیختن — رستن — رُستن — زدودن — هشتن — سفتن — آغشتن. **(133, 154)**.

(*b*) Conjugate پیوستن in the second person.

II. Derive the following with their meanings:— مدافعت ازدواج — اصطبار — منصب — تلبیس — مقصد

III. (*a*) What does ی denote in یافتی — کردنی — شبی زودی — فرمانروای روم — هندوستانی? **(229)**

IV. Give the plurals of the following and account for the difference in the plural terminations of the first three words, though each of them ends in ه: **(61)** — عاشق — سلطان — نفس — پادشاه — مورچه — کوه رعیت — طفل

V. What do you understand by the following:— فعل ناقص فعل مجهول - مخاطب - ضمیر - حرکات ثلاثه - مرفوع - تانیث?

VI. Name the pronominal affixes. How are they used? What change do they undergo when they are joined to ؟ ؟ (119)

VII. How is the genitive case formed? Give examples. (80)

VIII. What terminations are used to denote "*fulness*," "*resemblance*," and "*place*"? (105, 49)

1877.

I. Give the following forms of the verbs کاستن and فروختن Present participle. Future tense, second person. Perfect tense, passive, second person.

II. Write down the infinitives of the following Aorists with their meanings :— آید — هلد — سنبد — رهد — روید — گرید — ساید — افرازد. (183)

III. How is the صفت placed in a sentence with respect to its موصوف? (93)

IV. How are the comparative and superlative formed of Persian and Arabic adjectives? (98, 100, 101)

V. Derive or analyse the following words :—
اقارب — فرمان‌روا — مخلوق — متوجه — ستمکش — تولد — دیوانه‌وار — سرباز — اتفاق — تحقیق (Chap. XX.)

VI. Form words from the roots قبل and لزم on the following measures :— استفعال — افعال — فاعل (Chapter XVII).

VII. What do you understand by اضافت? When is it used? Give technical terms for the words connected by it. Notice the changes it undergoes in some cases. (80)

VIII. What is meant by :— یای قسمیه — الف دعا — الف ندا — یای لیاقت — ضمیر — فعل لازمی — امر? (222, 228, 229, 111, 135, 174)

1878.

I. (*a*) Give the Aorist 3rd person plural of گسیختن, 2nd person singular imperative of خفتن and دوختن (to milk.) (**154, 183**)

(*b*) Give the past potential and habitual past 1st person plural of خوردن—افگندن and بریدن and 2nd person singular pluperfect tense of آزمودن and افشردن (**167, 160, 162**)

II. (*a*) Give English equivalents of the following grammatical terms.—(**207, 200** *Note*, **215**)

مقدر — محذوف — مستثنی — مسند الیه — مبتدا

(*b*) What do you understand by ضمیر منفصل و ضمیر متصل and ضمیر مشترک ? Give examples. (**111, 127**)

III. Give the singulars of — اسرار — قواعد — حکما — اولیا
the plurals of زکی — حبیب — نور — عالم — شریف
the dual forms of زلف — خد — یوم — سنم. (**66**)

IV. (*a*) How are the comparative and superlative degrees of adjectives formed in Persian ? (**98, 100**)

(*b*) Give the superlative of منیر — کامل — شریف and عالم (**101**)

V. Show the difference between فعل ; اسم فاعل and فاعل ; مفعول ; نہی and نفی ; فعل مجہول and معروف and اسم مفعول (**136, 136, 137, 145, 173**)

VI. (*a*) Name and explain the *alif* in the following :—(**222**)

ستمگارا — سراپای — میرام — دمادم — بسا

(*b*) Give examples of — بای ظرفیت — بای استعانت بای علت (**223**) [examples (**46, III**).

VII. How are diminutives formed in Persian ? Give

1879.

I. Give the imperative of زیستن—رشتن, and the Aorist 3rd person singular of انباشتن—سردن and خفتن (**183**)

II. Give ماضی مطلق 3rd person singular of داشتن ; ماضی استمراری 2nd person plural of بردن ; ماضی بعید 1st person plural of فریفتن ; امکانی 1st person plural of سوختن (163, 159, 167, 162)

III. Give the etymology and meaning of the following words:— سبکتگین — دشنام — شپره — درودگر — ماهتاب — مرغابی and دشمن. (*Vide* Chap. XX.)

VI. Give اسم فاعل of the following Persian and Arabic words :— قدرت — عمل — کرد — سوختن — رفتن (186. *Note*).

V. Write in the Persian character the grammatical names of the '*alif*,' '*be*.' '*te*,' and *ye*,' in the following words :—

مست کند — رویت — بخاطراو — بسوتو — شبا روز — دانا حقی and دلجوی. (222, 223, 229)

VI. Give the grammatical name for each of the following:

دوازدهم — امروز — فردا — دوش — پنج — زیر — اسپ :- اسم

VII. Explain اضافت تخصیصی and اضافت توصیفی. (84,85)

1880.

I. How many Arabic letters are there in the Persian alphabet? What particular letters do not occur in Arabic? (11, 12)

II. Explain (*a*) ملفوظی, مکتوبی, مسروری and (27)

(*b*) How many and what letters are called شمسی and قمری and what are their characteristics? (32,33)

III. Explain فعل ناقص — فعل لازمی — فعل معروف — فعل متعدی — فعل مجهول. Give examples. (134, 135, 136, 137, 141)

IV. Give the Persian equivalents of :—Aorist, imperfect tense, pronoun, preposition and interjection.

V. Give English equivalents of the following:—حالت جری — صفت و موصوف — تذکیر و تانیث — حاصل مصدر.

VI. Write the Aorist of the following with meanings: سُفتن — آغشتن — جُستن — جَستن — گُسیختن. (153, 154)

VII. What is the difference between م and ن when prefixed to verbs, and give their grammatical names. (145)

1881.

I. How are ماضی شرطیه and ماضی متمنی formed? Give ماضی متمنی 1st person singular of شکافتن and ماضی شرطیه 2nd person plural of گسیختن. (166,165)

II. (a) How do you form the مُضارع ? (145)

(b) Give the مضارع of the following, with their meanings :— افراشتن — رستن — کافتن — کاستن — and سودن (153, 154)

III. Give the imperatives of آختن, خستن — آغشتن. (141)

IV. Give examples of کاف استفهام نفی — شین مصدری یای مفعولی, یای متکلم, یای لیاقت, یای فاعل (225, 226, 229.)

V. Explain ضمیر مشترک and اسم استفهام (125, 127.)

VI. Give the Persian grammatical terms for POSITIVE, COMPARATIVE, and SUPERLATIVE. (97, 98, 100)

1882.

I. How many forms of the ماضی are there in Persian? Give their names in Persian character, with their English equivalents, giving an example of each. (157)

II. What is the difference between the *alif* used in the following words: شبا روز — سراسر — تکاپو — دمادم (222)

III. By what process are حاصل بالمصدر and فاعل ترکیبی formed in Persian? Give an example of each (184, 188)

IV. Give the 2nd person singular imperative of the following infinitives and their meanings:—(183)
— فریفتن — سودن — انباشتن — خواستن — ربودن
هشتن and کشتن — خاستن — بستن

V. Analyse the following names, giving their English equivalents:—گژدم — خارپشت — خرگوش — سنگ‌پشت and درازگوش — خرچنگ (*Vide* Chap. XX.)

1883.

I. Give the grammatical meanings of اثبات, نهی, مصدر, نفی (180, 210.)

II. Give the Persian grammatical terms for:—reflexive and demonstrative pronouns, pluperfect tense, and copulative conjunction. (127, 128, 162, 196.)

III. Give the imperative forms of رُستن — باختن — ستودن and رَستن with their meanings. (183)

IV. Give the meanings of the following پیختن — کاستن — ریستن — افسردن and انگاشتن — مکیدن (183)

V. Conjugate برخاستن, گسیختن (1) 3rd per. pl. of the Aorist; (2) 2nd per. sing. of the future tense; (3) Present participle; (4) 1st per. pl. of habitual past.

VI. Define and illustrate کاف مفاجات — شین ضمیر اضافت یای تنکیر and شین مصدر (226, 229)

VII. Explain the meanings of the letters ب, ت and چ in the following, giving their technical names:—

(a) بدرخت گل رسیدم — بسبب درد بازماندم (223)

(b) مگر بوی از عشق مستت کند (224)

(c) چه برتخت مُردن چه برروی خاک (225)

1884.

I. Define حروف مُفرد and حروف مُرکب (190)

II. Give examples of یای لیاقت — الف دعا و تمنا

III. Give the imperatives of آمادن — ستودن — ستادن
جُستن and جستن — گزیدن — سختن — آمودن
with their English meanings. (183)

IV. Give the Aorist forms and English equivalents of خواستن and خاستن — زنودن — تنودن (188, 154)

V. What are the plural forms of the following words? Give reasons for the peculiarity of such forms :—
کارخانه — میوه — فرشته and نامه (61)

VI. Give Arabic plurals of حکیم — فوج — یوم — عضو — قول — فاضل (*Vide* Chap. XXIII.)

1885.

I. How will you divide letters according to the number and position of the dots? (29, 30)

II. What do you understand by the *servile*, the *solar*, and the *lunar* letters? Name all these letters. (32, 33)

III. How do you form the following? Give examples:—

(*a*) Substantives denoting an agent. (187)

(*b*) Diminutives. (46—IV)

(*c*) Abstract Nouns. (44)

(*d*) Adjectives denoting possession (105)

IV. What is علامت مصدر? Name all the letters that precede it. (180, 181, 182)

V. Give the technical term for, and name the auxiliary [verbs. (140)

VI. Mention briefly, and illustrate the different rules for the formation of imperatives. (183)

VII. Give the meanings and derivations of دارالضرب — دستار — ذوالقرنین — ترک تازی — حافظ (Chap. XX.)

VIII. Point out and give technical terms for all the حرف in the following:—

ای کہ بر مرکب تازندہ سواری ہوشدار
کہ خر خارکش مسکین در آب و گلست

IX. Explain fully
انگشت نماي جهان شدن—انگشت بدندان گزیدن*

1886.

I. Describe briefly the primitive vowel marks and show by examples that the meanings of words, vary according to the nature of these marks. (15)

II. What is the force of م in words like منزل? How is this force expressed with regard to Persian nouns? (48, 49)

III. What do the following suffixes denote? —سار—وار—زار—کار—فام and ور. Give examples. (49, 105)

IV. Distinguish between ضمیر منفصل and ضمیر متصل—اسم حالیہ and اسم فاعل (111, 186, 173)

V. How do you account for the various exceptions to the general rules for forming imperatives? (183 *Note.*)

VI. Give with meanings the imperatives of —گسیختن—کافتن—کاستن—گشتن—شفتن—غنون (183)

VII. Analyse the following compound words; give the meanings of their component parts:—خرچنگ—روزنامہ—خرگاہ—سخن چین—کامران—دارالشفا

VIII. (*a*) Explain clearly with examples the following kinds of:—اضافت ظرفی—:اضافت—اضافت توصیفی—اضافت مقلوبي (85, 87, 88)

(*b*) What do you understand by فک اضافت? (89)

IX. Give with meanings the plurals of —امام—فقیر—صندوق—جاسوس—قیصر—نقطہ—روح—عدد
(Chap. XXIII.)

X. What do you understand by:—حرف ختم کلام—حرف زاید—حرف تنبیہ (192, 197, 201)

1887.

I. Write down the rules that you would be guided by in determining the concord in number of nominative and verb. Give a short sentence to exemplify each rule. **(214)**

II. Conjugate بلیدن in the habitual past and the future perfect tense passive voice. **(160, 183)**

III. Mention any impersonal and defective verbs, and state how they are used in Persian. **(141, 142)**

IV. Cite a causal verb, and give the regular infinitive form corresponding to سفتن - کاستن - گشتن - سیختن - زادن

V. (*a*) Distinguish between مظلوم and ظالم; مدرس and مدرسه

(*b*) Trace the derivation of دیباچه — مرزبان — فیلسوف — خورشید (*Vide* Chap. XX.)

VI. Decline او and نامه and give the accusative dual form of مشرق and والده **(116, 66)**

VII. State the general principles which regulate the insertion of را as the sign of the accusative case. Under what circumstances is it omitted? **(74, 75)**

VIII. How do you form present participles and verbal nouns from گفتن — پرستیدن — فرمودن — سوختن — جستن

IX. Give instances of compound adjective or epithets formed by the union of two substantives. **(103)**

X. What is the grammatical name of the یای مختفی in زنانه — زوجه — and the numerical value of the expression خاک مصلی? **(228, 230)**

1888.

I. State the rules concerning the use of the pronouns هرکه هرچه — خود or خودش, giving sentences to exemplify them. **(124, 127)**

II. Define and illustrate.

چیم مساوات — کاف تفضیل — کاف تشبیه (225, 226)

III. Give examples :—(*a*) Of infinitives in شتن which form their Aorists irregularly. (183, Rule V. Exceptions) (*b*) Of verbs used both transitively and intransitively whose imperatives are regular. (143)

IV. (*a*) Put in the plural number and distinguish مُلک مَلِک — مُلک — مِلک (*Vide* Chap. XXIII.)

(*b*) Mention the feminine plural of — برادر — خروس

V. The Plural of علم is علوم; cite four nouns which form their plural after this model. (*Vide* Chap. XXIII.)

VI. Give as many meanings as you can of each of the following words :— تا — بر — رود — بار — دار

VII. Form adjectives from افسان — شرف — اندوه — عقل

VIII. Parse فغان — کاش — مرحبا — لهذا — خواه — سواي quoting a synonym for each. (200, 196, 197)

1889.

I. Translate into Persian :—

They shall arrive. We will come. You might speak. Thou wast reading.

II. Explain the following technical terms :— محذوف — حالت ندا — فعل ناقص — ضمیر متصل — موصوف — جملهٔ معترضه. (92, 215, 221, 79, 141, 117)

III. Give with meanings :— [*Vide* Chap. XXIII.

(*a*) The singulars of اطراف — علما — صحاری — غربا — نقود

(*b*) The plurals of منزل — قیصر — کسری

(*c*) The derivations of حکایت — مطبوع — مقید

(*d*) The synonyms of رفیق — فتح — لازم — دشمن

(*e*) The contrary terms of عنا — ادا — بقا — زبردست

IV. Form words from نظر on the measures of فاعل and فعيل.

V. Give the meanings and the imperatives of the following infinitives:— پیوستن — سفتن — سودن — عربده کردن — نوردیدن — افسردن — آشفتن (183)

1890.

I. Translate into Persian:—

(a) He and I were writing. (**214**, Rule VIII.)

(b) The man, the boy and the girl have entered the boat. (**214**, Rule II.)

(c) London is the largest and wealthiest city in the world.

(d) He was killed.

(e) Rama said that he would come. (**211**, Rule VI.)

II. Form the Plural of حیوان — گره — بنده — پا (**61**)

The singular of ملائکه — رسل — تکالیفات

The feminine of سید — کاوتر — بیگ (**57, 54, 56**.)

III. Give the diminutives of در — دختر (**48**, III.)

The verbal nouns of فرمودن — سوختن (**184**.)

IV. Give with meanings the imperatives of ضبط کردن — فرستادن — باختن — خواستن — رستن — شگفتن — گردانیدن — کشته شدن (**183**.)

V. Explain the following technical terms:— الف دعا و ندا — یای لیاقت — یای مفعول — یای زایده — اضافت تخصیصی — ضمیر منفصل — جیم مساوات — تجنیس تام — صفت مرکب (**222, 223, 229, 225, 111, 84, 103, 245**, I.)

VI. Explain the following proverb:—

کند همجنس با همجنس پرواز — کبوتر با کبوتر باز با باز

VII. (a) Give with meanings the synonyms for همت دیده — بندگی — ملاحظه نمودن — مدرس — قد

(*b*) The contrary terms for شادمان—نیک خُلق—مُقبِل

VIII. Write down the Arabic measures of بقّال — غالب — اِخراج—اکبر (237)

1891.

I. (*a*) Form the plural of بازو — نامہ — مُردہ — زن (61)

(*b*) Form the singular of — نوازشات — املاک — حیوانات (Chap. XXIII. and 61)

II. Give the feminine of—جاسوس- پسر- خان - خرگوش نر (54, 57, 56)

(*a*) Give the diminutive of طاق — مرد (48, III.)

(*b*) Give the verbal noun of — پیمودن — آموختن

III. Give, with meanings, the imperatives of نوشیدن— افراختن—پیراستن— خوابانیدن — ہلیدن — بافتن (183)

IV. Explain the following technical terms:—فعل معاون— ضمیر مشترک — مفعول ثانی — حروف زاید — ازمنہ ثلاثہ — حاصل مصدر — صیغہ امر ماضی امکانی (140, 127, 216, Note, 201, 150, 184, II. 174, 167)

V. Give, with meanings, the synonyms of محروم شدن— عبودیت — رفیق

VI. Give the contrary terms of مُدبر— بدخُلق — تہنیت.

VII. Write down the Arabic measures of معراض— بصیرت.

1892.

I. Give the meanings and the imperatives of — رسانیدن — کاشتن — زیستن — کاستن — نوشتن — پیمودن — معروف شدن — ہشتن (183)

II. Give with meanings —

(*a*) The synonymys of جنگ — منزل — تازہ

(*b*) The contrary terms for بزرگ - حق - موجود - نادان

(c) The roots of تطاول — تحمّل — مُنازعت.

(d) The Arabic measures of استعمال — عارف.

III. Explain the terms and give examples:— فک اضافت
جملہ شرطی و جزا — فعل متعدی — اسم ذات —
حروف استدراک — حالت جرّی — صفت و
موصوف — استعارہ — حروف علّت — ماضی
استمراری (89, 220, 134, 44, 196 III, 78, 91,
14, 159)

IV. Explain the following proverbs:—

(a) چو میدان فراخ است گوی بزن

(b) کار نیکو کردن از پر کردن است

V. Give some general rules for the arrangement of words in a Persian sentence. (211)

VI. Give technical terms for the particles, prefixes and suffixes occurring in the following lines:—

جوانا رہ طاعت امروز گیر ؞ کہ فردا جوانی نیاید ز پیر
من این روز را قدر نشنا ختم ؞ بدانستم اکنون کہ در باختم
قضا روزگاری ز من در ربود ؞ کہ ہر روزی از وی شب قدر بود *

VII. Give the singular and plural possessive cases of خانہ — بندہ.

1893.

I. Translate the following couplets and give technical terms for all words:—

چہ خوش گفت فردوسی پاک زاد
کہ رحمت بر آن تربت پاک باد
میازار موری کہ دانہ کش است
کہ جان دارد و جان شیرین خوش است

II. Give the meanings and the infinitives of — جہ — نواز
گسل — آفرین — رہان (183)

III. Give, with meanings, (*a*) The synonyms of—
پادشاه — رسم — پرہیزگار — معروف

(*b*) The contrary terms for نیک - صواب - عادل - شادی

(*c*) The Arabic measures of اکرام — رفیق

(*d*) The Arabic plurals of اسیر - حقّ - ساکن - فردوس

IV. Explain and give examples—
اعراب ثلاثه — کاف موصول — فعل مجهول —
فعل معاون — تشبیهی — خبر (15, 226, 137, 140, 208.)

V. Explain the following proverbs:—

(*a*) صبر تلخ است ولیکن بر شیرین دارد
(*b*). نیکان صحبت از نیکان کنند

VI. Write short sentences illustrating the meanings of the following expressions:— برخوردن — بسر بردن — تربیت کردن.

1894.

I. Give two examples of مصدر ترکیبی — اسم حالیه —
حروف استقرار — حروف سببیه — حاصل مصدر
(184, 185, 192, 197.)

II. Mention the gender, number and meanings of مدینتین -
تکلیفات — مشرقین — فقیره.

III. Give the causal verb, present tense, first person plural of نشستن — گُسستن — رستن — پروردن (139.)

IV. Distinguish between شدن and بودن regarding their usage.

V. Give examples of Benedictive Imperative, Desiderative (Optative) Past, and Denominative Verbs. (179, 165, 145 *a*)

VI. " Nouns of multitude, denoting rational beings, follow the same rule in Persian as in English." Explain and exemplify this remark. (214, VI.)

VII. (*a*) Name the Figures of speech commonly used in Persian. **(245)**

(*b*) Explain تجنیس تام and تجنیس مُرکب **(245, I, VII.)**

VIII. Derive and explain — بوستان — خونخوار — گلزار — خزانچي — دادگر — ماهتاب

IX. Give the meanings and Arabic plurals of — يتيم — بحر — وحش — حكيم — قلب — صندوق (*Vide* Chap. XXIII)

1895.

I. Translate the following couplet, naming the Figures of Speech in it:—

گرچه سیم و زر زسنگ آید همي
در همه سنگي نباشد زر و سیم **(245, X.)**

II. How do you express in Persian the relative pronoun with its antecedent? Quote two sentences in which a noun or pronoun is governed by a relative clause. **(122)**

III. What do you understand by the term قلب اضافت? Give four examples of compound substantives formed of two nouns by rejecting the اضافت **(88, 89)**.

IV. Write down the present indicative second person singular and plural of :— ایستادن , نمودن — بودن **(152)**.

V. Give (and translate) short sentences to illustrate the transitive and intransitive uses of :—

آموختن — آویختن — آمیختن — ریختن **(148)**.

VI. Attach an appropriate infinitive to each of the following words, and give the meaning of the compound expressions thus formed: — فراهم — باور — التفات — روا — سوگند — توقع — گمان — غم — **(148.)**

VII. How do you form verbal nouns from دانستن — دیدن -

- آفریدن — خوردن — لرزیدن — کردن — پرسیدن
— بیرون — ما and abstract noun from خواستن
خوب — تو — درون (184, II. 44,)

VIII. Give (*a*) the feminine of - اخ - شاه - داماد — خواجه
— خسر — معلم and (*b*) the plural of — نبی — گدا
کریم — ستر — عظیم (54, 56, 61, Chap, XXIII)

1896.

I. Explain the terms (*a*) حرکات ثلاثه (*b*) ازمنه ثلاثه
(15, 150,)

II. Enumerate and illustrate the different rules for the formation of the plurals of Persian nouns (61)

III. (*a*) Explain and give examples of :—
الف تحسین کلام — بای قسمیه — شین مصدر
(222, 223, 225, میم اضافت — یای نسبت
227, 229.)

(*c*) Distinguish between کاف تصغیر and کاف ترحم.
(226)

IV. Mention, giving examples, the different adjectival suffixes denoting possession (105)

V. State the different kinds of ماضی in Persian. Give examples (157-168)

VI. Give with meanings (*a*) the plurals of :—لسان-فتی-
قریب — عابد — فن (*b*) the imperatives of آغشتن —
چیدن — هشتن — کافتن — پیختن (Chap. XXIII, 183)

VII. Give Persian equivalents of the following proverbs:—
(*a*) Charity begins at home.
(*b*) All that glitters is not gold.
(*c*) To carry coals to Newcastle.
(*d*) Look not a gift horse in the mouth.
(*e*) He that will steal an egg will steal a horse.
(Chapter XXI.)

1897.

I. Give the singular or plural, as the case may be, of the nouns therein underlined :—

واکابربر صفحات دفاتر رقم فرموده اند که شش چیز فایده نتوان گرفت اول قول بی عمل دوم مال بی خرد سیوم دوستی بی تجربه چهارم علم بی صلاح پنجم صدقه بی نیت ششم زندگانی بی صحبت (Chapter XXIII)

II. Explain فک اضافت and اضافت استعاره. Give examples. (89, 86)

III. What are the exceptions to the rule that a verb agrees with its subject in number? (214)

IV. Give with meanings :—

(a) مضارع third person plural of فریفتن (154)

(b) امرنهی second person plural of شگافتن. (177)

(c) زمان حال first person singular of نگاشتن. (152)

(d) امرحاضر second person singular of سفتن. (175)

(e) اسم فاعل of افراشتن. (186)

V. Give the various readings (supplying the vowel or other marks, where necessary) and meanings of—

ملک — گرد — مهر — قوت — در (15)

VI. Explain clearly the ابجد system of enumeration. Find the numerical value of بسم الله الرحمن الرحيم (230)

1898.

I. How are the definite and indefinite articles expressed in Persian? (202, 203)

II. Show how double comparatives and superlatives are formed in Persian. Give examples. (102)

III. Give the meanings of the following words (1) as nouns (2) as verbs, with their infinitives :—

جوی — شوی — گرد — دوش — چین — گو — کار — کاه — ران — تاب (183)

IV. What rule would you observe as regards narrative construction in Persian? (211, VI.)

V. Write short grammatical and explanatory notes on the words underlined in the following sentences:—

(a) این تفنگ را چند خریدی

(b) برو منزل

(c) دو کتاب بیش ندارم

(d) از هجوم مردم تماشا چی این ممکن نبود

(e) این میوه‌ها را کُلاًّ در گرمخانه عمل می آوردند

(f) او شاهنشاه عالم پناه بود

1899.

I. (a) What kind of construction is used in reporting the speech of another in Persian? (211, VI.)

(b) Translate:—

(1) They said that they had gone to Shiraz.

(2) He asked the servant of whom he had heard the news.

(3) My brother told me that he would buy a book for me.

(4) He asked the gardener, "Oh, old man, do you except to reap its fruits?"

II. What are the rules for the formation of:—

(a) حاصلِ مصدر (184, II.)

(b) مصدرِ حقیقی or اصلی (184, I.)

(c) مصدرِ ترکیبی (185)

(d) مصدرِ معنوی (184, III.)

(e) اسمِ فاعلِ ترکیبی (188)

III. Explain with examples—

الف امالہ (222)- الف فاعلیت (222)- بای علت

(228)- بایِ ظرفیت (223)- نونِ نفی - میم نہی (227)

IV. (*a*) Distinguish between—

مونثِ حقیقی and مونث لفظی (54)

(*b*) Give, with meanings, the masculine of—

خانم - عمه - ماکیان - اخت - ام (56, 54)

(*c*) Give, with meanings, the feminine of—

اسپ — خسر — غوچ — داماد — بنده (54)

V. Explain the following idioms, and form sentences, illustrating their use :—

عنان از دست رفتن — گردن از طاعت پیچیدن — قلم بر اسمِ کسی کشیدن — از خواب در آمدن — ملامت کردن گرفتن — سخن درمیان نهادن

VI. Explain fully the following proverbs :— (*Vide* Chapter XXI.)

(*a*) توانا بود هر که دانا بود

(*b*) کار نیکو کردن از پر کردن است

(*c*) کسی نمی گوید که دوغ من ترش است مگر مشک
آنست که خود ببوید نه که عطار گوید

(*d*) نیاید به جوی باز آبی که رفت

(*e*) چو آهنگ رفتن کند جان پاک
چه بر تخت مردن چه بر روی خاک

(*f*) سعدیا دی رفت و فردا همچنین موجود نیست
درمیان این و آن فرصت شمر امروز را

VII. Give, with meanings, the plurals of the following words, giving all the different plurals where there are more than one, according to different vowel-marks :—(*Vide* Chapter XXIII.)

ملک - نفس - علم - بیت - ساقی - قوت - سنت

1900.

I. Give, with meanings, the following forms of خواستن :–

(a) زمانِ مستقبل مخاطب واحد

(b) صیغهٔ مجهول زمانِ مستقبل مخاطب جمع

(c) صیغهٔ امکانی با استمراری متکلم واحد

II. Explain, with examples:—

بای مفعول (223)—تای مفعول (224) - ہای مفعول (228)
یای مفعولی (229)— یای فاعلی(229) — الف فاعلیت (222)
میم فاعلیت (227) — واو معروف — ہای ملفوظی — حروف
جر (196) — فک اضافت (89) — اسمِ موصول (122)

III. (a) What do the terminations ان - تن and یت denote in Persian? Give examples.

IV. Give, with meanings, the masculine or feminine, as the case may be, of the following nouns:—

سلطان — دیوانه — جانور — خواجه — ام — عاشق —
درویش — غلام

V. Give the derivations of the following words, and give with meanings as many words as you know having the same derivations:—

استقبال — تصویر — میزان — تفاوت

VI. Explain the following idioms, and form sentences illustrating their use:—
(*Vide* Chapter XXII.)

چشم داشتن — بجان آمدن — پشت دست گزیدن —
بہم بر آمدن — دست از جان شستن — انگشت نمای
جهان شدن

VII. Explain fully the following proverbs:—
(*Vide* Chapter XXI.)

(a) هر عیبی که سلطان پسندد هنر است

(b) علاج واقعه پیش از وقوع باید کرد

(c) جوابِ جاهلان باشد خموشی

(d) نیک بخت آن کہ خورد و کشت
و بدبخت آن کہ مُرد و ہشت

(e) تونگری بدل ست نہ بمال
بزرگی بعقل ست نہ بسال

(f) ای دوست برجنازۂ دشمن چو بگذری
شادی مکن کہ بر تو ہمین ماجرا رود

VIII. (a) Explain the "Abjad" system of enumeration and give the numerical value of حسنآباد (230)

IX. Give the plurals, with meanings of:—
(*Vide* Chapter XXIII.)

حدیث - حکایت - طبیب - صدقہ - قلب - درخت - عابد - حُکم

1901.

I. Explain with examples—

الف اصلی (222) — شین مصدر (225) — میم تعین تعداد (227) — نون ضمہ (20) — ہای ملفوظی (24) — ہای مختفی (25)

II. Give, with meanings, the Aorist forms of—

رَستن - رُستن - رشتن - شکستن - کِشتن - کُشتن - کاشتن - کاستن - ہستن - ہشتن (183)

III. (a) Give, with meanings, the masculine or feminine of—

استاد — کنیز — پیل — پادشاہ (54)

(b) Give, with meanings, the singular or plural of:—
(*Vide* Chapter XXIII.)

عُلم — عِلم — احوال — ماہ — عالِم — عالم — نُواب

IV. (a) Give, with meanings, the adjectival forms of—

مال — جمال — مدت — درد

(b) Give the derivations of the following words and give, with meanings, as many words as you know having the same derivations:—

خیانت — تبدیل — قسمت — لطام

V. Explain the following idioms and illustrate their use:— (*Vide* chapter XXI.)

آہن سرد کوفتن — عینک زدن — تغافل کردن

VI. How many Arabic letters are there in the Persian Alphabet? Name them. What particular letters do not occur in Arabic and are purely Persian? (11-12)

VII. Enumerate ملفوظي — مسروري — مکتوبي letters. How many and what letters are called شمسي and قمري and what are their characteristics? (27, 32, 33)

1902.

I. (*a*) Find the numerical value of:— سفر نہ صد و ہشتاد
Write down carefully how you arrive at the result. (230)

(*b*) Enumerate the different kinds of اضافت. (83-89)

II. Mention with meanings—

(1) The masculine or feminine of بندہ—عم—پسر— شیرنر and آپا (54, 56.)

(2) The roots of درویش-قیامت-شمشیر-تقصیر and منظور (*vide* Chap. XX.)

(3) The imperative forms of :— نگاشتن — فریفتن— خفتن—آلودن and جوشیدن (183).

III. Illustrate with examples what you understand by :—

کاف تحقیر—جیم مساوات—بای ظرفیت—الف تمنا
یاي لیاقت—واو معروف — نون فند — میم نہي
(226, 225, 223, 222, 229, 23, 20, 227.)

IV. (*a*) State the general rule for the formation of imperatives when س precedes the termination تن Name some exceptions. (183, Rule IV.)

(*b*) Conjugate نواختن in

(1) ماضی قریب (161)

(2) ماضی استمراری مشکی (164)

V. Explain the following proverbs (*vide* Chap. XXI):—

(*a*) درخانهٔ مور شبنمی طوفان است

(*b*) چراغی که در خانه روا است بمسجد حرام

(*c*) مشک آن است که خود ببوید نه که عطار گوید

(*d*) نیاید بجوی باز آبی که رفت

(*e*) کار نیکو کردن از پر کردن است

(*f*) کند همجنس با همجنس پرواز
کبوتر با کبوتر باز با باز

VI. Explain the following idioms and form sentences illustrating their use (*vide* Chap. XXII.):—

سخن در میان نهادن — در سلک ازدواج کشیدن
جامهٔ زنان پوشیدن — انگشت نمای جهان شدن
بازار گرم ماندن — از سرخون در گذشتن

VII. Give the plurals with meanings of (*vide* Chap. XXIII):—
سطر — کتاب — رکن — دفتر — درخت — رعیت — کوه
نفس — علم

1903.

I. Form with meanings (*a*) abstract nouns from انسان — ما — خواجه — یک and رفیق (44)

(*b*) Diminutives from باغ — بط — پسر — کتاب and رود (46, III)

II. Distinguish between the meanings of the following, when used as nouns and as verbs:—کار — ساز — خر — گوی — نشان and مال.

III. (*a*) Quote, with examples, the rules for the formation of :—

ماضي بعيد — ماضي امكانى — ماضي and امر تنها (162, 167, 179)

(*b*) Give with meanings (1) امرحاضر second person singular of پختن (2) زمان مستقبل first person plural of خوردن (3) مضارع third person plural of دیدن.

IV. (*a*) Name the adjectival suffixes denoting "similitude." Give instances. (105)

(*b*) What is فک اضافت? Illustrate with examples. (89)

V. Write down, with meanings, the infinitives of—

بر and ریز — گزین — شناس — خسپ — ہل

VI. Mention with meanings (*a*) the singular or plural of:—

پردہ — حکام — نوشتم — غزل — جوانب — نیا — مکان and بحر — ورد — عنادل.

(*b*) The masculine or feminine of :—

اخت — خروس — آہو — مادیان — عروس — خان کدخدا and شاعر — راهبه — خاتون (54, 56)

1904.

I. State what you know of :—

حرکات ثلاثہ and ازمنہ ثلاثہ. Give instances (15,150)

II. Give the Persian terms for 'noun of agency' and 'diminutive' and cite rules, with examples for their formation. (186, 46, III.)

III. What do you understand by—

الف عطف — بای استعانت — کاف استفهام — واو تصغیر — ہای تانیث (222, 223, 226, 228)

IV. Quote, with meanings, the Imperative form of–(**183**)

خواستن — خاستن — جُستن — جستن — بریدن — بودن — کاشتن — کاستن — رُفتن — رفتن

V. Mention, with meanings—

(*a*) The singular or plural of—

عندلیب and نوشتہ — ایالی — بوزینہ — بذت

(*b*) The derivations of—

شہباز — ملاقات — کہربا — ماجرا — ارجمند

1905.

I. What are the forms of ماضی in Persian ? Give their English equivalents, illustrating each by an example. (**157.**)

II. (*a*) Give, with meanings, the second person plural Imperatives of—(**183.**)

بستن — انباشتن — آراستن — بریدن — بودن — کاستن

(*b*) What do the following suffixes denote ?—

گین — سار — گار — آسا — گون — وار (105)

III. How is حاصل بالمصدر formed in Persian ? Give instances. (**184**, II.)

IV. (*a*) Give, with meanings, as many synonyms as you can of the following :—

جنگ — شراب — تیغ — طاقت

(*b*) Explain the following :—

جملہ معترضہ — یای لیاقت — یای قسمیہ

کاف تصغیر — ضمیر متصل — حروف قمری — تنوین

V. Mention, with meanings, as many derivatives of the root عمل as you know. (**237**)

VI. Form adjectives from:—

شرف — انسان — صوفی — دلیر — فهم — عقل

1906.

I. Give, with meanings—

(a) The comparative of (101) عظیم — کبیر — عالی.

(b) The singular or plural, as the case may be, of—

قضاة — لیالی — ارض — لباس — قوی — نعمت

II. What does ی denote in—

شدنی — کردنی — فرمانروای روم — زودی

قوی — اصفهانی (229)

III. How are the following grammatical constructions formed? Give examples.

اسم فاعل ترکیبی — اسم تصغیر — حاصل مصدر

جنس تانیث — عدد تثنیه (188, 46, 184, 52, 66)

IV. Give, with meanings, the etymology of:—

خارپشت — ازدواج — مفتاح — مقابله — مشترک —

خرگاه — سکنجبین

V. Give, with meanings, the aorist second person plural of:—

آمادن — رُستن — رَستن — رشتن — زدودن — گزیدن —

گُزیدن — گسیختن — هشتن

1907.

I. Distinguish between فاعل and اسم فاعل, مصدر and حاصل مصدر. Give examples. (207, 186, 180, 184)

II. Explain the following :—

(۱) آنرا که حساب پاک از محاسبه چه باک

(۲) اول خویش بعد درویش — (۳) جو فروش گندم نما

(۴) چاه کن را چاه درپیش (۵) کس نگوید که دوغ من ترش است

III. Point out the exact force of the اضافت in

ملک شاه — اسپ سفید — تیغ نگاه — رستم زال — علم دوست — صاحب خرد

IV. What do you understand by the solar and the lunar letters? Name them **(32-33)**

V. How do you form امر of verbs when تن is preceded by (*a*) س and (*b*) ش? Give examples. **(183, IV, V.)**

VI. Quote suffixes forming اسم مکان. Give instances **(49)**

VII. (*a*) Mention, with meanings, the singular or plural of—

وقت — اشراف — علم — موجودات — خلیفه

(*b*) Derive the following :—

نوشیروان — معرفت — عابد — شمشیر — اصفهان

1908.

I. Give, with meanings, the aorist, 3rd person plural of—

آفریدن — رشتن — سکدن — سختن — فرستادن — کافتن

II. Name the various kinds of ماضی used in Persian. Give their English equivalents, illustrating each by an example **(157-168)**.

III. Give, with meanings, the singular of—

اقلیم — تماثیل — الویه — حیل — عناکب

IV. Give, with meanings, the plural of—

لولو — کسری — اسیر — جاسوس

V. Form sentences to illustrate the use of—

آسا — وش — لاخ — شن — آنہ (105, 49, 106.)

1909.

I. What letters precede دن and تن respectively in infinitives? State the rules for the formation of imperatives, giving examples. (181, 183.)

II. How are abstract and verbal nouns formed? Illustrate with examples. (44, 184.)

III. What suffixes are used to form diminutives (46, III.) and adjectives denoting (*a*) similitude, (105.) (*b*) fitness, (106) and (*c*) possession? (105.) Give instances.

IV. Give, with meanings, the plurals of—

قول — شمس — بحر — حدیث — نبي — طایفہ — بہیمہ — فردوس — عابد — دوا

V. Distinguish between—

ابد و عبد — اقارب و عقارب — الم و عُلَم — امر و عمر — جامہ و جامع — دُم و دَم — سر و سِرّ — شراب و سراب

VI. Enumerate the different kinds of اضافت. What do you understand by فک اضافت? (83-89.)

1910.

I. Give with meanings :—

(*a*) The singular or plural of :—

دکان — تاج — صنادیق — جام — خیم

(*b*) The imperative of :—

کاستن — رَستن — گزیدن — ریستن — جستن (183.)

II. Give, with meanings, the derivation of :—

خوردہبین — بوتیمار — ناخدا — کہربا — سرہنگ

III. Explain and illustrate the following :—(167, 225, 229, 32, 245, IX.)

ماضی امکانی — جیم مساوات — یای نسبتی — حروف شمسی — مشبہ بہ

IV. Name and explain the اضافت used in the following :-

سوختۂ آتش — ولی عہد — مرد خوب — آب رود — دہکان پسر

V. What do the following suffixes denote ? (105, 187 106, 49.)

فام — بان — آنہ — گین — گون — دان

Illustrate them with examples.

1911.

I. How are verbal adjectives formed ? Give examples. (189.)

II. Give, with meanings, the antonym of :—

ثواب — برقا — اقبال — تہنیت — زیبا

III. Explain and illustrate :—

ضمیر منفصل — کاف موصولہ — ماضی معطوفہ

میم نہی — اشتقاق — یای مجہول

IV. Enumerate the rules for the formation of imperatives. (183.)

V. Explain the ابجد system of enumeration. Find the numerical value of مغفر (230)

VI. (a) Give, with meaning, the Arabic plural of خادم —

مسجد — نور — سلطان — رعیت

(b) The synonym of—

گزدم — شمشیر — آسایش — علم — قلعہ

1912.

I. Enumerate and explain the different kinds of اضافت (83 to 89)

II. Give, with meaning, the Arabic plural of :—

اسقاد — سوال — قیمت — کاتب — شاعر

III. How is the Passive voice formed in Persian? (188)

IV. Show by diacritical marks the different readings of the following words, and give their meanings:—(15)

شعر — سحر — انعام — گرد — ملک

V. Translate into English freely :—

(۱) لوازم پیری در جوانی آماده کردن
(۲) آب که از سر گذشت چه بسیار چه کم
(۳) هرکه زر دارد زور دارد
(۴) در خانهٔ مور شبنمی طوفان است
(۵) اندر شوره زار تخم کاشتن
(۶) جای گل گل باش و جای خار خار

1913.

I. Give with meaning :—

(a) the Arabic plural of :—

فرمان — فریضه — دایرة — امام — رب

(b) the imperative of :—

کاشتن — هشتن — راندن — گرفتن — بستن

II. Explain and illustrate the following :—(20, 21, 33, 150, 225).

نون غنه — واو معدوله — حروف قمری — ازمنهٔ ثلاثه — چه مبالغه

III. How are abstract and verbal nouns formed? (44, 184)

IV. Construct short sentences, in Persian, illustrating the use of :—

منزل گرفتن — مجلس را گرم داشتن — گله کردن — گول زدن — روی درهم کشیدن

V. Find, according to the ابجد system, the numerical value of خاک مُصلّی.

1914.

I. Explain and illustrate the following:—

حروف ساکن — صفت تفضیل — فعل مشترک —
مضارع — ماضی مشکی (17, 98, 143, 154, 163)

II. Explain the following phrases, and frame short sentences to illustrate their use:—

رای زدن — چشم گماشتن — دل نهادن — کمر بستن
گردن کشیدن

III. Give with meaning:—

(a) The Imperative of—(188)

ستادن — پیراستن — رفتن — بریدن — شکستن

(b) The Arabic plural of—

باب — رسم — معنی — رقیب — ازل

(c) The antonyms of—

راستی — صبح — دوست — عالم — نور

1915.

I. Explain and illustrate:—

استعاره — تضاد — مصدر حقیقی — حروف استحقار —
زمان مستقبل (96, 184 I, 197 VI, 153.)

II. Enumerate the different kinds of اضافت. What do you understand by فک اضافت? (83 to 89)

III. Give, with meanings, the Arabic plurals of :—

ابن — عین — قریب — بیت — امر

IV. Translate into Persian :—

(a) His Majesty the King.

(b) Good Morning. Please come in.

(c) Are you hungry ? No, Sir, but I am thirsty.

(d) Do you speak Persian? Yes, I speak it a little.

(e) The sea is rough.

1916.

I. Explain and illustrate the following:—

جملۀ اسمیه — جملۀ فعلیه — مفعول به — یای فاعلی — تشبیه — اضافت مقلوبی (216 III, 229, 88)

(219, I. II)

II. Form the following:—

(۱) زمان حال مخاطب جمع of ربودن

(۲) ماضی شکی غایب جمع of آماده کردن

(۳) ماضی قریب مخاطب واحد of دیدن

(۴) صیغه شرطیه با حال متکلم جمع of آمدن

(۵) ماضی بعید مجهول غایب واحد of کشتن

(۶) ماضی تمنی متکلم واحد of خوردن

(۷) ماضی استمراری مجهول مخاطب جمع of پرسیدن

(۸) صیغه امکانی با ماضی متکلم واحد of کشیدن

III. Give, with meanings, the infinitives of the following:—

تاب — جه — کاه — کار — چین — سنب — شکیب — روی — روب — انگار (183)

INDEX.

Alphabet (Letters of), حروف تہجی

Abstract Noun, اسم ذات

Accidence, صرف

Accusative Case, حالت مفعولی

Active Verb, فعل معروف

Adjective, وصف or صفت

Adverb, حرف تمیز

Adversative Conjunction, حرف استدارک

Affixes, لواحق , ملحقات

Affirmative Adverb, حرف اثبات

Affirmative Sentence, جملہ خبریہ

Agent, فاعل

Alternative Conjunction, حرف تردید

Antecedent, موصول بہ

Antithesis, تضاد

Aorist, مضارع

Auxiliary Verbs, افعال معاون

Benedictive Imperative, امر دعا

Cardinal Numeral, عدد مطلق or ذاتی

Case, حالت

Causal Verb, فعل مجبور

Causative Conjunction, حرف علت

Clause, فقرہ , جملہ

Cognate Accusative, مفعول مُطلق

Collective Noun, اسم جمع

Common Noun, اسم عام

Comparative Degree, صفت تفضیل

Complex Sentence, جملہ مُرکب

Comparative Particle, حرف تشبیہ

Compound Adjective, صفت مُرکب

Compound Verb, فعل مُرکب

Concessive Conjunction, حرف جُملہ

Conditional Particle حرف شرط

Conditional Clause, جملہ شرطیہ

Conditional Conjunction, حرف شرط

Conjunctive Past, ماضی معطوفہ

Conjunctive Pronoun, ضمیر متصل

Noun, اسم [الجمع
Noun of Multitude, اسم
Noun of Agency, اسم فاعل
Noun of Time, اسم زمان
Noun of Place, اسم مکان
Noun of Instrument, اسم
آلت
Noun of Number, اسم عدد
Nominative Case, حالت
فاعلی
Negative Verb, فعل نفی
Neuter Gender, جنس غیر
ذی روح
Objective Case, حالت جری
Object (of a Verb), مفعول
Optative Imperative, امر
تمنا [دعا
Optative Sentence, جملہ
Ordinal Numeral, عدد
معین or وصفی
Parenthetical Sentence,
جملہ معترضہ
Past Tense, ماضی مطلق
Past Imperfect, ماضی
استمراری [ثلاثہ
Primitive Vowels, حرکات
Primary Tenses ازمنہ ثلاثہ
Particle, حرف [مفعول
Perfect Participle, اسم
Perfect Tense, ماضی قریب
Present Participle, اسم
حالیہ [مسند بہ
Predicate, خبر — محمول
Passive Voice, صیغہ مجہول
Pluperfect Tense, ماضی
بعید
Plural Number, عدد جمع
Potential Mood, صیغہ
امکانی
Preposition, حرف جر
Personal Pronoun, اسم
ضمیر
Possessive Pronoun, ضمیر
مُضاف الیہ [مضف
Positive Degree, صفت
Proposition, جملہ
Proper Noun, اسم خاص
Permutation of Letters,
حرف تبدیل
Radical Letters, حرف
اصلی [حروف زاید
Redundant Particles,
Reflexive Verb, فعل مشترک
Reflexive Pronoun, ضمیر
مشترک [موصول
Relative Pronoun, ضمیر
Regular Verb, فعل قیاسی
Relative Clause, جملہ وصفیہ
Second Person, مُخاطب

Servile Letters, حروف زایده
Singular Number, عدد واحد
Simile, تشبیهی [مُفرد
Simple Sentence, جمله
Strong Verb, فعل سماعی
Syntax, نحو
Subject, مُبتدا — مسند الیه
Subjunctive Mood, صیغه شرطیه [مبالغه
Superlative Degree, صفت
Suffixes, حروف ملحقات
Tense, زمان
Third Person, غایب
Transitive Verb, فعل متعدی
Verb, فعل
Verbal Noun, اسم مصدر
Vocative Case, حالت ندا
Vowel, حروف علت
Weak Verb, فعل قیاسی

OPINIONS.

"'Hints on the Study of Persian' is a very good Grammar, and a very useful and comprehensive work for the study of Persian. Though the book at first sight appears small, yet a judicious perusal of it will show, in a striking manner, that much thought, judgment, and labour have been bestowed on it, and that the Authors are deserving both public praise and patronage."

(Sd.) HAIRAT,
Professor of Persian,
Elphinstone College.

BOMBAY, *10th May 1892*

"'Hints on the Study of Persian' is an excellent manual of Persian Grammar. Many innovations have been introduced, and explanations of Arabic terms and expression also have been given. It ought to prove of great use to students taking up Persian as their Second Language in University Examinations. The framework of the book, the arrangement and the method of treatment are all excellent. It only needs a little more encouragement."

(Sd.) IMAD-UL-MULK'M.A. (*Calcutta University*),
Director of Public Instruction,
H. H. the Nizam's Dominions.

HYDERABAD, 12*th March* 1893.

"The compilers of 'Hints on the Study of Persian' have clearly reconciled theory with practice, without which no living language will be learnt promptly and thoroughly. The principles adopted by the compilers in the arrangement and the classification of grammatical materials are such as will enable students to acquire a practical knowledge of the Persian language in the shortest time possible. With respect to the grammatical rules, the compilers have kept in view the main object of communicating facts in the simplest and the most popular way possible. It is a peculiar advantage of this book that sufficient attention is paid to the treatment of Arabic words, Syntax, Idioms, Proverbs, Synonyms, Homonyms, etc. The compilers have the merit of giving a very intelligible arrangement of grammatical materials to students who want to acquire a thorough knowledge of the Persian language, and wish to speak and write it with fluency and facility. It must be observed that the book is excellently printed—a circumstance which will not fail to increase the popularity of this excellent manual. The best proof of its usefulness is the issue of the fourth edition in four years."

(Sd.) Dr. EUGEN WILHELM,
Professor of Iranian Languages
at the University of Jena.
(*Germany.*)

Jena, 22*nd January* 1893.

"I have no doubt 'Hints on the Study of Persian' will prove very useful to the students of the Persian language. I was particularly much pleased with the lists of Idioms, Proverbs, Synonyms, Homonyms, etc. It was a good idea to give a short account of the Arabic Grammar to enable the student to distinguish the two elements in modern Persian. The Authors have collected an amount of practical information quite necessary for the perfect knowledge of the language, and yet hardly to be found in our Grammars, at least those in use in Europe. As it is, this book is a very remarkable performance which will be as creditable to the Authors as useful to the readers."

(Sd.) JAMES DARMESTETER.

Paris, 21*st June* 1889.

"'Hints on the Study of Persian' is, indeed, a very useful and comprehensive Persian Grammar. It will be a very good *vade mecum* of the students wishing to have a clear idea of all the grammatical principles of the Persian Lauguage.

This book is specially valuable for full and correct explanations of all technical terms, useful examples, and very good model excercises. Messrs. Kangas' discussion of Syntax and Verbs with their conjugations is more complete and accurate than that of all other manuals of Persian Grammar. Moreover, the value of this excellent book is much enhanced by different Chapters on Proverbs, Idioms, and by model exercises, and the large number of important questions with references with which all chapters conclude. In short, I am so much satisfied with the utility of this valuable work that I have great pleasure in strongly recommending it to the students of the Persian Language of Central India and Upper India."

(Sd.) NIZAM-UD-DIN AHMED, M.A.,
(*Allahabad University*)
Professor of Persian, Rájárám College.

KOLHAPUR, 20*th October* 1894.

" 'Hints on the Study of Persian' is the most useful and comprehensive manual of Persian Grammar. It is a complete Grammar of the Persian Language for High Schools. It is at the same time brief, accurate and intelligible, and thus saves much time and hard labour. It is a desirable novelty, and it will be of great value to the students of the subject, who ought to be grateful to the Authors for their learned assistance. I shall recommend it confidently to all those who stand in need of a good Persian Grammar."

(Sd.) MOIN-UD-DIN AHMED, M.A.
(*Calcutta University*),
Professor of Persian, Holkar College.

INDORE, 13*th November* 1894.

"The Authors of 'Hints on the Study of Persian' have struck a new line for themselves and produced a book of considerable merit. A careful examination of the entire work satisfies me that great care and much labour have been devoted to its production. Regarded both from the teachers' and from the students' point of view, the book must be pronounced excellent. It is clear in statement and accurate in the rules laid down. The book has already made its way and will be found indispensable by the students of the Persian Language."

(Sd.) S. C. SHAHANI, M.A.,
Professor of Persian, Wilson College.

"'Hints on the Study of Persian' is a very useful and interesting production. The Authors seem to have bestowed much care and attention in the compilation of this Manual. The advantages of the systematic arrangement of its various parts are obvious. Its contents are judiciously selected. The book will certainly be a great help to the students of the Persian language, and the Authors deserve credit for thus trying to facilitate their work."

(Sd.) HOSHANG JAMASP DUSTOOR,
Professor of Persian, Deccan College.

POONA, 26th *June* 1889.

"This book at once bears testimony to the great labour the Authors must have undergone in order to make the book so very useful. Besides good and comprehensive grammatical rules, it contains many useful Proverbs, Idioms, and many other valuable things of which no trace is to be found in other Persian Grammars. It may with great advantage be introduced into High Schools."

(Sd.) ASRAF ALI, M.A.
(*Calcutta University*),
Principal, Mohobat Madressa.

JUNAGAD, 25th *February* 1890.

"'Hints on the Study of Persian' is a very good Persian Grammar and it will be very useful to the students of the Persian language preparing for the Matriculation Examination."

(Sd.) ABDUL FATTAH MOULVI,
The late Professor of Persian and Arabic,
Elphinstone College.

BOMBAY, 13th *January* 1889.

"'Hints on the Study of Persian' is very much the best Persian Grammar I have seen."

(Sd.) T. O. UNDERWOOD.

MADRAS, 20th *September* 1890.

" 'Hints on the Study of Persian' is, in fact, a complete Grammar 'Multum in Parvo.' The arrangement and get-up of the book are admirable. Each chapter is replete with useful information, and the subject handled is dealt with exhaustively and with precision. Questions on each chapter, as well as Matriculation Examination Questions with reference numbers to rules for solution, will be a great blessing to the students of the Persian language going up for the University Examination."

(Sd.) KARAMALI R. NANJIANI, B.A.
(*Bombay University*),
Educational Inspector, Cutch.

BHUJ, 26*th July* 1889.

" 'Hints on the Study of Persian' is the best Manual of Persian Grammar. It is replete with all sorts of practical information likely to contribute to the success of the students preparing for the Matriculation Examination. I can safely and cordially recommend it to every student of the Persian language. I have no doubt it will prove a very useful Textbook for our High Schools."

(Sd.) MAULVI SYED SIRAJUDIN, B.A.
(*Bombay University*),
The late Deputy Educational Inspector, C. D.,
Professor of Persian, Deccan College.

POONA, 1*st September* 1889.

" 'Hints on the Study of Persian' is indeed very valuable, and will be of immense use to the students of the Persian language preparing for the Matriculation Examination."

(Sd.) FARIDUDDIN AHMED, B.A.
(*Calcutta University*),
Professor of Persian, Boroda College.

BOMBAY, 12*th January* 1889.

" 'Hints on the Study of Persian' will be of great use to the students of Persian. The Authors seem to have taken great pains to make it as practical as possible."

(Sd.) SHAIK MOHAMED ISPAHANI,
Professor of Persian, Samaldas College.

BHOWNAGAR, 24*th June* 1890.

"'Hints on the Study of Persian' is a very useful and instructive publication. It is a work of great diligence and zeal. It will be very serviceable to both the beginners and the advanced students of Persian as it embodies all the important rules of Grammar. The compilers deserve every encouragement for their great interest and useful efforts in facilitating the means of the acquirement of the practical knowledge of this very useful and delightful language."

(Sd.) MIRZA MAHOMED JAFAR KHAN,
Professor of Persian, Sind Arts College.

KARACHI, *2nd September* 1889.

"The Authors of the 'Hints on the Study of Persian' have spared no pains in making it as useful and comprehensive as possible, and on the whole it is superior to any of those Manuals of Persian Grammar which have been prepared for use in our High Schools."

(Sd.) RUSTAM MEHERBAN AGA,
Persian, Arabic, and Hindustani Translator and
Interpreter, High Court, Bombay,
Professor of Persian, St. Xavier's College.

BOMBAY, *14th June* 1889.

"'Hints on the Study of Persian', is no doubt the most useful book for High Schools. It contains very good grammatical rules, definitions, illustrations, and a nice collection of Derivations, Proverbs, Idioms, etc. The learned and able compilers have bestowed great toil and care in preparing it, and I wish it every success."

(Sd.) SEYAD ABBAS HOSAIN,
Professor of Persian and Arabic,
Aligarh College.

ALIGARH, *8th March* 1891.

REVIEWS.

The Bombay Educational Record.—"Messrs. Pestonjee K. Kanga, and Jamsetjee B. Kanga the Persian Tutors have jointly published a text-book in Persian for the use of Standards VI and VII. in High Schools, which appears to be a disiinct advance on Manuals of this kind. It is entitled 'Hints on the Study of Persian,' is admirably printed, and is full of practical, valuable suggestions, and the best methods of teaching this popular language."—*December*, 1888.

The Times of India.—"We have much pleasure in strongly recommending this excellent 'Hints on the Study of Persian' to the students preparing for the Matriculation Examination. It is a nicely got-up book, showing great toil and care, and is exactly suited to the wants and comprehension of students. The definitions and illustrations have been judiciously selected, and the notes are admirable. The fact that it has been employed as a text-book in almost all the High Schools is a sufficient proof of the value of the work. In many previous manuals of Persian Grammar written for the use of schools, too little attention has been paid to Syntax, Derivations and Idioms, and a most valuable aid to the study of the Persian language has thus been comparatively neglected, but the Authors of this book have supplied this deficiency by introducing separate chapters on these subjects, and the students who wish to learn a simple easy style of writing Persian will find great help in this book. The Grammar is altogether a most useful one, and will be found a very suitable text-book for High Schools."—*December* 1*st*, 1888 and *May* 18*th*, 1889.

The Bombay Gazette.—"The Authors of this book are the Senior Persian Tutors of the two leading High Schools, and they have had therefore ample opportunities of thoroughly ascertaining the wants of Students. They have rendered excellent service to our High Schools by supplying the long-felt want of a suitable Persian Text-book. Every subject under treatment is systematically arranged, and at the same time expressed in a simple easy style. The book may be recommended to the students preparing for the Matriculation Examination as the best Persian Grammar."—*December* 5*th*, **1888**.

The Deccan Herald.—" 'Hints on the Study of Persian' is edited by Messrs. Kangas, the able and experienced Persian tutors, and this in itself is a guarantee of the accuracy and usefulness of the book. The general get-up and arrangement of the book are equal to those of any English work, while the matter contained in it is so varied and comprehensive and so skilfully and conveniently condensed in every chapter, that the work stands alone of its kind among all similar books. Not the least important feature of the book is the series of questions with references at the end of every chapter, which will, no doubt, prove a very valuable help to students. Its merits are so widely known and appreciated, and its importance and usefulness are so justly recognised that it has been regarded as an indispensable companion of the students of the Persian language. We really know of no other manual of Persian Grammar at once so good, so accurate, so handy and so inexpensive. We cordially wish the Authors the success they deserve."—POONA, *29th August* 1890.

The Indian Spectator.—"The compilers of the 'Hints on the Study of Persian,' both experienced Persian teachers, have jointly tried their best to give a complete course of the Grammar of the language in a condensed form. From the mode of treatment, the work appears to be based upon the model of a standard English Grammar. Again, it seems that the compilers have missed not a single authority to refer to, in order to make their publication as useful and instructive as could be made. The system of classification and arrangement is English, and therefore affords greater facilities to students to learn Persian Grammar in a regular course. The compilers have used their best knowledge and experience in collecting and explaining a large number of Idioms of the Persian tongue. They have done all they could to supply the desideratum of a Persian Grammar, and placed within the reach of students a cheap and easy manual of the kind. It is a very useful compendium for students of Persian."—*June 16th*, 1889.

Rast Goftar:—મી૦ પેસતનજી કાવસજી કાંગા અને મી૦ જમશેદજી બેજનજી કાંગાએ 'Hints on the Study of Persian' એ નામનું એક નાનું પણ અભ્યાસીઓને માટે બહુ કિમતી પુસ્તક પ્રગટ કીધું છે. તેની પેહેલી

આવૃત્તિ છપાયા પછી છ માસમાં બીજી આવૃત્તિ પ્રગટ કરવાની જરૂર પડી છે તેજ બિના એ પુસ્તક કેટલું ઉપયોગી અને કિમતી છે તેની મજબૂત સાબિતી રજુ કરે છે. જયારથી આપણી પાઠશાળાઓમાં ફારસી ભાષાનો અભ્યાસ દાખલ થયો છે ત્યારથી એ ભાષાના વ્યાકરણો અવારનવાર આશરે અરધો ડઝન જેટલાં નીકળ્યાં છે પણ અમો કશી શકશુબાત વિના કહિશું કે તે સર્વ કરતાં મેસર્સ કાંગાઓનું આ વ્યાકરણ ઘણી બાબતોમાં ચહડતું છે. બીજા વ્યાકરણ સાથ સરખાવતાં એક અભ્યાસી આ પુસ્તકમાં ઘણું નવું જોઈ શકશે. તેમના ગ્રંથની અમે ઘણી સ્તુતિ સાંભળી છે, અને તેની તારીફને તે યોગ્ય છે એવું અમારૂં મત છે–June 30th, 1889.

Kaiser-i-Hind:—હાલમાં આપણી મુંબાઈની બે નામાંકીત નિશાળોના બે અનુભવી ફારસી શિક્ષકોએ સાથે મળીને ફારસી ભાષાનું વ્યાકરણ બહાર પાડયું છે. તપાસ ઉપરથી માલમ પડે છે કે આ બંને સાહેબોએ એ વ્યાકરણ બનાવવામાં મેહનતની કશી બાકાત રાખી નથી. ખુબી એ છે કે તેઓએ પોતાનું પુસ્તક અંગરેજી વ્યાકરણના ધોરણ ઉપર રચ્યું છે અને તેથીજ તેઓ પોતાની નેમમાં ફતેહમંદ થયા છે. ચોપડી બનાવવાની રચના સેહેલ સમજ પડે તેવી સારી અને સાદી છે. આપણા બંને કાંગા ગ્રંથકારોએ પોતાના અનુભવનો ઘણો સારો લાભ અભ્યાસીઓને આપ્યો છે અને તેઓની ઘણી સારી સેવા બજાવી છે. આપણી મુંબઈની સરકારી તથા ખાનગી નિશાળોમાં એ પુસ્તક એક "સ્ટાનડરડ" યાને ખાસ અભિયાસને લાયકનું ગણાવું જોઈએ –June 30th 1889

Jam-e-Jamsheed:—ફારસીના વ્યાકરણમાં સબાબાર પુસ્તકો પ્રોફેસર લમ્સડન અને ફારબસના છે. તેઓ એક હાથ ઉપર મોંઘા અને કમયાબ છે તેમ બીજા હાથ ઉપર શરૂઆતના અભિયાસીઓ માટે તુલતવીલ અને મોટાં છે. 'Hints on the Study of Persian' એ બંને અંગ્રેજી ગ્રંથકારોનો જાણે અરક અથવા સાર આપે છે અને વળી વિદ્યાર્થીઓને લેવાને બની શકે તેવું છે. એ પુસ્તકમાં એક ખુબી એ છે કે જે મોટા પુસ્તકોમાં જોવામાં આવતી નથી તે એ કે એમાં શરૂઆતના અભિયાસીઓને નડતી મુશ્કેલી ટાળવાને પાછલા ભાગમાં પુષ્કળ જગા લીધી છે. એવા પ્રકારની આગળ નિકળેલી ચોપડીઓ ઉપર આ ચોપડી એક સુધારો અને વધારો છે એવા આ ચોપડીના બનાવનારા આપણી જાણીતી નિશાળોના ચડતા વર્ગના ફારસી શિક્ષકો છે અને તે કાબેલ હાથ હેઠળથી પસાર થઈ છે તે એ ઉપયોગી ચોપડીની વધુ શિફારસ છે.–June 26th, 1889.

Printed by B. Miller, Supdt., British India Press, Mazgaon, Bombay.
Published by Postonjee Kavasjee Kanga, Sir J. J. P. B. Institution, Hornby Road, Bombay.